GW00546672

JOSEPH

The Power of Persistence

First published in Nigeria by
Aslan L.I.F.E Publishers 2013

All rights reserved.

No part of this publication may be reproduced or
transmitted in any form or by any means electronic,
electrostatic, magnetic tape or mechanical, including
photocopying, recording or by any information storage
and retrieval system, without written permission from
the publisher.

ISBN: 978 095 727 440 2

Printed in Nigeria by
PRINTSERVE LIMITED
10, Makoko Road
off Herbert Macaulay Street
Ebute-Metta, Yaba
Lagos, Nigeria.
+234-1-7452222, 7453333, 7457777

JOSEPH

The Power of Persistence

O.M. Efueye

CONTENTS

DEDICATION

To my mother, Felicia Yetunde Gbejuade. I know that between Richard (my little uncle) and I, we gave you a good run for your money when we were young. I will never forget how you looked at me in the summer of 1979 as I graduated with my first degree and shook your head, marvelling that I had finally turned out all right.

The years have piled on, one on the other and you have seen your children grow. I now also have children of my own, (who will soon have children of their own!). Between you and my late father, you instilled in me the virtues of integrity, diligence, hard work and compassion, which have all guided me to where I am today.

Your gentleness and kind-heartedness continue to inspire me. I use this opportunity to tell you what you already know—I love you from deep within my heart.

ACKNOWLEDGEMENT

First, and most importantly, I thank my heavenly Father the God of gods and the Father of our Lord Jesus Christ. I still do not know what You saw in me or why, but I am so glad You chose me. Thank You for making it clearer with each passing day that I must die empty.

I would like to acknowledge Pastor Paul Adeolu Adefarasin, the senior pastor of House on the Rock, whom I worked with for 18 years.

From the moment I heard a message by one of my foremost mentors, Pastor Gary Garner of Ascension Life Ministries, it provoked a desire in me to investigate the life of Joseph and write a book on him. In a message titled "Jesus our Heavenly Joseph," Pastor Gary opined that there must be at least one hundred pictures of Christ in the Joseph story. I have found a lot more than that!

Pastor Gary, I have "borrowed" some of your thoughts and developed them and others into a treatise that explores Christ and Him crucified and what that means to us all. Thank you for your friendship and inspiration.

Apostle Lyn Hiles, I have never met you personally, but your messages have stirred up fires of revival in my soul. I know we will get together soon.

Jacque Heasley, your friendship is invaluable and we share a kindred spirit. One day soon, the Dreamer of Dreams will see them fulfilled.

Rev. Bob Alonge of Capital Assembly, Abuja Nigeria preached a message titled the Law of the Fifth, which forms the basis of Chapter 11 of this book. My dear friend and brother, thank you for being unselfish with the revelation God gave you, by letting me use it.

I love and appreciate you and your dear wife, Pastor Teju, and value our friendship.

Marta Kargbo, Beulah Iriele, Ndidi Okezie, Sharon Blankson and Dorcas Adenigbagbe: thank you for your tireless and often thankless commitment to the typing, editing and producing of the original manuscript.

House On The Rock, London Lighthouse Church office staff, what would I do without such a talented and hard-working bunch as you all? Pastor Kayode Adisa, Pastor Laolu Opebiyi, Pastor Alistair Frimpong, Beatrice Lawale, Eniola Dawodu, Monnique Waite; thank you all very much. May I also acknowledge volunteers who came into the office and were drafted into the project - Jenny Lee, Olaitan Oduwaiye, Joseph Taiwo and all others.

Tokunboh Agosu, thank you for your excellent contribution as always.

The manuscript was very professionally edited by Nancy Arant-Williams, who also edited my first book, A Word in Season.

Special thanks also go to the following dear friends, sons and daughters, without whom this project would never have seen the light of day: Toyin Salako (Craigo) who has been very active in all my creative endeavours; Joy and Irene Ainabe; Bidemi and Bukky Arowolo; Tosin and Lola Lanipekun; Uche and Ify Oti; Jazzy and Edith Orefuwa; Tosin and Damola Salako, Yomi and Ladun Omojokun and Mabinty Koroma. Sister Bims Alase, you are incredible and have been a blessing from the "beginning". Fidelis Pepple, Omo, you are a friend indeed. Orits Onuwaje, omere, mo dope, oh. May God abundantly reward you beyond your thoughts, desires and imagination.

Most importantly, I would like to appreciate my wonderful, loving supportive family, my precious wife, Carol who believes in me and stands by me through thick and thin. Shweety, you are the best! Dede and Marcel – you are model children and the pride of my heart.

FOREWORD

Pastor O's book, **_Joseph: The Power of Persistence_** explores one of the Bible's greatest stories, providing great insights as to God's dealing with his people. The story of Joseph spreads over 13 chapters of Genesis and draws us to the wonderful conclusion that God knows what He is doing, He is in control. Pastor O's reflections bring the story alive and will challenge us as 21st century followers of Christ.

Steve Clifford, General Director, Evangelical Alliance

INTRODUCTION

Joseph. What an enigmatic personality! His story is so compelling that it has captured the imagination of countless generations over the ages. He has fascinated Jews, captivated Gentiles, instructed the elderly, featured prominently in Sunday School for the youth, taken centre-stage in numerous musicals, drama productions, and has been the subject of countless literary and art works.

Joseph. It is obvious even to the unschooled and unlearned, to the spiritually bankrupt and inept, that there is more to his story than meets the eye.

Joseph's story begins in the thirty-seventh chapter of the book of beginnings –Genesis. Yet strangely enough it actually does not begin with him but with his father, Jacob. It sets the tone for how this story, like every other story in the Bible, unfolds on many levels. For the sake of this treatise, we will be exploring five of those levels.

Level one reveals the story at its literal level with its obvious implications.

Level two applies to the Jews, otherwise known as "natural Israel."

Level three, and perhaps the most important of all, points to Christ.

Level four offers practical application for the contemporary reader.

Level five challenges us with the truth that we need a Saviour—and that we are not to be mere hearers, but doers of the Word. (See James 1:25.)

In reality, it is the intention of its Author that sets apart the Bible from any other book. While others are meant only to educate, inform, entertain and recommend change, they lack the ability to transform.

The Bible, on the other hand, is profitable for doctrine, reproof, correction, and the equipping of the reader for every good work. (See 2 Timothy 3:16.) Jesus actually declared His words to be spirit and life, (see John 6:63), while Solomon proclaimed God's Word to be life to those who find it and health to all their flesh.

From our study we will discover how the remarkable story of Joseph is really a vivid picture of Jesus and His finished work on the cross, as well as what that means to us.

CHAPTER ONE

"I HAVE A DREAM!" (OR TWO)

In The Beginning

Joseph's story begins with a reference to his father, Jacob, who, according to the text, lived in Canaan. In Genesis 37:1 we see how three generations walked with God, and how He uses one generation to influence the ones that follow.

In Genesis 37:2 we are told, "These are the generations of Jacob. Joseph…" Strangely enough, the generations listed in Jacob's line begin with his youngest son, Joseph, instead of his oldest, veering from tradition. This purposely emphasizes the remarkably close relationship between father and son and actually points us to a picture (or type) of the relationship between Jesus and His Father. In his case, Joseph would have no story at all if Jacob had not been faithful to his heavenly calling. In his story we see that the greatness of the son is predicated upon the faithfulness of the father. The same is true of Jesus. John 14:28 say, "For my Father is greater than I." Yet John 10:29 goes even further, to say that, indeed, He is greater than all.

On our part we must realize that our walk with God cannot even begin till He Himself first beckons us and then empowers us to respond to His wooing. And lest we take any credit for such great wisdom John 15:5 reminds us: "…Without me ye can do nothing." In other words, He deserves all our praise.

In Genesis 37:2 we see that Joseph was seventeen years of age when this story begins. And while, at first glance that might seem like an insignificant piece of trivia, the truth is that the number seventeen is identified with victory. Let me give biblical evidence to support this assertion.

In Romans 8 Apostle Paul lists seventeen trials over which we are more than conquerors, in other words—victorious.

In a study of the story of David we see him taking five smooth stones when he went out to face Goliath. In 1 Samuel 17:45 he tells the giant, "I come to thee in the name of the LORD of hosts, the God of the armies of Israel, whom thou hast defied." Here we see David going to war in the power and authority of God's name. In biblical numerology, twelve is the number of divine rule, authority and power. Add twelve to his five stones (signifying grace) and victory is inevitable.

We see another illustration in the story of Elijah challenging the prophets of Baal on Mt. Carmel. Three times Elijah ordered four barrels of water to be poured over his sacrifice. (4x3=12.) After he prayed the fire of God fell and consumed five items: the sacrifice, the wood, the stones, the dust and the water. Add those five things to the twelve and we see that Elijah could not fail that day.

Finally, we recall that Jesus died on the day the Passover lamb was killed, the fourteenth day of the month. Then He arose three days later, on the seventeenth day, to give us victory over sin, sickness, poverty, hell and death. Hallelujah!

Returning to the story of Joseph, we see that from the beginning God is reassuring Joseph (and us) that no matter what we go through, God's thoughts concerning us are for peace and not for evil to bring us to an expected end—an excellent end. Jeremiah 29:11(KJV) says it this way: "To give you a future and a hope." Joseph's story begins with victory, because God always declares: "the end from the beginning, and from ancient times the things that are not yet done." Isaiah 46:10 further testifies of God, that His counsel would be established and He would bring to pass everything that was pleasing unto Him.

In this way Joseph represents a type of Christ who was sent by God, and introduced by John the Baptist as: "The Lamb of God that taketh away the sin of the world." The other John, also called the Revelator and the beloved, unveils the truth in Revelation 13:8, that this same Lamb was slain from the foundation of the world. This indicates that in the mind of God it was a finished work even before it began. By this I mean that just as a project manager would complete all his plans before the actual project begins, God also completes His plans in the spiritual realm before they begin in the natural, and thus brings it to a successful and glorious end. The victory was indeed assured because it had been won before the battle began.

You see, even in creation God followed this principle. Before God began to create He was at rest enjoying an endless, eternal Sabbath. Then at some indefinable point in time, He began to create the world. On the seventh day He again entered into His rest. Now we are called into rest as beneficiaries of the New Covenant. This rest, according to Albert Barnes in his Notes on the Bible, speaks of "heaven," a place of cessation from wearisome toil. By entering into God's rest we are to strive to live a life of faith that will culminate in heaven. Adam Clarke on his part says the rest refers not only to the gospel blessings but also to "eternal felicity." Anything God calls us to do or says about us is already and forever settled, that is, appointed, erected, fixed, and established in heaven. Like Joseph all your destiny stories must begin, and end in victory.

The Good Shepherd

Joseph, we are told next, was feeding the flock with his brothers, which means he was a shepherd. In fact, some of God's greatest chosen leaders were shepherds. Both Moses and David were shepherds; the sheepcotes have always been one of God's greatest leadership training facilities.

Luke 2:8 tells us that it was to shepherds watching their flocks by night that angels announced the Saviour's birth. That group may seem like a random choice till much later on when we see Jesus rebuking the Pharisees after He healed the man born blind. He was angry because they stubbornly refused to believe that He was God's Son and the only Mediator between God and men. In John 10:11 He told them: "I am the good shepherd..." Twice He stressed this theme in His teaching, instantly solving the mystery of why the shepherds were chosen to herald the birth of Christ. Because He is the chairman of the shepherd's union, the rank and file shop members were the first to hear the announcement of His birth. God always uses familiar things to make His point; in this case, the society of the day was mostly agricultural and pastoral so shepherds were the perfect choice. It also explains the nature of many of His parables.

In the same way we as believers must have the heart and qualities of a shepherd.

The twenty-third Psalm is truly one of the most well known and popular of all Scripture passages, because of its amazing word pictures with which everyone can identify. First of all, we see ourselves as vulnerable sheep tenderly cared for by a nurturing heavenly Shepherd. But more importantly, God offers us the exciting prospect of understudying His Son, so that we can become like Him, reflecting the marvellous love of our amazing God.

There is a shepherd in each of us and our sheepcote is our workplace—the primary training ground for greatness. Here we are secretly trained to fight bears and lions and to make our mistakes out of the public eye. Here we are purged of every vestige of arrogance and whatever pride our achievements have brought us. Here we are clothed with the garments of a servant, the only appropriate dress that prepares us for future greatness.

An Evil Report

In Genesis 37:2 we are told that Joseph was "with the sons of Bilhah, and with the sons of Zilpah, his father's wives: and Joseph brought unto his father their evil report" (Genesis 37:2). The word "evil" means naturally or morally bad or of inferior quality. It also refers to wicked thoughts or actions. It is used to describe malignant, noxious or injurious activities. Note that this does not mean that Joseph was an evil man. On the contrary, it shows a distinction between Joseph's character and that of his brothers who though older, were definitely not wiser. Joseph could only bring an evil report if his conduct was different; otherwise he would have been a hypocrite, exposing himself as well. Another implication is that Joseph not only knew and pursued his father's will, but also shared with him warm and intimate fellowship.

This aspect of Joseph's relationship with his brothers typifies Christ and His relationship with the spiritual leadership of His generation. Jesus outlines this fact clearly when He tells His blood half-brothers, "The world cannot hate you; but me it hateth, because I testify of it, that the works thereof are evil" (John 7:7).

Oftentimes people are offended when we are just going about our Father's business. Our mere presence can convict unbelievers who then become aggressive and even confrontational, without cause. Even when we do not realise it, they see Christ in us—and this nearly always sparks a reaction, whether good or bad. So do not be weary and do not murmur; after all Jesus said a disciple is no greater than his master. As such we cannot expect to be immune from the persecutions, misrepresentations and indeed, even the malignant hatred of the world. Joseph learned this lesson early, and we would do well to do likewise.

Just as Joseph knew the will of his father and was desirous to see it fulfilled Jesus declared in John 5:30: "I can of mine own self do nothing: as I hear, I judge; and my judgment is just; because I seek not mine own will, but the will of the Father which hath sent me" (John 5:30). At Lazarus' tomb Jesus emphasized the fact that the communication lines between Him and the Father were always open, as evidenced by John 11:41-42: "Father, I thank thee that thou hast heard me. And I knew that thou hearest me always..."

The point here is that the most important thing in life is the will of our heavenly Father. We were not placed on this earth to pursue hedonistic, secular, humanist or even philanthropic pleasures. We are neither here for religious endeavours, nor to save the environment, which has now become mankind's latest idol; by all means we are to care for our environment but not worship it. Rather it is your duty and responsibility to preserve it for your children and their children. In fact, God actually promises to destroy those who destroy the earth. (See Revelation 11:18.) However, He frowns at those "who changed the truth of God into a lie, and worshipped and served the creature (environment?), more than the Creator, who is blessed forever. Amen" (Romans 1:25).

As the story progresses, we find that Israel (Jacob) loved Joseph more than his other children, because he was the son of his old age..." (See Genesis 37:3.) To understand the relationship between them we must review his background to learn how Jacob came to start a family in the first place. It's a familiar story—how Jacob fought with his brother for dominion even in the womb, and ended up holding onto Esau's foot even while Esau was being born--and how later he bought his brother's birthright with a bowl of stew. And while we acknowledge that he robbed Esau of his father's blessing, that will not be our primary focus here.

Rather we will focus on Esau's murderous wrath, which forced Jacob to run for his life, to the home of his uncle Laban. It was there that he discovered the eternal principles of sowing and reaping. Genesis 8:22 tells us: "While the earth goes on, seedtime and the getting in of the grain, cold and heat, summer and winter, day and night, will not come to an end." It had to feel like the ultimate irony when, after living a life of fraud, treachery and manipulation Jacob finally realized he had fallen victim to a another, even greater master manipulator, whose own cunning made Jacob's antics look decidedly amateur.

Jacob's first ten sons were born of Leah, after Laban tricked him into marrying her instead of his true intended, Rachel. Just in case the story is unfamiliar to you, let's review: Jacob met and fell in love with Laban's younger daughter, Rachel, and he agreed to work seven years for Laban in exchange for her hand in marriage. On their wedding night, however, he was deceived into sleeping with and thereby, marrying her older sister, Leah. In effect, and also in type, all ten sons of Leah were the fruit of the flesh, and represent the flesh and the Law, which John 1:7 tells us was given by Moses. As far as Jacob was concerned, Joseph was his firstborn, because he was the firstborn of his beloved Rachel. But on another level this story is a type, representing a preview of Jesus, the beloved Son in whom God was well-pleased. (See Matthew 3:17; 12:18, 17:5, and Isaiah 42:1.)

As a special gift for Joseph, Jacob made him a coat of many colours, symbolizing his paternal favour. In the same way, Jesus (see John 2:40 & 52,) enjoyed the Father's favour, as well as the favour of men, even as He grew in wisdom and age. In Joseph's case this gift engendered the terrible hatred and jealousy of his brothers who thereafter, refused to "speak peaceably unto him" (Genesis 37:4).

The religious and political leaders of Jesus' day, who were also Jews, brethren in the flesh, were also jealous and hated him because others, including His Father, loved Him. No wonder John 1:11 says, "He came unto His own and His own received Him not." In fact, when Jesus was teaching in the temple the chief priests and elders questioned Him regarding the source of His authority. After confounding them, with a no-win question of His own, Jesus went on to tell them parables. In the second parable He spoke of a certain householder who planted a vineyard and fenced it off and added a winepress, erecting a tower within the confines of the vineyard. He rented it out to vinedressers and journeyed to a distant land.

When harvest-time came the landowner sent his servants to claim the fruits of the vineyard. Strangely, the tenants either beat or stoned every messenger. Finally the owner decided to send his son, reasoning that they would surely respect him. However, their response was worse in that they recognized him as the heir and decided to kill him, so that they could receive his inheritance. In the end, they did exactly that. Jesus then asked His listeners what they thought should be the fate of the guilty parties. Their judgment was instantaneous and critical. In Matthew 21:41 (LITV) we see their response. "Bad men! He will miserably destroy them and will rent out his vineyard to other vinedressers who will give him the fruits of their seasons." In fact, Jesus went even further when He added, "Did you never read in the Scriptures, 'The stone which the builders rejected, this One has become the head of the corner; this is the Lord's doing, and it is marvellous in our eyes?' Therefore I say to you, the kingdom of God shall be taken from you and given to a nation bringing out its fruits."

When the chief priests and elders heard the parable they knew He spoke of them. In the same way Joseph's brothers envied and hated him because of his father's love, the Jewish leaders envied and hated Jesus because of His Father's love. Matthew 27:18 says that even

Pilate was able to discern this and tried hard to release Jesus during the kangaroo court proceedings that saw the same leaders prefer a seditionist murderer to Jesus when they were given a choice. (See Matthew 27:19-24.) No other religious group attracts as much ire and opposition as true practicing Christians. To understand such hostility we must remember that, like Jesus, who gave that revelation to the world, we dare to call God our Father.

That truth is evidence of deep intimacy which no other world religion can offer, and that reason alone produces envy. We are also different because we claim the inheritance already set aside for us as sons and daughters of the Most High God. And not only that, but Christianity actually demands a lifestyle change. In the end, it is the submission to a higher authority that goes against the old nature's desire to be a "god" unto oneself as exemplified by secular humanism. The agnostic, the atheist and other religious people all hate us because they are irritated by our unquenchable, iridescent glow, which is fuelled by the incandescence of Abba Father's love.

"All I Have To Do Is Dream..."

As if Joseph's situation wasn't already bad enough he had a dream and excitedly told his brothers about it. He was clearly expecting them to share his excitement, but instead it only increases their ire. It is obvious that he is naïvely unaware of their negative response. In the dream he and his brothers were binding sheaves when suddenly his sheaf rose and stood upright, while his brothers' sheaves bowed down to his. In the process of explaining the dream he used the word "obeisance," which means to prostrate in homage to royalty or to God. However, it wasn't often used in the sense of worship.

In fact, in his notes on the use of the word, Spiros Zodhiates says it meant to "specifically bow down to prostrate oneself as an act of respect before a superior being" (Spiros Zodhiates Lexical Aids to the Old Testament Hebrew-Greek Key Word Study Bible, p. 1660).

Obviously Joseph's brothers understood all too well the meaning of the word. They responded with disdain, "Shalt thou indeed reign over us? Or shalt thou have dominion over us?" It was clear that they grasped the spiritual nature of the dream, and felt desperate to silence once and for all the rants of the dreamer.

If they had perceived the dream as mere youthful flights of fancy it would have been discounted and ignored. But they understood that Joseph had found favour with God, and that he would eventually prosper and reign over them, and it only infuriated them further. Who could have nudged him toward such unrealistic ideals? Who, indeed?

Meanwhile Joseph had another prophetic dream and again, naively related the same to his envious siblings. In this dream the sun, moon and eleven stars made obeisance to Joseph. We know that Joseph discerned the meaning of this dream, because he shared the first dream that pertained to his brothers with them only. He however went as far as to share this second dream with his father, who responded with amazement, "Shall I and thy mother and thy brethren indeed come to bow down ourselves to thee to the earth?" Here we get a clue that Jacob, who had a prophetic gift, had not only been encouraging his young son's dreams, but sought to ensure that Joseph was exalted to a position of prominence. In fact, he would do all he could to nurture his God-given vision towards fulfilment.

All Power...

The dreams are related in that they both speak of dominion. The first refers to dominion in the field. Jesus' parables of the Sower, the Wheat and Tares, and the Mustard Seed, all refer back to the phrase in Matthew 13:38 where we see that "the field is the world." In Joseph's dream the sun, moon and stars represent the heavens, thus guaranteeing Joseph dominion over both the heavens and the earth.

Notice the reactions to this information. The wise observed, or received the saying, while fools were envious, unaware that wrath kills the foolish man and envy destroys the silly one. (See Job 5:2.) Proverbs 14:30 also reminds us that a sound heart is the life of the flesh; but envy the rottenness of the bones. Here we see that Joseph's brothers still had not caught the revelation that God is not partial, plays no favourites, and will do for all what He has done for one. They did not realize that Joseph was simply a forerunner pointing the way to Christ.

Jesus, The Forerunner

In all these things Joseph typified Christ. And just as dreams foretold Joseph's incredible future, so angels prophesied about Jesus' greatness, while shepherds stood witness. Like Jacob, Jesus' Father spoke to His Son about the greatness that lay ahead. Isaiah 45:23 says: "I have sworn by myself, the word is gone out of my mouth in righteousness, and shall not return, that unto me every knee shall bow and every tongue shall swear." These very words were attributed to God Himself by the Prophet Isaiah. God, in turn, empowers His Son with those words. Paul explains this to the Philippians (in Chapter 2 verses 9-11, BBE) when he says, "For this reason God has put Him in the highest place and has given to Him the name which is greater than every name; so that at the name of Jesus every knee may be bent of those in heaven and those on earth and those in the underworld, and every tongue may give witness that Jesus Christ is Lord to the glory of God the Father."

Paul makes it clear that Jesus' dominion was in heaven, on earth, and under the earth. In the same way, Jacob's words and Joseph's dreams all prophesied of Joseph's dominion, which would manifest, but not till he had suffered, and learned obedience through suffering. (See Hebrews 5:8.) What a perfect picture of Christ.

The Plot Thickens

As the story goes on we see Joseph's brothers seeking pastures for their father's flock. Their search takes them to Shechem, and it isn't long before their father sends Joseph to check on their welfare. In spite of their previously envious, scheming behaviour, their loving father does not give them what they deserve, but rather deals with them according to his tender mercies, and sends someone to ask after their welfare.

You will notice that, in this story Jacob is called by that name the first two times he is mentioned. The third time, (note that the number three is the number of resurrection) he is called by his covenant name, Israel," which signifies not only his love for his son, but is also symbolic of God's love for Jesus.

In our story, "Israel" now says to Joseph, "Come, and I will send you unto them" (Isaiah 6:8). Echoing this phrase, the Prophet Isaiah demonstrates how God spoke those same words to Jesus, as a result of the plan designed before time began, that would offer salvation to mankind. In fact, in the year that leprous King Uzi died, Isaiah saw a vision of Jesus, as the King on His glorious throne. As a result Isaiah saw his own wretchedness. Then he heard the Lord say, "Whom shall I send, and who will go for us?" Instantly and enthusiastically Isaiah responded, "Here am I; send me" (Isaiah 6:8).

Note here that Isaiah's response is exactly the same as Joseph's—"Hinneh," which in the Hebrew, means, "Behold, lo! See, I am at your beck and call."

This is so important because it is designed by God to answer a common argument against the divinity of Christ by suggesting He was just a good man or a guru, an opportunist who saw a need and a vacuum and was "sharp" enough to fill it. In John 3:17 (KJV) we read: "For God sent not His Son into the world to condemn the world, but that the world through Him might be saved." In that most famous of night encounters Jesus told Nicodemus about being born again. The fact that Jesus was sent by God is reiterated at least another thirty times, two-thirds of these in John's writing. David's messianic prophecy puts the last nail in the scoffer's coffin when he acts as an oracle for the Christ, who states that in keeping with what was previously written about Him in the entirety of the holy writ, He had come to do the will of Father God. (See Psalm 40:7.) In fact, the Messiah's coming was planned so well in advance that it actually involved the preparation of a physical body for Jesus' earthly ministry. (See Hebrews 10:5.)

So Joseph was sent by his father, out of Hebron to Shechem where his brothers were supposed to be. They had, however left and gone on to Dothan. Hebron means "alliance or partnership" while Shechem means "back or shoulder" and Dothan means "two wells or cisterns."

All this is designed by God to tell a story: Joseph, a type of Jesus, was sent out of the vale of Hebron, that is, in partnership with his father, Jacob, a type of God, to secure the peace of his ten brothers, who were a type of natural Israel under the Law. They were supposed to be in Shechem, which we recall means "back or shoulder." Isaiah helps us understand that the government was to be on the shoulder of the Messiah. (See Isaiah 9:6.) Since the shoulder is a part of the body and not the head, this is a veiled way of declaring that the dominion and headship of Jesus is to be executed by His body. Shechem is then the place of dominion. So instead of staying in the place of dominion, they had wandered off to the place of two wells, two cisterns, or two pits. This is a picture of double-mindedness, which leads to instability, as outlined by the Apostle James. (See James 1:8.) Like Adam, they had wilfully left the place of obedience and dominion and fallen into the place of servitude to sin and Satan. Not surprisingly, it was in this place of two pits that they received the incitement (inspired from the pits of hell) to shed the blood of their brother. Guess where they decided to put him? You are right--the place where they now dwelt and drew inspiration, the well, the pit, the empty cistern!

The symbolism of this despicable act is again relived in the life of the Prophet Jeremiah who, because of his prophecies, a type of Joseph's dreams, was cast by his brethren, the Jews into the dungeon of Melchior. In the dungeon (ber) which incidentally is the same word used for pit, cistern or well, we are told there was no water and Jeremiah sank in the mire. (See Jeremiah 38:6.)

In yet another era, David would, in his Psalm of deliverance, declare that he waited patiently for the Lord who inclined unto him, heard his cry and brought him up also out of a horrible pit, out of the miry clay! (See Psalm 40:2.) Again the word "pit" is the same as it was with Joseph and Jeremiah. The writer of the Book of Hebrews explains that this Psalm is messianic and that David's experience was only recorded because it was a prophetic picture of Christ's descent to the pit after His crucifixion. It was also from this pit that He was subsequently resurrected. (See Hebrews 10:5-7.) Paul also alludes to this in his letter to the Ephesians declaring that as He arose He gave the fivefold ministry gifts to members of His body. (See Ephesians 4:8-10.)

Perhaps right now you cynically ask: "How do all these pit-stops affect me today?" How do they help me with my unpaid bills and my lonely single life, unemployment, marital strife, wayward offspring or failing business? The Prophet Zechariah telescopes into the future, our future, when he records the Father's assurance to Jesus: "As for thee also, by the blood of thy covenant I have sent forth prisoners out of the pit, wherein is no water" (Zechariah 9:11). And to us he says, "Turn you to the stronghold, ye prisoners of hope; even today do I declare that I will render double on to thee" (Isaiah 9:12). We are thus guaranteed that no matter how deep the pit we are in, we will overcome by the blood of the Lamb's covenant and the word of our testimony. (See Revelation 12:11.) We will also receive double for our trouble. (See Isaiah 40:2 & 61:7.)

Jealousy was the motivation for what his brothers did to Joseph. It was also the reason for Saul's relentless pursuit of David, for what the leaders did to Jeremiah, and what their counterparts did to Jesus. In Matthew 27:18 we see Pilate acknowledge that much: "For he knew that for envy they had delivered him." Later on, the Apostle Paul would be pursued and dragged before councils and rulers for the same reason. And in Matthew 5:10-12 and John 15:20 Jesus warned us to expect persecutions for our faith's sake.

Today in modern day Europe, liberalism and religious freedom is extended to Muslims, Eastern occultic religions, the magical arts, mediums, and nearly everyone else. However, the moment you mention the name of Jesus Christ, you suffer opposition, discrimination and outright scorn. Nowhere in the world is it politically correct to be a Christian.

Back to our story: for all his other faults, Reuben is primarily responsible for saving Joseph's life. The pit was his compromise till he could devise a method of getting Joseph out of the hands of his other siblings in order to return him to their father. He was not a part of the plot first to kill, then to sell Joseph. However he did not possess the moral fibre and strength of character to stop his younger brothers from doing the wrong thing. This is what I call the Eli complex--that is, knowing what the right thing to do is, but being too spineless, too partisan or too selfish to do it. In the end this would cost Eli the rulership of Israel and the death of both his sons in one day. In the same way Reuben suffered the loss of his rights and privileges as the firstborn. Although this was mostly for sleeping with his father's concubine, his lack of backbone also contributed in no small measure, to his fate.

Having been dissuaded from killing Joseph, they stripped him of his coat of many colours, as if that could strip away his father's favour. But that was impossible, because, coat or no coat, he was truly the apple of his father's eye. No doubt you have heard the saying, "Clothes do not make the man." That was certainly true in this case. In fact, Joseph would go on to fulfil his dreams without the coat!

In the same way Jesus was stripped of his coat by soldiers who then cast lots to see who would win it. Yet, the coat made little difference to that soldier, because with or without that coat, the Father still favoured His Son.

In Genesis 37:25 we read that once his brothers tossed him in the pit they "sat down to eat bread." This is the height of callousness and symptomatic of their hard hearts. At this point Joseph, in anguish of soul, tried to appeal to their better judgment, but they were too far gone to care.

Like the children of Israel in Exodus 32:6, we see that when Moses went up to the mountain, "...the people sat down to eat and drink, and rose up to play." In his letter to the Galatians, the Apostle Paul described the reprobates of that day, saying their god was their belly, meaning they put their fleshly desires above all else. This is exemplified by the fact that they lifted up their eyes and saw only a company of Ishmaelite's, the carnal product of Abraham and Sarah's biggest mistake.

When their brother had lifted up his eyes and looked up, in contrast, he saw the sun, moon and stars and sheaves that arose. Ishmael was Abraham's seed, Isaac's brother after the flesh and "...as then he that was born after the flesh persecuted him that was born after the Spirit, even so it is now" (Galatians 4:29). The New Testament application is that it was Jesus' brothers after the flesh who sold Him into the hands of the Gentiles.

That said, the Ishmaelites were coming from Gilead, the hill of witness, to where Joseph was, with their camels, which represent transportation through the wilderness, bearing spices, balm and myrrh. This immediately speaks to me of the visit of the magi at the birth of Jesus when they brought treasures of gold, which speaks of Jesus' divine nature; frankincense which points to his priestly office; and myrrh which was to prepare Him for his sacrificial death. (See Matthew 2:11.)

Immediately, another icon leaps out at me as I recall another incident where Jesus is invited to a meal in the house of Simon the leper. (See Matthew 26:6 & Mark 14:3-9.) As He eats, a woman with an alabaster box of spikenard, a rare and expensive ointment of pure fragrant liquid, breaks her box and pours its contents over the Messiah's head.

This unusual act evokes indignation among others, who decry the apparent waste of valuable resources, saying it could have been sold and the proceeds given to the poor. Jesus, however, defends her action, and praises her, but most importantly He reveals the spiritual import of what she did: "She hath done what she could: she is come aforehand to anoint my body to the burying" (Mark 14:8). Another clue to the spiritual significance of this woman's action is the fact that spikenard is also defined by Strong's as meaning "trustworthy, i.e. genuine (unadulterated)." What she did was an act of genuine, pure, and unadulterated worship borne of complete confidence in the trustworthy nature of the object of her worship.

Did you know there is an Old Testament equivalent of this woman? The Shulamite woman, who was the king's sweetheart, is a perfect picture of the bride of Christ, and is described this way in the Song of Solomon 1:3 (KJV): "While the king sitteth at his table, my spikenard sendeth forth the smell thereof. A bundle of myrrh is my well-beloved unto me..." So like Mary, the Shulamite woman poured the sweet fragrance of her spikenard on the king while he reclined at table. Awesome! What is that costly thing in your life that you must sacrifice for the King and His kingdom's sake? What price, are you willing to pay to honour God and to comfort even the most insignificant member of His body?

In the same way that Joseph was carried by the Ishmaelites in the midst of spicery, balm and myrrh down to Egypt, so Jesus was anointed by Mary unto His burial and descent to the grave, the pit. In the end the woman's act would be an eternal witness, a memorial wherever the gospel is preached.

In the same way we will do many things by the leading of the Holy Spirit that will outlive us and continue to testify of us long after we have gone to glory.

Judah took up where Reuben left off in that he served as an advocate for the preservation of Joseph's life. Judah's name, of course, means praise. A praiser's conscience is always more sensitive than others around him because of his rapport with God. This is because praise leads to depths of intimacy with God that makes the praiser privy to aspects of God's character, will and purposes not available to the casual bystander or the lukewarm believer. Thus the praiser will exert influence and leadership over his peers, siblings and compatriots. God had decreed that the sceptre of rulership would not depart from Judah, the house of praise till it gave birth to God's fullness in the person of His Son. Judah's brethren, it is written, were content. In the Hebrew this literally means they hearkened. Though they did not hearken to Joseph's cry or to the voice of their consciences, they hearkened to Judah. Judah therefore should have used this influence positively. Though he failed this test, he would later be tested again along the same lines when Joseph was prime minister in Egypt.

Joseph was sold to the Ishmaelites for twenty pieces of silver. In Bible numerology twenty is the number of redemption and silver is the metal that denotes redemption. This is exemplified by an instruction given to Moses in the thirtieth chapter of Exodus. Everyone above twenty years of age was to give an offering unto the Lord. The prescribed offering was half a shekel of silver, which worked out to– not surprisingly--twenty gerahs. Because each soul was of equal value in the sight of God, and the price of the atonement or redemption for each soul was the same; the rich could not give more, and the poor could not give less. (See Exodus 30:12-16.) Thus we see the combination of the number twenty and the silver metal symbolising the cost of atonement for an adult Israelite.

Armed with this information, it begins to make more sense that one of the twelve disciples, Judas Iscariot covenanted with the chief priests to betray Jesus for thirty pieces of silver. One wonders why there appears to be a disparity between type and anti-type, between shadow and reality. In other words, if twenty is the number of redemption, why did Judah betray Jesus for thirty, not twenty pieces of silver? Types, shadows and symbols suffer from the obvious weakness of not being able to completely portray what they represent. For example, on the Great Day of Atonement, because the goat could not typify both the death, and resurrection of Christ, two goats had to be used.

Judas' actions were pointing to much more than the price of redemption. Thirty, as a number, in its secondary application, is the number of maturity as evidenced by the fact that traditionally that was when Jewish leaders were considered of suitable age to assume most positions of authority. This was the age when Jesus began His ministry, and when Joseph became prime minister and David became king of the whole of Israel. In the Bible, thirty is primarily the number for the price of blood.

Judas Iscariot, after betraying Jesus, did regret his action, but selfishly was more concerned with how its adverse consequences would affect him. In that frame of mind he returned to the chief priests to voice his feelings that what was done, could be undone. So though there was regret and possibly remorse, it was a vain repentance with no effective change of heart. (See Matthew 27:3.) This can be contrasted with Peter's repentance, and indeed that of all the other disciples who also denied the Lord but whose hearts were broken over their behaviour.

We must always check our hearts whenever we have missed the mark spiritually. We must ensure that we are not just repenting because we are afraid to face the consequences. Rather, there must be heartfelt sorrow at the pain we have caused our heavenly Father, a conscious effort to detest the actions that have broken His heart, and a resolve, unlike the dog that returns to its vomit, never again to repeat the sin. We are to "go, and sin no more" (John 8:11).

Judas' plea met with absolutely no sympathy from the chief priests, so he threw down the pieces of silver in the temple, departed and went and hanged himself. The response of the chief priests is mind-boggling. In the religious sense it was clear that the money could not be put into the temple's treasury because as they themselves said, it was "the price of blood." In effect they were calling it blood money, thereby testifying against themselves that they were complicit in, if not outright responsible, for the shedding of innocent blood. Hypocritically, they would not pollute the temple by putting dirty money into its treasury, but they could murder an innocent man with no compunction whatsoever! No wonder Jesus had earlier heaped woes upon their heads and called them children of those who killed the prophets and those who would themselves kill, crucify, scourge and persecute those He would yet send to them. After they considered the matter they used the money to buy a potter's field in which strangers would be buried.

It is always fascinating to see how God uses everything, even those intended for evil by malicious, vile and degenerate men, for His good purpose. Since thirty is the number of the price of blood, and silver denotes redemption, this means the betrayal of Jesus caused His blood to be shed as payment for the redemption of the world. The mention of the field ties in with Jesus' parable in which He explains: "The field is the world" (Matthew 13:38).

The issue of the potter has a dual application. First, as Jeremiah explained, God is the potter and we are the clay. Second, after the fall of man in the Garden of Eden, God declared that unregenerate man is dust, and dust would be the serpent's food all the days of his life. In effect, the unsaved man is always food for the devil! Clay, also, is literally dust and water. The water of the Word mingled with the dust of the earth, makes good material from which the Divine Potter can fashion vessels unto honour, particularly as the field has been bought by the blood of the Lamb. The strangers, that is those estranged from God by sin, and buried in this field of the world have been redeemed and set free. Alleluia! Jesus' blood purchased, redeemed and set us free, therefore we have no right to be bound, and the enemy, his agents, and the travails of life are not at liberty to keep us bound. We have been bought with an invaluable price and we no longer belong to ourselves; nor can anyone else lay claim to us. (See Colossians 3:3.) It is therefore incumbent upon us, as God's Word advises, to glorify God in our bodies and our spirit, which are His. (See 1 Corinthians 6:20.)

Once Joseph was sold, he was brought into Egypt. Similarly, once Jesus was betrayed, He was brought before the worldly rulers--Pilate and Herod who symbolised Egypt, the pinnacle of carnal, worldly power. Reuben returned to the pit where he had persuaded his brothers to keep Joseph temporarily, only to find him gone, sold by his siblings. Reuben's apparent distress eloquently testifies to the fact that he was neither a part of the plot to kill Joseph nor the plot to sell him. The plot, in all likelihood, was the brainchild of the sons of the maids, Bilhah and Zilpah. This hypothesis may be corroborated by the assertion at the very beginning of Joseph's story that he "was with the sons of Bilhah, and with the sons of Zilpah, his father's wives: and Joseph brought unto his father their evil report" (Genesis 37:2).

No doubt, these boys grew up with a feeling of inferiority premised on the knowledge that they were the children of slaves, maid-servants. They would further share the insecurity of all the other sons who, in their father's eyes, were little more than second-class citizens. Joseph was his "only begotten son"! And though it was in his power Reuben did not do enough to deliver Joseph. Like Pontius Pilate had before him, merely washing his hands was not enough to absolve him of the brutal murder of the innocent Christ. Like Eli, the protest of his sons' evil actions was, in itself, not enough when he had the power to do more. Reuben had a character flaw, a moral weakness that kept him from taking a bold stand against sin. Two incidents prove this point: he went along with the lie his brothers told about Joseph's fate, and, he slept with his father's concubine, Bilhah. As the firstborn, he should have been highly motivated to do the right thing. The same is true of us; if we want the double portion blessing, we must accept double the responsibility. It is little wonder then, that Jacob's blessing was not passed on to Reuben.

Of Goats, Blood, And The Like

This brings us to the next part of this interesting multi-faceted saga. The brothers killed a kid goat and dipped Joseph's coat of many colours in the blood. Here, many icons begin to pop up. The Hebrew word for "killed" is sachet, which means to slaughter (in sacrifice or massacre). By using that choice of words God introduces and highlights the central principle—the principle of substitution, which resonates both overtly and subtly throughout the Scriptures.

The brothers thought they were merely killing the goat, but it was actually a sacrifice designed to take the place of Joseph who had to lay down his life for the ministry that lay ahead of him, to ultimately save the lives of his brothers as well as the fledgling nation of Israel. And while he had done nothing wrong and did not deserve to die, he was, nevertheless, sentenced to death by his own brothers. It is not surprising that the word chosen is that for a "he-goat." Note also that the coat was dipped "in the blood" (an alternate rendering of the word dipped is "plunged." (See Strong's Dictionary of Hebrew and Greek.)

All these immediately bring to mind the Great Day of Atonement when two goats were chosen by the High Priest who cast lots to determine which would be sacrificed as a sin offering for the people, and which would be the scapegoat, released into the wilderness. The blood of the slaughtered goat was to be sprinkled upon and before the mercy seat "to make an atonement for the holy place, because of the uncleanness of the children of Israel, and because of their transgressions in all their sins" (Leviticus 16:16). Jesus became the fulfilment of all these Old Testament types when He initially became the sin offering whose blood was shed for the atonement of mankind's sin-nature. Secondly, He became the innocent scapegoat whose Father transferred the sins of the world upon Him, in a manner of speaking. Little wonder then that when John the Baptist saw Jesus by the Jordan, he said, "Behold the Lamb of God that takes away the sin of the world" (John 1:29 KJV).

The word "atone," is a compound of two English words which clearly reveal God's intention to reconcile fallen man to Himself so they would again be "at one." Today, even as believers our greatest challenge is dealing with the guilt and condemnation of our past sins. The knowledge that our "garments" have been dipped or plunged in the blood of the scapegoat who is our Saviour, should reassure us that: "There is therefore now no condemnation to them which are in Christ Jesus, who walk not after the flesh, but after the Spirit" (Romans 8:1).

Joseph's brothers then took Joseph's coat to their father claiming they found it and asked him to determine whether it belonged to Joseph. Their motives were probably twofold: deferring suspicion away from themselves and getting back at their father for his favouritism.

Israel's reaction was predictable and only enraged them further, justifying their evil act. "It is my son's coat," he lamented, "an evil beast hath devoured him; Joseph is without doubt rent in pieces" (Genesis 37:33). He then proceeds to rip asunder his own clothes and to clothe himself with sackcloth, the traditional mourning garb. If his sons thought that Joseph's absence would open their father's heart to them they were badly mistaken. In fact, all attempts to comfort Israel met with stubborn resistance and a pledge that only death would end his pining for "my son."--a grating phrase he continuously used as though the others were not his sons!

Israel instantly recognises the coat as a gift he had given Joseph. This coat represents favour, blessings, and all that comes with the anointing of the Father. John the Baptist throws light on the nature of these things when he testifies: "A man can receive nothing, except it be given him from heaven" (John 3:27). Paul says it is because of God that we are blessed, which is why we have no reason for pride or arrogance. (See 1 Corinthians 4:7.) Hebrews 5:4 says no man takes the honour of priesthood upon himself, because, it is only given by God. Lastly, James 1:17 tells us that every good and perfect gift comes from God. Jesus is the antitype of all these gifts. Israel's lamentation over Joseph is loaded with pictures that bear closer examination. "An evil beast hath devoured him..." (See Genesis 37:33.) This was a prophetic statement whose significance unfolds in the New Testament. In 2 Peter 2:12 Peter refers to false teachers as beasts. Jude verse 10 calls them irrational brute beasts.

So just as an evil beast was supposed to have devoured Joseph, the evil beast of mankind's reprobate nature devoured our heavenly Joseph, Jesus the Christ. This fact was corroborated by Jesus Himself when the scribes and Pharisees asked Him for a sign to prove He was the Messiah; His response was that no sign would be given to their wicked and adulterous generation except that of Jonah in the belly of the whale for three days and three nights. (See Matthew 12:38-40.)

By this Jesus meant that, just like the whale swallowed Jonah, the evil beast of death swallowed Jesus, holding Him captive three days. A whale is--wait for it--a big fish! Joshua, the Greek transliteration of whose name is Jesus (see Hebrews 4:8), was the son of Nun. Nun in the Hebrew means fish. Joshua "the son of fish" who divided the Promised Land for the children of Israel, is a type of Jesus Christ, "the

Son of Man." Recall that Jesus always referred to Himself as the "son of man." So as Jonah was swallowed by a big fish, so Jesus was swallowed by a big fish, the evil beast, the reprobate nature of Adam. Thus, God made He who knew no sin to become sin for us, so that we could become God's righteousness in Him, Jesus Christ. Without realizing it Israel was thus speaking prophetically, like Ananias and Caiaphas did, about the Christ. Because he was functioning in his prophetic office, Joseph could not die till his father had declared him dead. On the cross, Jesus would never have died till He gave up the ghost in obedience to the Father's will: "Father, into thy hands I commend my spirit" (Luke 23:46).

The good news is that Jesus, being innocent, "...God hath raised up, having loosed the pains of death: because it was not possible that He should be holden of it" (Acts 2:4, KJV). Therefore like Paul in 1 Corinthians 15:57 we can boldly declare: "But thanks be to God, which giveth us the victory through our Lord Jesus Christ." The depth of Israel's grief over the "death" of his son is, no doubt, a good picture of the intense anguish God the Father felt when His Son had to endure an agonizing and undeserved death on the cross.

Worse still, nothing could assuage the despondency God felt about being separated from His Son. Such a thing had never occurred before and will never occur again. Even if someone understood the impact of this incident (and no one did!) there could be no comfort for the Father till resurrection morning. "Thus his father wept for him" (Genesis 37:35). The application of this for the believer is that once we have experienced the incredible "bottomless-pit" feeling that occurs when sin separates us from God we have a strong incentive to flee from sin and run back to God. If we fall into sin, we are to repent by confessing and forsaking such sins, so that fellowship with our Father is restored as soon as possible. (See 1 John 1:7-9.) Joseph's story ends at this point with the assertion that the Midianites sold him in Egypt to Potiphar, a courtier in Pharaoh's employ, a captain of the guard, which literally means, chief of the slaughter men, or executioners.

A closer examination will reveal the symbolism of these things. Midian means strife; Egypt means black, Pharaoh is the sun and Potiphar means belonging to the sun. Recall that we were told "...and his brothers envied him..." (Genesis 37:11). James 3:16 tells us: "For where envying and strife is, there is confusion and every evil work." Matthew 27:18 says that Pilate "knew that for envy they had delivered Him,"--that is Jesus.

Putting it all together, a spiritual picture emerges: envy and strife led to the evil work of selling the Lord Jesus Christ into the blackness of death and hell for three days and three nights by the pharaoh of hell, who assigned the chief of the executioners and his subordinates to ensure that He did not escape. Nahum 1:9 assures us that affliction will not arise a second time. This is good news for the believer: Jesus was sold to the blackness of death so we will never again be separated from God. Alleluia! His death was my death; now His story is my story. As Paul said, "I have been put to death on the cross with Christ; still I am living; no longer I, but Christ is living in me; and that life which I now am living in the flesh I am living by faith, the faith of the Son of God, who loved me and gave His life for me" (Galatians 2:20, BBE). What a powerful truth on which to end the first part of the Joseph saga.

CHAPTER TWO

WHEN PRAISE BETRAYS

In a change of scene we see the story shift to focus on Joseph's brother Judah. Many biblical scholars believe that Judah's story is not a chronological one directly following Joseph's journey to Egypt, but a parenthetical sidetrack to address some issues of divine interest. We are told that it came to pass that "Judah went down from his brethren, and turned in to a certain Adullamite, whose name was Hirah." (Genesis 38:1). The New Testament uses the Old Testament to demonstrate why the children of God are not to be unequally yoked with unbelievers, in the same way the children of Israel were not to be yoked with Gentiles. It is important to note that the issue is not one of racial superiority or segregation, but of moral and ethical purity.

Here God was trying to make the point that if you lie down with dogs you will get up with fleas. Admonishing the Corinthian church Paul quotes the Greek poet and comic Menander when he declares: "Stop being led astray (figuratively--being deceived); Evil associations corrupt good habits (or morals)" (1 Corinthians 15:33, ALT). Proverbs 13:20 warns that: "He that walketh with wise men shall be wise: but a companion of fools shall be destroyed."

God went to great lengths to emphasize that the Jews were a holy people, chosen to be separated unto Him. He uses the word "peculiar" which in Hebrew, implies, "a private possession or property, which one has personally acquired and carefully preserves." No doubt, Peter had this in mind when he postulated that the Church is a chosen generation, a royal priesthood, a holy nation, a peculiar people, called to show forth the praises of He who called us out of darkness into his marvellous light. (See 1 Peter 2:9.) Titus 2:15 bears witness that Jesus' death was to "redeem us from all iniquity, and purify unto Himself a peculiar people, zealous of good works." The argument as Paul outlined it is that if we were purchased at great cost by God, we are fully accountable to Him and are thus not at liberty to do anything that would grieve Him.

In other words, it is out of the question for a believer to marry, or have close association with those who are not of like mind. Now that does not mean we refuse to associate with unbelievers, otherwise how will they see our light if we hide it under a bushel?

Judah, we are told, went down from his brethren. The Hebrew word used for down is yarad, which according to Strong means to descend to a lower region such as the shore, a boundary, the enemy, etc. But it also has a figurative meaning, which is, to fall. It is obvious that Judah's is neither a geographical nor a topographical descent but a moral one. The departure from God's Word and people, whether by disobedience, rebellion, foolishness or even ignorance, will always cause a downward spiral. The implications are clear when we see that God said to Isaac, using the same word: "Go not down into Egypt..." even though there was a famine in the land and in direct contrast to his father Abraham who had, under similar circumstances, gone "down to Egypt" with near-disastrous consequences.

The spiritual implication is best illustrated in the story of Samson in Judges 14:1-12: "And Samson went down to Timnath, and saw a woman in Timnath of the daughters of the Philistines." The level of the moral descent becomes clear when we see that the Philistines were not only "uncircumcised" idolaters but were also the imperial and feudal lords over God's people. To relate with her, Samson had to go down. Reading on: "And he came up, and told his father and his mother..." In effect, to relate to his parents, he had to ascend to their spiritual heights. Samson's parents tried hard to discourage him and educate him on the dangers of an unequal yoke. They even used a word to describe the Philistines that David would later use to describe Goliath--"uncircumcised." We see that Samson refused to heed his parents' pleas: "Get her for me; for she pleases me well" (Judges 14:3). This phrase in the literal Hebrew could be rendered: "She is right in mine eyes." The Book of Proverbs warns us about such lustful, carnal desires: "There is a way which seemeth right unto a man, but the end thereof are the ways of death" (Proverbs 14:12, KJV). When they failed to convince Samson, they decided to cause it to work for good and reluctantly accompanied him to Timnath. Judges 14:5 then says: "Then went Samson down, and his father and his mother, to Timnath..." Here we need to note that our actions, whether good or bad, affect not just us but those around us. The text goes on: "And he went down, and talked with the woman; and she pleased Samson well." Finally, the spiritual descent is complete when we are told: "So his father went down unto the woman..." (Judges 14:10), and all that is left is the consequences of his rebellion, ignorance and disobedience.

In the same way, Judah's descent caused him to make friends, and keep company with a certain Adullamite named Hirah, whose name means "nobility" or "splendour." Being of spiritually noble stock himself, could it be Hirah's splendour and nobility that attracted Judah? If it was, Judah soon realised that all that glitters is not gold, and there is a vast difference between natural glory and spiritual splendour. In fact, the things that are most highly esteemed with men are nothing before God. Hirah's nobility was meaningless without faith in the God of Israel. Once Judah had begun his journey down this slippery slope, it was only a matter of time before he went the rest of the way. "And Judah saw there a daughter of a certain Canaanite, whose name was Shuah and he took her, and went in unto her" (Genesis 38:2). Shuah means a halloo, a cry, riches and depression. The picture God is painting here is that no matter how rich you are depression will always lead to a cry for help. Also, depression often gives birth to suicide. Note that there is no mention of marriage but simply that Judah took her and went in unto her. Those who go down do not fear God and have little or no regard for the institution of marriage; fornication and co-habitation are therefore rife in their lives. Eventually, Judah probably legitimized the relationship because later in the narrative, she is referred to as "Judah's wife." (See Genesis 38:12.)

Judah's wife bore him three sons, Er, Onan and Shelah. It is said of Judah that he was in Chezib when his wife bore Shelah. Chezib means false or falsified. Judah was in the place of falsehood and did not even realise it! But God's presence would not depart from him; in fact he was convicted of his sin. His reawakened conscience dictated that he not allow his sons to make the same mistakes he had made. From that point on Judah did all he could to legitimise and secure the heritage of his sons, even searching to find a good wife for his first-born. The woman he found was called Tamar, which means to be erect, a (palm) tree, which would symbolize, as the very first Psalm declares, a righteous person, or as Prophet Isaiah declared "a tree of righteousness, the planting of the Lord" (Isaiah 61:3). However, because God considered Er to be a wicked man, He killed him. The word for evil is rah which means bad, naturally or morally evil. The word is also used for calamity, mischief, misery, sorrow, wrong and wretchedness. Though we do not know the details of Er's misdemeanours, any one of these terms show that he was evil enough for God to put him to death.

Now, it's important to know that there was no inherent wickedness in Judah's lineage; his great grandfather Abraham, was the father of faith; his grandfather was the willing sacrifice at Mount Moriah, and his father Jacob being a "plain" man. (See Genesis 25:27.) [The word "plain" is the Hebrew word tam, which according to Strong's Hebrew and Greek Dictionaries, means "complete; usually (morally) pious;

specifically gentle, dear:--coupled together, perfect, plain, undefiled, upright."] Since everything brings forth fruit after its kind, where then did Er's wickedness come from? Moses gives us a clue when he says in "...but for the wickedness of these nations the LORD doth drive them out from before thee" (Deuteronomy 9:4). The seed of wickedness was from Er's Canaanite roots. In effect, some of the dangers of unequal yoking which God had warned Moses about on Mount Sinai were manifest in Er. His younger brother, Onan was of the same stock and orientation, and proved to be equally as wicked. The tradition was that if an older brother died without offspring, his younger sibling was to marry his wife to raise children unto his name. This custom was later given legal backing when it was incorporated into the Mosaic laws. (See Deuteronomy 25:5.) This is closely allied to the concept of the Redeemer-kinsman which is highlighted in the story of Ruth and Boaz. Onan realised that by marrying Tamar, any children born to their union would be termed his brother's, and he did not want this. Instead of stating his objection like the nearer kinsman did to Boaz in the Book of Ruth (See Ruth 4:6), he consented. However to prevent Tamar from conceiving, he practiced coitus interruptus spilling his semen on the ground each time they had sex.

It is instructive that this method of birth control has come to be known as onanism! This displeased the Lord and He killed him as He had his brother before him. No doubt it was the pharisaic nature of Onan's actions that displeased God. To the casual observer, he appeared to be noble and to be doing the right thing, but this was a façade. Onan actually wanted power without accountability; pleasure without pressure; command without demand; authority without culpability; ability without dependability. This incidentally also has close ties with "the masturbation complex" and explains why God equally hates that activity, because it is sin and it is hedonistic, advocating pleasure without productivity.

Judah was now faced with a dilemma: he could give Tamar to his third son, Shelah as the custom required and thereby risk his death also or... the options were few. Like most men faced with tough choices Judah decided that, "procrastination is the better part of valour," (if I may be permitted to mix my metaphors!) "Procrastination is the thief of time." "Discretion is the better part of valour.") He promised Tamar that she would be married off to Shelah when he was older, though it appears that in his heart, he had no intention of keeping that promise, fearing that Tamar might " kill" or be responsible for the death of her new husband as with the former two. At some point Judah's wife died. After the traditional mourning time was complete he took comfort in his work. We are told he went up to his sheepshearers in...wait for this...Timnath, the same Timnath that Samson went down to, to seek his first wife who was of Philistine extraction. Judah, on his part, went down with his Canaanite, unbelieving friend, Hirah, the Adullamite.

There seems to be more to Timnath than meets the eye. It is not specifically mentioned, but it would appear that Judah, assisted by his friend, went illegally to Timnath to relieve his sexual tensions. Could this explain why his daughter-in-law, to whom he had made the promise he never intended to keep, decided to dress up as a harlot? Was whore-mongering a secret vice of Judah's, known only to members of his inner circle? Tamar hatched a plan that was both cunning and devious, like many people who dwell in accursed lands and cultures. Now, please know that the brilliance of a plan in no way implies the endorsement of God. James 3:15 expounds: "This wisdom descendeth not from above, but is earthly, sensual, devilish." This devilish wisdom was what moved the princes of this world to crucify the Lord of glory. Is this not reminiscent of the logic of Lot's two daughters, which caused them to orchestrate incestuous relations with their father and subsequently bear those two wicked nations of Moab and Ammon? Tamar justified her behaviour by saying she was merely frustrated after waiting indefinitely for a broken promise: "For she saw that Shelah was grown, and she was not given unto him to wife" (Genesis 38:14).

Food for the Devil

What is it that could possibly motivate Judah, a first-born of promise, and a man of praise, to go out and sleep with a harlot (See Genesis 38:23.) especially since he understood the deep shadow of shame the discovery of his iniquitous act would cast? What makes us as believers do equally shameful things even as born-again, blood-washed saints? The answer to this is our agamic nature, which if not put to death in Christ, can put us to death. In Romans 3:10 Paul warns us that there is none righteous, not even one! It is that same spirit that would make Judah's namesake betray the Messiah many years later. We must be on guard against the spirit of the son of perdition--the praise that betrays--and instead exalts the self. The Devil knows that we as humans are predisposed to wanting our own way, so he gives it to us, knowing it will ultimately lead us in the way of death.

Before Christ, we as human beings became proficient at sinning. From the time of the fall in Eden, the unregenerate person, by default, has belonged to Satan. From creation Adam was made the god of this world, but when he disobeyed God's command not to eat of the forbidden tree, he committed a great act of treason and handed over the title deed to his kingdom and his life, relinquishing the certificate of occupancy, to the Devil. And nothing has changed; when we surrender to fleshly lusts, to the self, it is, in essence, a surrender to sin and Satan. Romans 6:16 CEV tells us: "Don't you know that you are slaves of anyone you obey? You can be slaves of sin and die, or you can be obedient slaves of God and be acceptable to Him." So all Satan has to do to make you worship him is to encourage you to do what you like, what feels good: to be answerable to no one in your morality, least of all, God. This is the height of idolatry and the essence of Satan-worship. This explains why witchcraft, Baalism, and every form of occultism has at its crux, bacchanalian orgies and riotous, licentious and frenzied revelry, or more simply put, loose, immoral, self-indulgent behaviour.

We should also remember that when God judged Satan for instigating the fall of mankind He told him: "Dust shalt thou eat all the days of thy life..." Genesis 3:19). The man outside of Christ, the unregenerate man, the unsaved man, is dust and is therefore food for the devil! On the other hand, what was on Tamar's mind? What were her motives? Was she aware of the Abrahamic promise; was she intent on being a part of it at any and all costs? This would make her action one of faith albeit via misguided means. Was she simply self-seeking and self-serving, with the natural human (and particularly female) desire not to be alone? Was it a long-repressed or restrained desire for intimacy and/or sex? Whatever her motives, she was brilliant in her planning and flawless in her execution. She certainly had Judah (no pun intended)--hook, line and sinker. Luke 16:18 tells us: "For the children of this world are in their generation wiser than the children of light." Not only did she get Judah where she wanted him, but she also took out an insurance policy for when the consequences of her action would inevitably become manifest. Judah played right into her hands and like his uncle, Esau had done many years before, was ready to part with the emblems of his birthright, his authority, his status and his calling, for a moment of pleasure. No wonder God called Esau a profane man and a fornicator. (See Hebrews 13:6 KJV.) For sex and in place of the agreed payment of a kid from the flock, Judah left his signet, bracelets and staff!

After each action comes a consequence. Yes, we can choose our actions but we cannot choose their consequences, as these are preset.

Yet it is a measure of the grace of God and the enduring power of His love that even consequences can be alleviated by repentance and the calling upon the name of the Lord with a sincere heart. Judah sent the kid to "the harlot" to redeem his emblems. Guess who he sent it by-- "His friend the Adullamite." This phrase is a subtle but damning indictment of Judah, but his sending Hirah also shows you why he made friends with Hirah in the first place. They were obviously comrades-in-arms. When Hirah went, of course, he could not find Tamar since she had disguised herself as a whore and used a strategic but temporary location. The area citizens further certified that there was no resident harlot there, and Hirah reported this back to Judah. It is ironic that Judah, first of all, recognises that if he makes too much of a fuss about getting his emblems back, shame and disgrace would inevitably follow when his illicit deed is revealed. The second irony is that he makes a lame attempt to appear "honourable" by stating that he at least tried to redeem his pledge to the whore, and only failed only because of her disappearance from the agreed rendezvous spot. Three months later, as an African proverb puts it, the peel of the banana Judah ate underwater, began to float. In other words, the fruit of his deeds (or misdeeds) was revealed. When he learned that his widowed daughter-in-law was pregnant, he and others concluded that she had been sneaking out to play the harlot, engaging in prostitution. Judah's hasty reply to the accusation was (Genesis 38:24): "Bring her forth, and let her be burnt!" In other words he assumed the accusations to be true. It has been said, and wise men would scarcely disagree that assumption is the lowest form of knowledge, and most unreliable.

The Bible admonishes us to investigate and double-check every accusation and not to make a decision till we are very sure we have reached the truth. Even then, Deuteronomy 17-2-5 demands that it must be corroborated at the mouth of two or three witnesses. In the Sermon on the Mount Jesus warns that if we judge, we will inevitably be judged; because with the judgment we judge, we shall be judged and with the measure we use, it will be measured back to us. In other words, " what goes around comes around". He further warned that most times when we are concerned about the speck in other people's eyes, that is, their relatively minor faults, we ourselves are usually guilty of much greater faults (that is, the log in ours). (See Matthew 7:1-5.)

At this point Tamar played the ace up her sleeves. Judah acknowledged that she may have been justified because he had made her a promise he never intended to keep. In addition, he actually declared her to be more righteous than he was. The word for righteous is tsadaq, and it means "to be morally or forensically right; to clear oneself, to cleanse, to be straight, just, true, upright, righteous, to justify or be justified, to be restored, vindicated, on exonerated from wrongs." (Strong's Dictionaries of Hebrew and Greek)

This is not to suggest that Tamar's actions were morally right. Judah was suggesting that relative to his actions, she was in a sense vindicated. The story would have ended here but for the magnitude of God's loving kindness, and amazing grace. If God were a mere man this incident would have marked the end of both Judah's and Tamar's destinies. I believe it is only God's company that employs people whose job-performance histories declare them to be known serial failures, people with questionable parentage, established moral failings, obvious weaknesses and no lofty historical pedigree; in fact-- people acknowledged to be foolish! Instead Judah gets the right to become the forefather of the Messiah as we will discover on Israel's deathbed, later in our narrative. As for Tamar, she bears twins and with her son, Pharez, she is inducted into the genealogy of the Lord Jesus Christ as one of the few women alongside Rahab, Ruth, Bathsheba and Mary.

The Judah epic ends with the birth of Pharez and Zarah. Once again we see a repeat of conflict in the womb that took place between their grandfather and great uncle. Here again, the younger gets the birthright and the older must serve him. The point is that the battle is not always to the strong nor the race to the swift; it is never by might or power, but by God's Spirit. (See Zechariah 4:6.) This poem encapsulates the thought succinctly:

No matter your personal background

No matter where you were once found

No matter what your eyes have seen

No matter where your legs have been

No matter what your antecedents

No matter what the precedents

Whether released from life's dustbin

Or controlled by a life of sin

There's power mighty in the blood

To get you through fire and flood

God keeps no record of wrong

He'll turn your mourning into song

He doesn't mark iniquity

Though He enjoys ubiquity

To all members of the human race

He daily extends limitless grace.

One Cross is Enough © 2009 O.M. Efueye

Since the Judah chapter is considered to be parenthetical to the story, it stands to reason that God is trying to establish a contrast between the life of Judah and that of Joseph. Judah willingly went down from his father and brethren. He was thus a type of Adam who also, as an act of his will, went down from his Father.

This contrasts with Joseph who would never have been separated from his family but for the deception of his brothers. In this, he was like Jesus who would never have been separated from His heavenly Father, but for the sins of His brethren, mankind. Yet, Jesus was also like Adam and Judah in that He willingly went down from His Father, to graciously bring up or redeem His people. But while they went down for their own lusts and pleasure Jesus went down at great cost to Himself and to fulfil the good pleasure of the Father. Thus Jesus was separated from God so that God by His Spirit would never leave us or forsake us, and would indeed be with us till the end of the age. (See Hebrews 13:5 & Matthew 28:20.)

This assurance builds our faith even in the middle of our worst challenges. From that we can conclude that if He will never leave or forsake us, so it would be the height of ingratitude to abandon Him when the going gets tough. Judah pitched his tent with the people of the land to satisfy his personal lusts and desire. Joseph, on the other hand, joined himself to the people of the land to redeem his brethren and fulfil God's larger plan. Jesus joined Himself to His bride, the Church to redeem, sanctify, cleanse and perfect her. This is what the institution of marriage symbolises: a husband is to love his wife just as Christ loved the Church and gave Himself for her so that He would sanctify her by the Word which acts as a cleansing agent. It is that love that ultimately presents the wife to her husband without spot, wrinkle, blemish or any such thing. (See Ephesians 5:25-27.) If more men married for this reason and with this understanding, what a glorious difference the world would see!

Judah was tempted sexually and fell, while Joseph was sexually tempted but withstood the temptation and came out on top. In this, he was a picture of Jesus who was "in all points tempted like as we are, yet without sin." We can likewise overcome the temptations of an increasingly sex-crazed society, for: "There hath no temptation taken you but such as is common to man: but God is faithful, who will not suffer you to be tempted above that ye are able; but will with the temptation also make a way to escape, that ye may be able to bear it" (1 Corinthians 10:13 KJV). Judah bore two wicked sons whom God killed. Joseph bore two righteous sons whom God promoted, prospered, and inducted by grace into the family line of the Saviour. Jesus had two sons, the Jew and the Gentile, and both fell short of God's righteousness and deserved to die like Judah's sons. Jesus, however, died in their place thereby reconciling them to His Father and to one another, contrary to their natural, cultural, religious and historical inclinations.

Judah failed the moral test. Joseph passed the moral test. Jesus at the very beginning of His ministry faced the moral dilemma of taking the so-called shortcut offered Him by Satan, to regain the lost dominion over the earth by simply worshipping Satan. But Jesus passed that moral test by putting the deceiver to flight, reminding him that worship only belongs to God. No doubt Potiphar's wife offered Joseph a shortcut to freedom through the proposed affair, but nothing would sway him in the direction he knew to be wrong. We will always be lured by the prevalent fallacy of this generation, which believes that the end justifies the means. With God, however, motives are always more important than results. Men judge by externals and results, but God weighs the heart motives, as the Lord Himself informed Samuel when he was sent to anoint a king of one of Jesse's sons. (See 1 Samuel 16:7.) Finally, in spite of his very bad decisions and actions, Judah repented and God turned it around so that it worked together for good. On the other hand Joseph only did the things that pleased

God. If God raises the comparison, it is only because it is important to Him. The question is are you more like Judah or Joseph? Does your praise betray or does it do what it is designed for, to exalt the name and character of the Lord?

CHAPTER THREE

THE LORD WAS WITH JOSEPH

If you were to ask me to name the theme for the thirty-ninth chapter of Genesis, I would without hesitation say "...the LORD was with Joseph." For continuity's sake the story of Joseph resumes with the same information with which it ended before the diversion to Judah's story: Joseph was brought by the Midianites/Ishmaelites to Egypt and was bought by the Egyptian, Potiphar. Potiphar is said to be an officer (a word that in the Hebrew means among other things, a eunuch, chamberlain, courtier or officer) of Pharaoh. He was also said to be the captain of the guard, literally chief of the slaughter men or executioners. If I were to choose to whom I would be sold as a slave, I doubt if the chief executioner would win my vote!

The first new information we are given is: "And the LORD was with Joseph" (Genesis 39:2). This statement is poignant and relevant because in the light of the modern Christian's comfort theology, if God is with you, you do not suffer or encounter any hardship. However, one might question whether a person who was loved by his father but hated by his brothers, was truly favoured. Most Christians would not choose to be the target of an elaborate murder plot. Nor would they choose to be part of a plan where their own siblings conspired to eliminate them. Most of us would have felt long-forsaken had our brothers ignored our passionate pleas for mercy. Being sold like cattle for twenty pieces of silver would only have confirmed that conclusion. Yet, what lay ahead would be far worse. This is why it was necessary for Joseph to be fully persuaded that the Lord was with him.

When the angel Gabriel appeared to the virgin Mary, his salutation was "Hail, thou that art highly favoured, the Lord is with thee" (Luke 1:28).

> A woman of very modest means, but the Lord is with you!
>
> Pregnant in mysterious circumstances, but the Lord is with you!
>
> About to lose your fiancé, but the Lord is with you!
>
> The object of ridicule, but the Lord is with you!
>
> Grossly misunderstood, but the Lord is with you!
>
> Your plans capsized and discarded, but the Lord is with you!

Before listing seventeen things that will separate us from the love of God in Christ, Romans 8:31 assures us that if God is for us, no one can stand against us. After spying out the land with ten other spies who brought back an evil, discouraging report, Joshua and Caleb (see Numbers 14:9), urged the camp of Israelites, saying, "Only rebel not ye against the LORD, neither fear ye the people of the land: for they are bread for us: their defense is departed from them, and the Lord is with us: fear them not." The crux of their argument is that the size of the enemy or obstacles is irrelevant to those who have Almighty God on their side. On his part the Psalmist declares that "The LORD is on my side; (literally in the Hebrew "for me") I will not fear: what can man do unto me?" (Psalm 118:6)

It is therefore crucial to start every journey knowing that the Lord is with you. Joseph's story, if you recall symbolically started with victory, at the age of seventeen. Now the second phase begins with the assurance of God's presence and its consequence: "The LORD was with Joseph, and he was a prosperous man" (Genesis 39:2). The word "prosperous" also translates as profitable, that is to "push forward," literally or figuratively. At this juncture, a dichotomy seems to arise between God's idea of prosperity and ours. Naturally, we would expect that if God was with Joseph, he would be empowered to prosper. However, we are told: "He was in the house of his master the Egyptian" (Genesis 39:2). How, we reason, can I be blessed and still be in captivity; and not just captivity, but to an Egyptian, of all people? What happened to "And the LORD shall make thee the head, and not the tail; and thou shalt be above only, and thou shalt not be beneath?" (Deuteronomy 28:13). The clue lies in the alternate definition of the word "prosperous," which is to be profitable. Here it is important to note that many times we may be serving the purposes of God, and even blessing other people, but not personally seeing or reaping the benefits immediately. There is usually a period, according to the Prophet Isaiah, of taking root downward, and bearing fruit upward. This agrees with that most prevalent and eternal of principles: the law of sowing and reaping. One of the central pillars of this law is that you have to sow in order to reap. Once you sow however, you will also reap what you sow; but that will come later, and when it does you will reap more than you sowed. There is always the passage of time between seed-time (or sowing the seed) and harvest. Many in our day struggle with this concept, because we are accustomed to instant gratification, but the truth is that a smile is the only thing in life that brings instant rewards. If you are the impatient type and you cannot wait for your rewards, I recommend you go around planting smiles everywhere you go and you will enjoy the instantaneous fruit. For everything else, "You have need of patience" (Hebrews 10:36).

As we soon discover, Potiphar was an astute businessman and an extremely prudent man. It was not long before he realized that the Lord was with Joseph and therefore blessed and prospered everything he did. This is an awesome testimonial to Joseph's character. Potiphar was an Egyptian who had no relationship with Jehovah. So how did he know, that the Lord was with Joseph and "made all that he did to prosper in his hand"? (Genesis 39:3). Obviously it must have been because he observed the apparent favour on Joseph's life, and upon asking him the secret of his success, Joseph probably always attributed the glory to "the Lord."

Having seen divine favour upon Joseph, no doubt, Potiphar tested him with little things and he proved faithful with these. Potiphar then decided Joseph was trustworthy enough to oversee all his endeavours. This move had the expected results for we are told that from that point, "The LORD blessed the Egyptian's house for Joseph's sake; and the blessing of the LORD was upon all that he had in the house, and in the field" (Genesis 39:5).

Joseph could have reasoned, "Wait a minute! I am the blessed one, so why are the blessings manifesting in the life of my Egyptian master rather than in mine?" Scripture clearly states that it was on account of Joseph or for Joseph's sake that the house of the Egyptian was blessed. The subtle undercurrent here is that the Egyptian was being blessed but it was accruing to Joseph's account! This interpretation will prove to be accurate, as we will soon discover. On another level, though, recall that a vital component of the Abrahamic blessing was that: "thou shalt be a blessing ...and in thee shall all families of the earth be blessed." (Genesis 12:2-3). We must learn to be content with fulfilling this vital part of the Abrahamic covenant. God's original plan for the nation of Israel was that they be a priesthood to the nations and that through them God would channel His blessings to a needy world. This mandate, rejected by the natural Jews, has been transferred to the body of Christ, the Church of the Living God, as Peter clearly explains in 1 Peter 2:9, KJV: "But ye are a chosen generation, a royal priesthood, a holy nation, a peculiar people; that ye should show forth the praises of him who hath called you out of darkness into his marvellous light."

The mistake we make is to believe that God promised first to bless us before making us a blessing. The truth is if God were to use perfect vessels the temptation would be for us to take credit for our achievements. Apostle Paul says the reason God uses fragile, imperfect, vessels like us is so that the glory of God will be clearly manifest, never to be mistaken for anything else. (See 2 Corinthians 4:7.)

Clearly, God often makes us a blessing before we are blessed. Perhaps you are thinking that you cannot give what you do not have. While that is technically true, we must realize that not all blessings are material in nature. Jesus warned that one's life does not consist merely in the abundance of one's possessions, no matter how bountiful. (See Luke 12:15.)

After the death of Jesus, Peter, John and the other disciples were hiding in terror in the upper room till the day of Pentecost. When the Holy Spirit came upon each of them, their timidity gave way to courage, and fear gave way to faith. Shortly after they entered the temple via the Beautiful Gate the congenitally lame man asked alms of them, and they caught the vision that though they had no silver or gold to offer, they were still blessed and empowered with something infinitely better–the name of Jesus. (See Acts 3:6.) Alleluia! With that name, they did what money could not do; with that name they became a blessing to their generation with no immediate prospect of a reward. But that was no longer an issue because Peter had already earlier settled the matter. He had asked Jesus what would be their reward for leaving all and following Him. Jesus guaranteed them a hundredfold returns on most things in this world along with persecution, and eternal life in the world to come. (See Mark 10:28-30.) The early disciples were content to live with eternity in view--a lesson we, too, would be wise to learn.

Joseph's ongoing stewardship training was perhaps a more important reason why Potiphar was visibly blessed while Joseph was not. He had to learn the dynamics of stewardship and service before he could access the glorious destiny that God had prepared for him.

Four Principles of Stewardship

The story of Joseph exemplifies a parable on stewardship that Jesus taught to His disciples. The parable was prompted by the Pharisees and scribes, who murmured that Jesus kept company with sinners. After teaching the parable of the Lost Sheep, the Lost Coin and the Lost Son to the Pharisees and scribes, (see Luke 15), Jesus then turned to His disciples and outlined the parable of the Unrighteous Steward. (See Luke 16:1-13.)

This parable is the subject of much theological debate, and many cannot agree as to what exactly some aspects of it mean. However, Jesus made four clear conclusions, and they translate to four basic principles of stewardship that we will focus on here. But before we do let me point out that the heart of stewardship is faithfulness. Objectively, to be faithful means to be trustworthy, while subjectively, it is to be trusting, true and sure. This means that first of all a steward must be a believer, a man of faith, because this is what enables him to be faithful.

Integrity, fidelity and reliability are other ideals associated with faithfulness and therefore with stewardship. In Luke 12:42 KJV Jesus emphasized to Peter the importance of faithfulness to stewards whether they were disciples or not. Paul ties this concept and its ideals together in 1 Corinthians 4:2 when he says, "Moreover it is required in stewards, that a man be found faithful." The first principle of stewardship has to do with your attitude toward position or positioning. Nobody becomes a success or a failure overnight. The importance of references when one is applying for greater responsibilities is that you have proved yourself on a smaller scale or at a lower level (and are thus ready to move higher). This indicates that you will do the same when faced with bigger challenges. Jesus put it this way: "He that is faithful in that which is least is faithful also in much: and he that is unjust in the least is unjust also in much"

(Luke 16:10). There is an African proverb that declares that the indicators for how your day will turn out are to be found at dawn. That is to say that no one becomes an overseer without first working on the shop floor. This is the meaning of the saying "From little acorns grow mighty oaks." The Prophet Zechariah warns us not to ridicule the day of small beginnings. (See Zechariah 4:10.) In 1 Timothy 5:22 the Apostle Paul admonishes Timothy not to lay hands suddenly on any man. By this Paul was telling Timothy to watch, try and test potential leaders before appointing them as deacons, pastors or in other leadership positions.

As a wise leader Potiphar was aware of this stewardship principle. First, he recognized Joseph's divine favour for what it was. In corporate terms this is the equivalent of natural giftedness, training or exposure. Potiphar also noticed that Joseph had the "Midas Touch," because God prospered everything he touched. But as good as that was it did not automatically mean Potiphar could trust him. To test his trustworthiness Potiphar made him his personal aide. Once Joseph proved his faithfulness Potiphar made him overseer of all his affairs.

Joseph thus pointed to Jesus who was faithful in the execution of His earthly father's business, and this convinced His heavenly Father that He was worthy of greater trust. He duly discharged all that the Father commended to His care all the way to Calvary. It is for this reason that we as believers must never despise our modest beginnings as they are designed to determine our future level of promotion.

The second principle of stewardship has to do with your attitude toward money or resources. In the aforementioned proverb of the Unjust Steward, Jesus proclaimed in Luke 16:11 KJV: "If therefore ye have not been faithful in the unrighteous mammon, who will commit to your trust the true riches?" "Unrighteous mammon," "unjust riches," "unrighteous worldly wealth" and "wealth that is tainted with fraud" are all synonyms for money, resources and personal possessions. Jesus taught in His first sermon that money has the potential to rule your life in a way that only God should. "No man can serve two masters:" Jesus warned; "for either he will hate the one, and love the other, or else he will hold to the one, and despise the other. Ye cannot serve God and mammon" (Matthew 6:24). In 1 Timothy 6:10, Paul said: "The love of money is the root of all evil," though most married couples agree: "The absence of money is the root of all quarrels," but that is an altogether different matter! A faithful steward will put money in its place and make it a servant to his greater purposes. He will make it do anything for him, but he will not do anything for money. He will keep accurate accounts and will under no condition divert or misappropriate his master's resources. He will not take advantage of the fact that he is the sole signatory and thus "borrow" his master's resources "just for a few days" with the shameful objective of returning it "even before he knows it was borrowed." Joseph exemplified this by treating his master's resources as a sacred trust. Later on, as prime minister, Joseph would turn over all the riches and land to Pharaoh with not a thought of gain of any kind for himself. For Joseph, purpose and destiny were much more important than possessions and pleasure. Jesus said his food was to do the will of the Father and to finish His work. Every mite or denarius that came into Jesus' hands was channelled toward the realisation of God's calling on His life. Our attitude toward wealth will determine what spiritual responsibilities God ultimately commends to our hands.

The third principle of stewardship has to do with your attitude toward trusteeship. Jesus asked, "And if you have not been faithful in that which is another man's, who shall give you that which is your own?" (Luke 16:12). Diligently applying yourself to the back-breaking, sweat-inducing task of tilling the arid, semi-barren land of someone else's cabbage patch, is a dress rehearsal for becoming the proprietor of an efficient, fruitful, fully-mechanised ranch of your own. Ask Ruth about working in a field which was soon to become hers! She went from gleaner to owner. It took David the better part of thirteen years to enter into his own promise. After he was anointed by Samuel, David spent the time in-between serving Saul and refusing to subvert him even when he had the means, motive, opportunity and external encouragement to do so. This acute sense of propriety and stewardship contributed to God's favour and is why he was described by God as a man after His own heart. (See 1 Samuel 13:14; Acts 13:22.) Joseph was found faithful at every stage of his life, from caring for his father's sheep to being second only to the King of Egypt. Our heavenly Joseph is no different and He calls us to serve those in authority over us as though we are serving the Lord. This is the seed that ensures that in the end we will have our own blessing, to which others will then be faithful.

The fourth principle of stewardship pertains to vision. Joseph was a single-minded man, a man with a focus. Matthew 6:24 applies here as well: "No servant can serve two masters, for either he will hate the one, and love the other; or else he will hold to the one, and despise the other. Ye cannot serve God and mammon." To give of your best to an assignment you must have no distractions. You cannot have your own agenda and serve someone else's effectively. You will also be a poor steward if your goal is to advance your personal agenda using someone else's platform. Drawing disciples after you while supposedly working for someone is nothing short of what can only be called the "Absalom complex." It is an exercise in futility to imagine, as many erroneously do, that we can serve God with all of our hearts and still be able to covetously pursue riches in the way the world does. If you have a chance to choose your master, make sure your vote goes to God rather than money. The preacher explains why when he says: "Wisdom is a defence and money is a defence: but the excellency of knowledge is that wisdom giveth life to them that have it" (Ecclesiastes 7:12). In every place of his assignment Joseph served only God but was aware that he could only do this through faithfully and diligently serving the men placed over him. This principle of focus is encapsulated aptly in Jesus' initial teaching to the disciples when He asks them to seek first the Kingdom of God and His righteousness, then all other things, which the non-believers hanker and chase after, would be added unto them as bonuses. (See Matthew 6:31-33.) Even in terms of modern technology, the secret of the laser beam's success is its ability to focus.

"A Man's Gift Will Make Room for Him…"

Moving on, it is vital to remember that Joseph was a bond-servant, and a slave. The reason Potiphar bought him in the first place, was Potiphar's perception that Joseph would be a good investment that would in turn, attract good returns. If that were not the case, then he would have been much like the proverbial salt that had lost its savour, which was good for nothing but to be trodden under men's feet. (See Matthew 5:13.) As children of God, we must realise that wherever we are, we are supposed to be blessed in order to be a blessing. This blessedness is the basis of your usefulness, your "sought-after-ness," your indispensability to those around you. One must therefore never stop being a blessing even when there is no apparent gain. It would appear that Joseph's "fruitfulness" was what spared his life when his master's wife falsely accused him. After all, Potiphar was the chief executioner and Joseph was his slave, with no rights or privileges. Joseph's execution would not have made news in even the most inconsequential local gazette, let alone raised any notable eyebrow.

The Preacher, one of the wisest men who ever lived surmised in Proverbs 18:6 KJV: "A man's gift market room for him, and bringeth him before great men." There was a notable difference in the affairs of Potiphar's household, livestock and other businesses after Joseph took over. The challenge many people face is that they imagine they cannot be effective or be a blessing unless they are overseers, managers, supervisors, executive managing directors or chief executive officers. Joseph, however, did not start as an overseer. It was only after his master discerned that the Lord was with him and blessed all he did, that he was confident to commend little things to Joseph's hands. Consequently, "Joseph found grace in his sight" (Genesis 38:4). Grace is a gift, which can be frustrated, abused, misused or even ignored, but Joseph properly appropriated this grace by serving his master faithfully. Bear in mind Paul's admonition in 1 Corinthians 4:2 KJV: "Moreover it is required in stewards, that a man be found faithful." Potiphar, having wisely tested Joseph, could now promote him to overseer. If you are a blessing to me, it is in my best interest to promote you and give you greater responsibilities so that you do not just continue to be a blessing, but do so at a higher level. This is because you have proven that you will be faithful no matter what your position.

As mentioned earlier, Potiphar was an astute businessman. He bought the slave primarily because it was cheaper than hiring a local Egyptian at minimum wage, with union privileges. Potiphar's entrepreneurial portfolio was impressive with interests both inside and outside his home. This we deduce from assertions like "...Joseph went into the house to do his business; and there was none of the men of the house there within" (Genesis 39:11). In Strong's the word house (bayith in the Hebrew) is defined as a house as it regard to a family. But it also refers to a court, dungeon, palace, prison or temple. So Joseph did not just go to a small residential home but a grandiose, palatial edifice, headquarters for several enterprises. The use of the word "house" can be equated to such contemporary applications as The House of Chloe, The House of Rothschild and The House of Gucci. The word used for business is one that implies deputyship, ministry, livestock, industry, and work and its results, though it never refers to servile employment. It is also clear that Potiphar had a lot of staff as our text talks of "men of the house." Moreover, it is said that, "The blessing of the LORD was upon all that he had in the house, and in the field." The world "field" is used to describe land that is spread out, to include the country and the wild. Potiphar presided over a business empire that had manufacturing and cottage concerns, livestock, and real estate. In fact, Joseph proved so trustworthy that his master left the entire responsibility of the business to him, knowing he would not usurp it as he would later prove even with Pharaoh. What a man!

The Dynamics of Service

Joseph's character is also a prime example of the dynamics of service. Since God is a God of purpose, everything He does or permits to happen is designed to work together for our good and to reveal a more excellent weight of glory in us. When God puts you under someone to serve them, it is actually designed ultimately to serve you and God's greater purposes in your life. Joseph's life exposes these dynamics very succinctly as outlined below:

1. The inferior (lesser) always serves the superior (the greater).

2. When you serve effectively, you spend a significant amount of time with the one you serve.

3. This means the one you serve makes many demands on your time and ability, to ensure continued effective service.

4. While you are in his service, your employer teaches you all you need to know for your effective service to him.

5. You also pick up things he did not teach you.

6. Effective service is therefore training for leadership, in a disguise. By its very nature, service postures you for leadership.

7. Working with people whom you do not like, or who are not like you, who may not even like you and who are not your type, will take you to places you would not normally go to, and expose you to things, information and places you would not normally be exposed to.

8. When you are effective in service, you free your boss to go to the next level so that you can legitimately take his place.

9. You generally do not get your full reward in the place of your training. This is partly because there, your true worth is not yet known, and the tendency is for you to be taken for granted. Your attitude and response to being overlooked will determine how far you will ultimately go, as this is part of your training.

Now let's look at how these dynamics played out in Joseph's life and the way they reflect the type of Christ.

Though Joseph was superior by covenant to Potiphar and even to Pharaoh, he humbled himself and became as the lesser in order to serve the greater. Just like Jesus in Philippians 2:3-4, Joseph esteemed his masters better than himself in lowliness of mind. He looked not on his own things but on the things of his masters." At no point did he feel like he was running out of time to "do his own thing." Neither did he subvert his masters or divert their resources to his personal ends in what is known as private practice. As a seed of the patriarchs he himself was a patriarch in the making, and yet he did not seek equality with his master. Rather, like Christ, he made himself of no reputation and assumed the status of a servant, humbling himself and becoming obedient to a type of death. On account of this, God also highly exalted him and gave him a name, which was above every other in Egypt, and "they cried before him, Bow the knee..." (Genesis 41:3).

Joseph, to serve effectively, spent what would appear to be an inordinate amount of time with Potiphar in his house.

Similarly, Joshua had to spend the better part of his life with Moses once he received the call. In this way, he learned all that Moses deemed to teach him. However he also learned many things Moses did not teach him, which he picked up by observation and the sheer privilege of being close to the leader who was very close to God! He certainly learned not to make the same mistakes Moses had made. For example, Moses chose twelve spies for a covert mission, a mission that was doomed to failure from the start, because it is impossible to get three people, let alone twelve, to agree on any one thing.

When it was Joshua's turn he hand-picked two men and gave them clear instructions as to their mission. Though word still leaked out of their arrival, it was easier for the faithful prostitute, Rahab, to hide them. There are some things you can only learn by inspiration while there are others you must work out by perspiration. Generally, ideas, innovations and concepts come by flashes of inspiration. The administration, detailing, workability, fine-tuning, and planning, however, require careful, time-consuming, nose-to-the-grindstone involvement, dedication and industry. For example, Moses could only learn of the heavenly tabernacle by inspiration. Building it though, required many skilled artisans dedicating several months of disciplined, committed, man-hours. It is also ironic that he was given the right of rulership and the design of the Tabernacle by divine mandate and revelation, but he nearly burned himself out because he did not know how to delegate. It took Jethro, his father-in-law who had none of Moses' inspiration, but many years' "perspiration," to come up with an alternate administrative strategy. (See Exodus 18:17-23). He was a successful shepherd, running the family business with his girls. He was also the Priest of Midian, which meant he also had to administer a religious organisation and system. That in itself speaks volumes. The advice he gave Moses was personal, gleaned from a system he had obviously tried, tested and found effective. In fact, it was so good that it formed the basis of Jewish government from that time forward. Clearly, Potiphar made inordinate demands on Joseph's time; we glean this from the assertion that: "He left all that he had in Joseph's hand; and he knew not aught he had, save the bread which he did eat" (Genesis 39:6). Isn't this, the heart's cry of every manager that he would find a self-motivated, reliable staff member to run the business as the manager himself would?

The word oversee is paqad in the Hebrew. Its diverse meanings give one insight into the incredible character qualities of Joseph that elicited such faith from his employer. Among its many connotations according to Strong, are "to visit, inspect, review, muster, number, care for, look after, entrust, charge with, and to deposit." Spiros Zodhiates says: "a strong undercurrent in the meaning of paqad is a positive action by a superior in relation to his subordinates." He further surmises that it could also be "an action on the part of God which produces a beneficial result for his people" (Spiros Zodhiates, Hebrew-Greek Key Word Study Bible–Lexical Aids to the Old Testament Page 165). Joseph himself testifies that Potiphar put everything he had, which would of course include knowledge, understanding and wisdom, at his disposal, when he said, "Neither hath he kept back anything from me..." (Genesis 39:9). Not unexpectedly, Joseph also picked up on other things from Potiphar that he did not teach him. It was this effective service that prepared Joseph to serve in prison, which in turn would later commend him to Pharaoh and catapult him into leadership in the most influential economy of its day. Even that "unpleasant" journey exposed Joseph to people and experiences he would otherwise never have met or had respectively. As the adage goes, travel truly does broaden the mind (and this is true even of reluctant or forced travellers). So far, Joseph had been exposed to Ishmaelite/Midianite modus vivendi, Egyptian culture and some other lifestyles that will be explored in detail a little later. He went to places he would otherwise never have visited and was exposed to information and experiences, which his brothers could only read of in books. So Joseph became overseer in a relatively short time because of his faithfulness in service, but more importantly because God was with him and prospered all he set his hands to.

The Great Temptation

"It came to pass after these things that his master's wife cast her eyes upon Joseph and said, 'Lie with me.'" (Genesis 39:7). Wow! It appears that after every promotion comes another test. Why was it "after these things"? Was she jealous of Joseph's ascendancy in Potiphar's esteem and his rapid promotion in the entrepreneurial hierarchy? Was he more attractive now that he wielded more power? Or had it been for her "lust at first sight"? After all, it was said of Joseph that he was "well-built and handsome" (Genesis 39:6 GW). Or was her lust growing with each day till it got to this point? Or perhaps it was simply because the devil was alarmed by Joseph's meteoric rise to his God-given destiny in spite of the many obstacles he had so methodically and persistently strewn in Joseph's path. This was therefore likely to be the latest in the devil's efforts to subvert him in his course. We as believers must realise that a word from God, a divine vision, mandate or instruction, does not insulate us from temptation, trial, test, or tribulation, but is a guarantee of ultimate success in spite of these things. Joseph was now faced with the greatest temptation of his life so far. Dictionary.com defines temptation as:

1. "The act of tempting, enticement or allurement; and

2. The fact or state of being tempted, especially to evil."

The same source defines the word "tempt" as "to entice or allure to do something often regarded as unwise, wrong or immoral."

For this to be a temptation, it had to be enticing, alluring, attractive, and had to offer some kind of advantage apart from the obvious sexual gratification. Joseph was a virile young man with active sexual urges; only eunuchs are not subject to such temptations! Mrs. Potiphar had to be very beautiful and must have gone out of her way (or most of her clothes!) in order to be enticing to Joseph. Moreover, she no doubt suggested the possibility of his freedom, or her bed, which had to appeal to the "prisoner" Joseph. However, there is absolutely no substitute for doing the right thing—in fact, the alternative is death. Joseph did his best to reason with her, arguing that he held a position of such absolute trust that he could not betray his master. "How can I do this great wickedness, and sin against God?" (Genesis 39:9)

David came to an understanding of the nature of sin, when he repented before God over the Bathsheba scandal saying, "Against thee, thee only, have I sinned, and done this evil in thy sight..." (Psalm 51:4 KJV). Joseph likewise knew that every sin is first a slight against God even when it directly affects men more than it appears to affect God. Our primary obligation is to God, and that affects how we treat our fellow human beings. That Potiphar's wife did not desist is an indication of how far gone, how degenerate, she really was.

Rather, Potiphar's wife piled on the pressure. "It came to pass as she spake to Joseph day by day," the text suggests she continued to entice him into a sexual liaison on a daily basis, in what we would now call an "affair." This is one of the deceptive modern words used to sugar-coat and lend legitimacy to the sins of adultery and fornication. The scenario might have gone something like this: "We can elope," or "We can secretly poison Potiphar and get all his property," or maybe "I can negotiate your freedom, stay married and we remain secret lovers," are all probable arguments Mrs. Potiphar may have employed. In all these things, Joseph neither succumbed, nor did he buy her arguments. He not only refused to sleep with her, but, wisely refused to even be around her. How unlike many of us today who even when we have no intention of embarking on an illicit physical relationship, enjoy the flirtation and attention of an outsider to our marriage, and thus commit emotional adultery. Others of us by being with such a person, slowly have our resistance worn down daily till we one day find ourselves in the nasty throes of regret.

Realizing that she was getting nowhere with this "goody-two-shoes" Mrs. Potiphar literally took things into her own hands and grabbed him; hell hath no fury like a woman scorned. At this point, most of us would have yielded; but not Joseph. Remember that from an early age, he had shunned the evil and sinful paths that his older siblings had wilfully trodden. The power of his God-inspired, purpose-laden, vision-driven dreams were no doubt constantly before him, and there was no way someone else's carnal desires would stand in his way. But Potiphar's wife found an opportune moment when none of the other staff was present; she may have gone to great lengths to orchestrate the situation. Catching him by the garment, she tried to force him. "Lie with me." At this point, Joseph recalled that the Word commands us to resist the devil and he will flee from us. When it comes to sexual immorality, however, our Holy God does not ask us to resist, but to flee! 1 Corinthians 6:18 tells us to: "Flee fornication." This is because a good run is better than a bad stand. A living dog is infinitely superior to a dead lion; and he who fights and runs away will live to fight another day. And finally, you decidedly cannot, as the Bible warns, "take fire in your bosom and not have your clothes burnt" (Proverbs 6:27).

When Potiphar's wife saw that Joseph had left his garment and fled, her devious brain immediately concocted a new plan. Obviously, she was embarrassed by his rejection, convicted by being corrected, terrified of being exposed and unsure of what Joseph would tell

Potiphar. She need not have feared; after all he had not said anything all this while because he was a man of prudence, wisdom and integrity. Not taking any chances she called to the men of the house and reported that Joseph had tried to rape her; she had only escaped to raise the alarm. And what was more, she had proof—he had left his garment in her hand. After gathering witnesses to corroborate her story she just had to wait till her husband came home. She had plenty of time to think—to change her mind and tell the truth, but how does anyone reverse the lies they have already spread far and wide? A wise man once said the problem with a little lie is that it never stays little.

We can all testify to spontaneously telling a lie, which was ill-thought out; but upon closer interrogation, we had to tell more lies to prop up the rather shaky original, and this continued till we were completely entangled in a self-spun web of deceit. Ironically, the truth is so much less complicated as it can and always stands alone; it always stands upright and stands the test of time. Potiphar's wife did not have such a dilemma. In fact, she took the time to fine-tune her fabrication, unconcerned with its potential consequences. It did not bother her that this lie, at the least, had the potential to cost Joseph his freedom, and possibly his very life. How could she pretend to be unaware that a man cuckolded, is more dangerous than a bear robbed of her whelps. In fact, the wise writer of Proverbs says, "… a jealous husband can be furious and merciless when he takes revenge" (Proverbs 6:34). Many scholars have wondered why Joseph did not protest and point an accusing finger at her. But he understood the truth, that vengeance belongs to the Lord and He will repay. (See Hebrews 10:30.)

When Pharaoh chased the children of Israel upon their exodus from Egypt, when three mighty nations came against Jehoshaphat, and at sundry other times when the enemy came against God's people like a flood, the admonition was always the same; "… the battle is not yours but God's…Ye shall not need to fight in this battle…stand ye still, and see the salvation of the LORD with you...for the LORD will be with you" (2 Chronicles 20:15-17 & Exodus 14:13-14).

More importantly, Joseph understood the principle of authority and how to handle errant, recalcitrant, tyrannical or unjust leadership.

In fact, if you are wise you dare not tackle authority head on and expect to win. You must approach leaders with caution and great wisdom. Samuel displayed this understanding when he arrived at Jesse's house to anoint the new king, but provided a good cover story to protect himself and Jesse's household should news of this event leak to Saul who was, incidentally, still king. In their epistles Peter and Jude contrast the apostate false teachers with the holy angels in heaven; the former disregard and disrespect authority while the latter, Michael the Archangel, even when in the right, trod cautiously in dealing with errant authority figures.

In contrast, John the Baptist boldly confronted rebellious authority, ended up in prison, and ultimately lost his head. The truth is that when you metaphorically lose your head in dealing with authority you could literally lose your head! Therefore the lesson here is to be wise when dealing with authority figures. What do you think would have happened if Joseph had begun to loudly protest his innocence? When Potiphar was (mis)informed of the situation it is said that his wrath was kindled; this is an old English term meaning he was incensed or furious. Joseph's protestations of innocence would have turned the kindled wrath into a raging inferno that would, no doubt, have swept him away. Not to mention that Mrs. Potiphar, to protect her " sullied honour", would have requested his execution. Because he was a man without rights he would have been summarily executed. It must never be forgotten that Potiphar was the chief executioner. It was actually only by God's mercy that he was not consumed. Most importantly though Joseph was reflecting the character of Christ, who "was oppressed, and he was afflicted, yet He opened not His mouth: He is brought as a lamb to the slaughter, and as a sheep before her shearers is dumb, so he opened not His mouth." The next phrase predicts Joseph's end: "He was taken from prison and from judgment..." (Isaiah 53:7-8). Of course, for this to happen, he would have to go to prison first. Joseph also understood another important truth—that time is the great revealer of secrets. Job said "All the days of my appointed time will I wait, till my change come" (Job 14:14). The Psalmist says of Joseph: "Till the time that his word came: the word of the LORD tried him" (Psalm 105:19). In Ecclesiastes 3:17 we find the third witness, the Preacher who said: "God shall judge the righteous and the wicked: for there is a time there for every purpose and for every work."

Joseph understood that his life and times were in God's hands. Just as John 3:17 tells us God did not send His Son into the world to condemn the world but to save it, so Joseph would tell his brothers repeatedly that God sent him before them to preserve lives. This is how Joseph came to end up in prison. By divine ordination and favour, Joseph was put into the "V.I.P." prison with cabinet ministers and other such dignitaries who had temporarily fallen from grace. Had he chosen to be vindictive and petty, Potiphar could have sent Joseph to the "commoners" prison. So even in his wrath, Potiphar was still extending favour to Joseph because: "When a man's ways please the LORD, he makes even his enemies be at peace with him" (Proverbs 16:7). Do not imagine for a second that it was a bed of roses. After all, it was still prison. Joseph also had to face a fresh challenge. He must have felt out of his depths in this new, unfamiliar environment--not being Egyptian, not being nobility, not even being a citizen, but a slave. Sometimes God will take you out of your comfort zone in order to bring you into your sovereign zone!

Scripture tells us for the third time that the Lord was with Joseph. This is such an important fact that God chose to establish it at the mouth of two or three witnesses. It was crucial to establish this fact because in the natural realm the opposite appeared to be the case. If you had been sold into foreign slavery by your own blood brothers, then been falsely accused and incarcerated indefinitely without a fair hearing or trial you would doubt that man was with you, let alone God! Psychologically, one of the most difficult aspects of Joseph's prison predicament was the realisation that his term had no definite end point. Even those serving life sentences are sometimes eligible for parole after a specified time. When you have seemingly been tossed into prison and the key thrown away, you might tend to suffer more mentally, as a sense of hopelessness and despair sweeps over you and threatens to drown you in its wake.

But Joseph was revived by the power of a dream that burned inside him and shattered the vice-like stranglehold of injustice, while dissipating the deep fog of depression and despair. He victoriously realised with great relief that a man with a vision cannot die (and certainly not in prison).

It was this same realisation that kept Simeon alive in a crooked and perverse generation. He survived, though suffering and affliction continued, and evil men ruled. (See Luke 3:1-2.) The Holy Ghost was upon him and had assured him he would not see death till he had seen the Lord's Christ, the consolation of Israel. Indeed till Mary and Joseph brought Jesus into the temple to present Him to the Lord, Simeon did not die. (See Luke 2:25-35.) How then do you know that the Lord is with you? Naturally, we imagine that if God is with us we will find ourselves in pleasant places, enjoying only justice, equity, truth, kindness, fairness and goodness. However, the truth is God looks at things another way; that is: in whatever situation you find yourself, He will cause you to prosper, and to excel in an apparent fashion. God's presence causes you to obtain mercy from men around you. This explains why though it was in Potiphar's power to kill Joseph, and that would have been the most logical and expected thing, he did not. The text also tells us that the presence of the Lord in

Joseph's life caused him to have favour with the keeper of the prison. (See Genesis 39:21.)

Note that the phase in Potiphar's house was over and Joseph had passed that examination with flying colours. Observe that Potiphar's influence over his life was now minuscule to non-existent, but he had learned that, even in his servile position he could learn something from Potiphar. If he had been slack or had procrastinated, he would have missed the season of his visitation and all that phase was meant to teach him. He would also have had to retake the exams as no one ever gets promoted till they pass the appropriate tests. His new phase was life in prison and his new boss was the keeper of the prison. Joseph's response in his previous tests accounted for where he was now, and his response to this test would determine where he would go next. Again this phase begins with the assurance that: "The LORD was with Joseph" and as a result, He "showed him mercy, and gave him favour in the sight of the keeper of the prison" (Genesis 39:21). This scripture would have been better translated kindness, rather than mercy, because mercy means "not getting" what is deserved, while favour was a result of God's kindness. The truth is that favour is a gift from God. It is thus God who causes people to like you without a reason or cause, just as Satan moves people to hate you without a cause. Interestingly enough, it did not take as long for the keeper of the prison to commit everything to Joseph's hand as it had taken with Potiphar. This is because he had proven himself faithful. Thus, Joseph immediately became overseer of the prisoners and all their activities. He had again risen to the pinnacle after being catapulted by the slingshot of destiny to an undesirable destination. Most times, we have little or no choice as to where we find ourselves, but we can determine how high we climb when we are there. Joseph, by industry, intuition, ingenuity and integrity, not to mention a good attitude and most importantly, grace, swiftly rose to the top in prison just as he had in Potiphar's house.

The former South African President, Nelson Mandela, found himself a guest of the defunct apartheid government, against his will. His attitude ensured he would not be kept in prison indefinitely. His positive attitude made him one of the world's greatest living statesmen. It is your disposition rather than your position, that will determine your elevation. Many times, we find ourselves in the captivity of a loveless and troubled marriage, an unfulfilling and tedious job, dealing with children whose behaviour is reprehensible, with a thwarted destiny, facing a trust betrayed, or in a cycle of failure. And because it is not where we want to be or think we should be, we develop a bad attitude. We allow our condition to determine our disposition, and our environment, our temperament. Yet God expects it to be the other way around: whatever circumstances life throws at you are temporal, while your destiny is the product of your attitude. A good attitude will propel you to the place of lasting victory while a bad attitude will sink you lower and lower till you are entrenched in your worst fears. Job 3:25 KJV captures it accurately when he says, "For the thing which I greatly fear is come upon me, and that which I was afraid of is come unto me." Indeed, "The fear of the wicked, it shall come upon him: but the desire of the righteous shall be granted" (Proverbs 10:24).

In a dark situation, everyone looks out for a bright spot, a light at the end of the tunnel, the silver lining to the cloud, the hope of a better future, the solution to the problem. When you are moulded to conformity by the situation, you are perceived to be a part of the problem. However if your demeanour and attitude show optimism, joy, buoyancy, cheerfulness, confidence and positivity, then people will look to you as a light in their darkness. This is partly what Jesus meant when He told His disciples that they were the light of the world, comparable to a mountain-top city which, despite the best of efforts, could not be hidden. (See Matthew 5:14.) When you watch all those action/disaster movies with people in impossibly tight spots, they usually turn to the optimist and ask, "Do you think we are going to come out of this alive?" Are the people around you so attracted to your positive nature that they are asking you the same question regarding the issues they face? Being asked such a question gives you the opportunity to share with them the testimonies of the many times in the past when God delivered you from far worse situations, giving you the assurance that He will inevitably do it for them also.

Peter tells us to set our hearts apart to the Lord (not to our problems) and always to be willing to respond to those who ask us the reason for our hope (optimism, in other words). (See 1 Peter 3:15.) Joseph's faithfulness caused the entire prison to be committed to his supervisory care; and his influence was so pervasive that nothing was done there without his being consulted. The chapter ends with this observation: "The head jailer gave Joseph free rein, never even checked on him, because God was with him; whatever he did God made sure it worked out for the best. (See Genesis 39:19 MSG.) Joseph walked in the grace of God and it in turn caused him to enjoy favour and to do such impressive work that he was given rule, authority and dominion, even in prison, just as it had been in Potiphar's "empire." Faithfulness will give you the privilege and liberty to exercise initiative and to rule. You cannot however be faithful unless and till grace gives you the opportunity.

As this chapter comes to a close consider that a man's skills and giftings will secure for him a job, a position or an opportunity. His faithfulness will sustain him and keep him at that job. Nevertheless, it is his integrity that will promote him and make him a director and a shareholder. We all have much to learn from Joseph!

CHAPTER FOUR

THE BAKER HAD TO DIE!

The next phase of the Joseph chronicles begins with the same familiar phrase used to introduce his encounter with Mrs. Potiphar–"And it came to pass after these things…" This implies that it was imperative, crucial, and inevitable that these things had to occur before the next phase could begin. It also implies a supernatural orchestration of certain events to bring the hero to a pre-ordained destination. There is also the subtle suggestion that Joseph's training programme was coming to an end. For the next phase of his life he would have to draw upon all that had gone before. With the gift of foreknowledge, we know Joseph is still a full two years away from freedom! ("And it came to pass at the end of two full years…") (Genesis 41:1). Yet, even he could sense that he had traversed the most difficult part, the uphill stretch of his journey. Though he had not yet arrived at his destination, the worst was behind him. He would later realize that there was one more crucial training programme that he had to undertake. "And it came to pass after these things that the butler of the king of Egypt and his baker had offended their lord the king of Egypt" (Genesis 40:1, KJV). At this point in Joseph's story, we see some very deep parallels between him and the Christ as God begins to unravel the mystery of His divine plan of redemption for mankind.

It is very instructive and symbolically significant that of all Pharaoh's courtiers, chamberlains and eunuchs, the butler, responsible for bearing the cup that holds water and wine, and the baker, responsible for baking meats and bread, are the ones involved in this incident. The word offend (chata in the Hebrew) is to sin, to incur guilt and to condemn. It is the most important Old Testament word for sin. It is very similar to the Greek word hamartano. The word expresses the idea of being off target, getting lost, coming short of the goal and, breaching civil law as well as sinning against God by falling short of His standard. So Pharaoh was very upset with two of his officers--the chief of the butlers and the chief of the bakers. This particular king, like all Pharaohs was the supreme ruler of Egypt. Nothing negative is ever ascribed to him in the entire Joseph saga. In fact, his benevolence towards Joseph, his father and brothers is impressive. For example, in a show of outstanding beneficence, he gives of the choicest, lushest, most verdant of pastures to the fledgling Israelite nation. Furthermore, this Pharaoh is contrasted with a new one of whom it is said, "Now there arose up a new king over Egypt, which knew not Joseph" (Exodus 1:8); and that was the hard-hearted Pharaoh who would not let God's people go! The altruism of this Pharaoh Joseph met with, strange as it may seem to the religious, suggests that he is a type of Jehovah God. His pronouncements in relation to Joseph on the other hand, show Joseph as a type of Christ, but we will look at that later.

Back to our story: Pharaoh was wroth with his servants because they had sinned, missed the mark, and thereby attracted the wrath of their master. The spiritual implication is that even doing our best as "servants" under the Law, the old Mosaic covenant, we will always miss the mark, for which our only entitlement is God's wrath and eternal spiritual incarceration. James casts light on the dangers of trying to live by the Law as servants instead of by grace as sons: "For whosoever shall keep the whole law, and yet offend in one point, he is guilty of all" (James 2:10, KJ). No wonder Jesus told His disciples that He no longer considered them servants who had no knowledge of the affairs of their Master, but friends who were an integral part of their Father's business. (See John 15:15.) Moreover, the servants' predicament was a picture of mankind adjudged by God to be under sin, with the following consequence: "...The wrath of God is revealed from heaven against all ungodliness and unrighteousness of men, who hold the truth in unrighteousness" (Romans 1:18, KJV).

So, we are told the butler and the baker ended up in the very prison--
"the place where Joseph was bound" (See Genesis 40:3.) It is
wonderful to observe though, that like Jehovah, Pharaoh's anger was
tempered with restraint and mercy. He could legitimately and
instantly have had them both killed; rather, he put them in prison, and
not even the commoners' jail, but the prison of privilege. The lesson
here: in every trying situation, there is always room for praise.
Incarceration in the same prison as Joseph would also turn out to be a
blessing, for one of them at any rate. Furthermore, "The captain of the
guard charged Joseph with them, and he served them: and they
continued a season in ward" (Genesis 40:4).

As the butler or baker isn't it nice to know that:

- You lost your position, but someone is still serving you!

- You are in prison, bound, but someone is still serving you!

- You missed the mark, but someone is still serving you!

- Your boss is angry, but someone is still serving you!

- Your promotion is delayed, but someone is still serving you!

It seems unfair that even in prison, the class system persists.
Admittedly, as Jamieson, Fausset and Brown observe in their
Commentary on the Bible the butler was more than just a cupbearer,
but was also an overseer of the royal vineyards and cellars with
hundreds of people under him. They also observed that both butlers
and bakers in ancient Egypt were always persons of great rank and
importance. They concluded that because of the sensitivity and
confidentiality of their posts and their access to the throne, they were
usually the highest nobles or blood princes, and one might have
assumed that prison would be the great "leveller" where everyone was
treated equally. However, anyone who understands the prison system

knows that the class system is most pronounced there. Thus the Captain of the guard committed the butler and the baker to Joseph's care. At this point, Joseph could have chosen to be totally frustrated and wonder why all these "negative" things "always" seemed to happen to him. On the other hand he could choose to realise that he was taking his final examinations and if he passed them, he would graduate into a glorious destiny that he could scarcely imagine. The word bound used in relation to Joseph's imprisonment is a give-away clue (see Genesis 40:3) to a hidden message. It is the Hebrew word, asar, and on one level it means to yoke or hitch, to fasten; by analogy to bind, fast, gird, harness, hold, keep, imprison, or to put in bonds. But the same word also means to make ready, prepare, or set in array! So next time you feel bound by situations and circumstances, or the enemy tells you, you are in prison, harnessed, tied or yoked to life's frustrations, let him know that God is at that moment preparing your destiny and arranging your victory. Alleluia!

"...He served them..."

As Joseph had served his father and brothers, the Ishmaelites, Potiphar, the captain of the guard, and the keeper of the prison, he was now being called to serve his fellow prisoners. Just as before, he humbled himself in service knowing God would exalt him in due season. In so doing, Joseph was reflecting the character of Jesus who served the will of His father and then went on to His brothers who rejected him and sold Him into the hands of the wicked. He went on to serve the Gentiles, was then sent to the depths of the earth, where He served His fellow prisoners, by liberating them at His resurrection.

There is a part of this story that one could easily gloss over. It was the captain of the guard, Potiphar, not the keeper of the prison, who charged Joseph with the care of the butler and the baker. These were

Potiphar's fellow courtiers who had offended their lord, Pharaoh. Potiphar would feel for, and identify with them and would want to make life as comfortable as possible for them, without incurring Pharaoh's wrath upon himself. Having proved Joseph's faithfulness, diligence, industry, prudence, discretion, etc., he could safely commit his colleagues to Joseph's personal care knowing it was the very best they could get under the circumstances. Could this imply that Potiphar had begun to be reconciled to him and was now (and probably always was) convinced of Joseph's innocence but could not release him for fear of displeasing his wife? As an aside let me say here that men should exercise great caution in yielding to their ungodly wives' whims and caprices for it was such that led to the fall of Adam, and indeed that caused Herod to behead John the Baptist, a man he knew to be righteous, to please his illegitimate wife, Herodias. When confronted with their wives' indiscretions, "dirt" and bad judgments, God expects husbands to "sanctify and cleanse (them) with the washing of water by the Word" (Ephesians 5:25), thereby lovingly restoring them to the path of righteousness, as opposed to sliding with them down the slippery slope to perdition.

It is interesting to know that on one particular night, the butler and the baker, while incarcerated, both "dreamed a dream" (Genesis 40:3&8). And because the dreams were too cryptic to easily decipher, each one needed his own interpretation. What are the odds? Is this not the hand of God at play, or is it at work? Awake or asleep, even the hearts of kings are in God's hands, and he can "turn it where he likes, like water courses" (Proverbs 21:1). In the morning, Joseph came in unto them early in the morning, just after sunrise. From this we can conclude that though weeping endures for the night even for believers amid trials, that same dark night gives way to joyful sunrise. (See Psalm 30:5.) Furthermore, anyone who serves cannot afford to sleep indefinitely and without discipline. Great statesmen, athletes, entrepreneurs, even cleaners, shop stewards and traders have to rise before the sun to ensure that they maximise their opportunities. In fact, there are several warnings to the indolent, lethargic and work-shy in the Book of Proverbs, which we cannot explore in detail in this treatise. Suffice it to say that Proverbs also demonstrates that the end of a sleeper/sluggard is poverty and lack. (See Proverbs 6:6-11.) Please note that the word "sleep" also refers to repeatedly passing up opportunities. Someone aptly defined P.O.O.R as: "Passing Over Opportunities Repeatedly." It is not an absence of opportunities that makes folks poor. It is their inability, first of all to recognise opportunities for what they are; secondly, and perhaps even worse, is their unwillingness to take the opportunities even when they recognise them as such. Describing this attitude, the Book of Proverbs says "The hater of work puts his hand deep into the basin: lifting it again to his mouth is a weariness to him." Another translation says: "Some of us are so lazy that we won't lift a hand to feed ourselves" (Proverbs 26:15 BBC and CEV).

The reason Joseph "came in unto them" was because he had been given charge over them and was serving them. Did he perhaps come to make their beds, set out their clothing, fetch water for their baths, or inquire about their needs for that day? For whatever reason, he came as a servant. It is possible to serve and not be too concerned with whether your boss, colleague or subordinate is happy or sad. But Joseph was compassionate and tender-hearted toward his two wards. Noticing they were sad, he asked "Wherefore look ye so sadly today?" (Genesis 40:7). Please note that the word translated "sadly" is ra or ra,ah the same word used to describe the lean ill-favoured oxen in Pharaoh's first dream. (See Genesis 41:3.) The subtle implication here is that their sadness was a symptom of their leanness of soul that resulted from Pharaoh's ire. The practical application is this: were Joseph to be a manager, he was not to make work his primary and only consideration. The welfare of his wards and staff was to be of equal or even greater importance to him. We are to observe and be concerned with, and do something about the welfare of our staff or those placed under our care. After all, it was the Almighty's concern for the welfare of fallen humanity that led to the incarnation of the Word of God. Though Joseph, too, was imprisoned, he stepped out to minister to the needs of his charges, fulfilling the injunction to: "Rejoice with them that do rejoice and weep with them that do weep" (Romans 12:15). As a fellow prisoner he took their trials and heartaches upon himself. When he heard their problems were borne of their dreams, he was on familiar ground, for he too was a dreamer of dreams, and knew that dreams could cause problems. Joseph here typifies our High Priest who is not untouched by the feelings of our infirmity because "in all points, he was tempted like us but remained without sin" (Hebrews 4:15). No one, least of all Joseph, had any idea how or when his situation would change. Yet, as we discussed earlier, God's counsel tells us: "The Lord controls the mind of a king as easily as He directs the course of a stream" (Proverbs 21:1 GNB).

Similarly Proverbs 16:1, KJV, CEV states that:

"The preparations of the heart in man and the answer of the tongue, is from the LORD." In effect, "We humans make plans, but the Lord has the final word." It is also important to note that God can and does speak by dreams and other means to people who are not even His children, as Pilate's wife could aptly testify! Matthew 27:19 says: "Have thou nothing to do with that just man: For I have suffered many things this day in a dream because of him." She said this to her ignorant husband as he sat down at the judgment seat to hear the "case" against Christ. And if God speaks to unbelievers, how much more will He speak to us, His beloved children? Once he discovered that the dreams had caused their sadness, and knowing that no one but God could interpret them, he shared this truth with them. This strongly implies that they were not among soothsayers, astrologers, tarot, palm and tealeaf readers, magicians, wizards or necromancers, whether in Egypt or elsewhere. Joseph was confident that if they told him the dreams God would give him their interpretation. This is because God knows and declares the end from the beginning, and from antiquity the things that have not yet happened. (See Isaiah 46:10.)

Joseph's confidence was based on his intimate relationship with God. He was aware that if he asked, he would receive, if he sought he would find and if he knocked, it would be opened unto him. (See Matthew 7:7-8.) The butler then told Joseph that he saw in his dream a vine before him. The vine had three branches that budded and blossomed, and its clusters ripened into grapes. Next he saw Pharaoh's cup in his hand and he took the grapes and squeezed them into Pharaoh's cup, and gave the cup to Pharaoh. Joseph quickly responded that the three branches were three days, and that within that time frame, His head would be lifted up. The word "lifted up" means to accept, advance, forgive, pardon and magnify. After the butler's pardon that Joseph predicted, then would follow a restoration unto his "place" (i.e., a pedestal or station-base, estate, or office), and he would once again deliver Pharaoh's cup into his hand as he had done before he fell out of favour.

Because he was confident that the butler's days in captivity were numbered, Joseph, by faith, began to imagine a life outside the prison and asked that the butler put in a good word for him before the king. This is the first time that Joseph hints about what has transpired and declares his innocence. Yet he takes care not to bring a railing accusation against his brothers or to portray them in a bad light before the king's courtiers. What a lesson for us as believers. Imagine how difficult it would have been to reverse people's negative opinions of his brothers later, if he had first stooped to denigrate them.

The Cup Of Blessing

The butler's dream is so loaded with symbolism of the finished work of Christ that even the spiritually blind cannot fail to see them.

"In my dream, behold a vine…," the butler commenced. In John's gospel Jesus tells us He is the true vine. (See John 15:1.)

"And in the vine were three branches," the butler continued. (Genesis 40:10). Jesus connects the link when He says, "I am the vine, ye (His disciples in every age) are the branches" (John 15:5). Joseph helps us understand that the three branches are three days. (See Genesis 40:12.) The butler then went on to declare: "And it was as though it budded, and her blossoms shot forth; and the clusters thereof brought forth ripe grapes" (Genesis 40:10).

The uncanny similarity of imagery and choice of words reminds me of the story of Aaron's rod that budded. That text reads: "And it came to pass, that on the morrow Moses went into the tabernacle of witness; and, behold the rod of Aaron for the house of Levi was budded, and brought forth buds, and bloomed blossoms, and yielded almonds." The background to this interesting event was a leadership dispute in the newly emerging nation of Israel. Several leaders of some tribes had come together to rebel against the authority and leadership of Moses and Aaron. To put the matter to rest, God decided to make manifest His chosen leader. Each of the twelve tribes was to bring a rod bearing the names of princes and the tribes they represented. Aaron's name was etched on Levi's rod. All twelve rods were laid in the tabernacle in front of the Ark of the Covenant. The next day, as in our quoted text, Aaron's rod, representing the House of Levi, had sprouted; it had budded, blossomed with flowers and produced ripe almonds. The parallels between this story and the butler's dreams do not end here. All twelve rods were identical in the sense that they had long been severed from their parent donor-tree even as the butler had been severed from the privilege of service to his great king and master, Pharaoh. The rods, after being cut and treated, were in many ways also like the dead, dry bones that Prophet Ezekiel saw in the valley in his vision.

Common sense, logic, science and experience all point to the fact that they could not live again, let alone bud, bloom and yield fruit. John 15:4 says: "The branch cannot bear fruit of itself, except it abide in the vine." Yet Aaron's rod not only budded, it bloomed, blossomed and even yielded almonds. The message was that he and his household were elected, chosen and approved by the Almighty as the priestly lineage, as indicated by the resurrection of the rod. It was not by any achievement, qualification or goodness on Aaron's part, but election by resurrection. Likewise, John points us: "unto Him that loved us, and washed us from our sins in His own blood, and hath made us kings and priests unto God and His Father" (Revelation 1:5). The message to us is that by His death and resurrection, Jesus washed us from our sins and thereby empowered us to be kings and priests. Consider that the rod was once alive and connected to the vine. Then it was cut off and was therefore dead. Now it was alive again. This typifies "Jesus Christ, who is the faithful and true witness" (Revelation 1:5, 3:14), (a witness is one who has seen, heard and experienced something of which he can boldly testify). Jesus thus testifies, "I am He that lived, and was dead; and, behold, I am alive for evermore, Amen..." (Revelation 1:18).

The budding of the rod is a picture of "the first begotten of the dead." It is this resurrection that gives Jesus the power, and the right to the title, "Prince of the kings of the earth" and "King of kings and Lord of lords" (1 Timothy 6:15; Revelation 17:14; 19:16). Paul is a second witness when he tells the Church in Rome that Jesus Christ was: "declared to be the Son of God with power, according to the Spirit of holiness, by the resurrection from the dead" (Romans 1:4). Moses and Aaron were thus an Old Testament picture of king and priest. The goal was to bring to God the Father "glory and dominion forever and ever." (Revelation 1:6). As kings and priests, we as believers are expected to show forth God's glory and exercise dominion over all the works of His hand.

Finally, as Aaron's rod pictures election by resurrection, remember that both the butler and baker had offended their master and lord, the king of Egypt, and at the time of the dreams they were both under the sentence of death. It was the vine before the butler along with its fruit, which he squeezed into the cup and gave into Pharaoh's hand that secured him favour and restoration. In the same way, Jesus' shed blood and the cup, which He drank of, secured life, favour and access to God, for us as believers. If this Pharaoh is a type of the King of kings, Pharaoh's cup into which the ripe grapes are squeezed is the road to the cross, which had been marked out by God the Father for Jesus–His crucifixion, death and burial.

Jesus Himself testifies to this when He asks James and John if they were able to drink of the cup of which He would drink. (See Matthew 20:22.) Later on in the Garden of Gethsemane, He would refer to the cup again, asking that if it were possible, God would cause it to pass from Him. (See Matthew 26:39 & 42). Finally in John's account of the gospel, Jesus tells Peter to sheath his sword because He, Jesus, would have to drink the cup His Father had given Him. (See John 18:11.) From John's references in Revelation 14:10; 16:19 & 18:6 we can see that this cup is also identified with the fierce wrath of the judgment of God against sin and its originator and father, Satan. The beauty of the message is that this wrath was assuaged by the atoning death of Christ. Pressing the grapes into Pharaoh's cup represents primarily the Gethsemane experience. Here, like the grapes, Jesus was squeezed by what He was going through, such that His sweat was like great droplets of blood falling to the ground" (Luke 22:44).

It is significant to note that the word for blood (dam) is also translated by analogy as the juice of the grape. It is used as such by Jacob in his prayer of blessing for His sons, and Judah in particular. (See Genesis 49:11.) It is also used in the same way by Moses in his own farewell message to Israel. (See Deuteronomy 32:14.) The ultimate goal of this well-chosen word is to highlight the spiritual imperative of the butler's salvation by blood. Paul the Apostle signifies it for the New Testament believer when he says, "For if, when we were enemies, we were reconciled to God by the death of His Son, much more being reconciled, we shall be saved by His life" (Romans 5:10).

Remember also that Gethsemane represents an oil press. In effect, Jesus had to go through the same pressing process that a seed goes through before the oil is extracted from it. As the butler's head was lifted up by reason of the squeezing of the grapes into the cup, so are we lifted up by reason of Jesus' sufferings. The phrase "lifted up" also signifies that we are accepted, exalted, forgiven, helped, held up, honourable, magnified, raised up, respected, and best of all--that we arise. After this squeezing, the butler was restored to his former "manner" (this word means a favourable verdict pronounced judicially, as a sentence or formal decree). All that Adam caused us to suffer and lose was reversed, and we by reason of Jesus' death, are restored to a place of honour with a favourable, irrevocable verdict of "not guilty" and "justified." By Jesus' resurrection from the dead, Paul tells us "God has put all things under the power of Christ, and for the good of the Church he has made him the head of everything" (Ephesians 1:22 CEV). He further tells us that Jesus is "the head of the body, the Church; He is the source of the body's life. He is the first-born Son, who was raised from death, in order that He alone might have first place in all things" (Colossians 1:18 GNB). Thus, as the raising of the butler's head restored him to his place (of grace, honour and favour), so the raising of our Head, Jesus Christ, through the "lifting up" of the cross and the resurrection from the dead, restores us, the Church to our place of grace, honour and favour. Alleluia! (See John 12:32.)

Remember the butler was being restored to his place, which he lost by transgression. In Acts 1:25-26 Apostle Peter observes that Judas by transgression fell from the ministry to, and service of God, and Matthias, whose name implies "grace" (the gift of God), took his place. The butler's restoration is thus a picture of the Bible's central theme of "restoration through redemption." Joseph asked the butler to remember him when it was well with him, and to show kindness to him and make mention of him to Pharaoh so that the injustice repeatedly done him could be reversed. Being in Christ means it is well with us, and we are to remember those who are less-fortunate and less-privileged, showing them kindness in diverse ways, and interceding for them before our Great King, before whom we have the privilege of access, and reverse any injustice done to them. Isn't it ironic that Joseph could foresee the chief butler's imminent parole, but he could not foresee his own. "Physician, heal thyself," thus becomes the misguided taunting reproach of those who do not share Joseph's, Jesus', or our, faith. Most times in the midst of our own issues, God calls us to be a blessing unto others. Many times, it is to people who have wronged us or totally do not deserve to be blessed (at least not in our thinking and certainly not by us!). Yet God is not unfaithful and will not leave us as He did not leave Joseph without the comfort of a witness. From early on God had given him dreams of his honour and the respectful homage of his brothers, and that had not, and would not change.

Just like Jonah's three days in the belly of the whale, the butler's three days typify Jesus' three days in the belly of the earth. (See Matthew 26:61 & John 2:19-21.) It is interesting to note that the character of the chief baker is revealed by the fact that he waits to hear the butler's dream favourably interpreted before he shares his own. In his dream, he had three white baskets on his head (Strong's Dictionary defines the word "white" as white bread). It is exciting and certainly not an accident to see this allusion to bread. Observe also that he was a chief baker (aphah–to cook, especially to bake). In the uppermost basket were all manner of baked items for the king, Pharaoh, and the birds ate of this bread basket from the baker's head. Again the three baskets are the three days of Jonah in the belly of the whale. They represent the three days Jesus referred to in his discourse with the Scribes and Pharisees about the destruction and raising of the temple. Naturally, they mistook this for the physical temple in Jerusalem, but Jesus made it clear that He was talking about the temple of His body. In fact, when this scripture was fulfilled at Jesus' resurrection, it formed a focal point for the disciples' faith as they remembered that He had prophesied it to them well before it happened. (See John 2:19-22.)

Just as Joseph told Pharaoh his two dreams were one, so indeed the two dreams of the butler and baker are one. We shall look more closely at this shortly. (See Genesis 41:25, 26-32.) Joseph's message to the baker was that the three baskets were three days and that in three days Pharaoh would "lift up thy head from off thee" (Genesis 40:19). In the Hebrew this literally means that Pharaoh "would reckon thee, and take thy office from thee." He would be hanged on a tree and the birds would feast on his flesh. In what Jesus implied to be the mother of all parables, (see Mark 4:13), the parable of the Sower, Jesus teaches that the "fowls of the air" which came and devoured the seed by the wayside are none other than a picture of Satan, the "wicked" one. (See Mark 4:15; Matthew 13:19.) David uses a similar metaphor when he declares: "When the wicked, even mine enemies and my foes, came upon me to eat up my flesh, they stumbled and fell." (Psalm 27:2). In effect, the birds are like the thief who comes to steal, kill and destroy. (See John 10:10.) The baker, according to Joseph would thus be hanged on a tree and his flesh would be devoured by scavenging birds.

If the baker represents the crucifixion, death and burial aspects of Christ's atoning sacrificial death, we can see why the baker had to die. His being hanged on a tree is also deliberate in divine predestination: "For he that is hanged is accursed of God" (Deuteronomy 21:23), as the Law of Moses clearly states. Lest skeptics imagine that this correlation is a figment of one's imagination or a "stretched-to-fit" application of the Scripture, Paul expounds it to the Galatian Church when he tells them that "Christ hath redeemed us from the curse of the law, being made a curse for us: for it is written, Cursed is everyone that hangeth on a tree…" (Galatians 3:13). Thus to fulfil the typology of Christ's passion, the baker did not only have to die but he had to be hanged. There is yet one aspect of the baker's dream that needs to be considered. The baker relayed the fact that he had three white bread baskets on his head with all manner of baked items and birds ate them out of the uppermost basket on his head.

Remember when we saw that the baker did not relay his dream till he heard the favourable interpretation of the butler's dream? This is a picture of a carnal-minded believer, that is one who is guided by his flesh or feelings and who does not walk by faith as the butler did, but by sight. In writing to the Romans Paul contrasts the law of sin and death, with the Law of the Spirit, which brings us life in union with Christ Jesus. Apostle Paul explains: "What the law could not do, because human nature was weak, God did. He condemned sin in human nature by sending His own Son, who came with a nature like our sinful nature, to do away with sin. God did this so that the righteous demands of the law might be fully satisfied in us who live according to the Spirit, and not according to human nature. Those who live as their human nature tells them to, have their minds controlled by what human nature wants .Those who live as the Spirit tells them to, have their minds controlled by what the Spirit wants." (Rom 8:3-5GNB)

The point Paul is trying to get across is that "to be controlled by human nature (The KJV-says to be "carnally minded") results in death; while to be controlled by the Spirit ("spiritually minded") results in life and peace" (Romans 8:6.). The lesson to the Church is that the devil will devour the carnal believer and ultimately kill him or her. The death of the baker is thus a picture of the death of Jesus delivering the saint from carnality and the law of sin and death and granting him access to the law of the spirit of life in Christ Jesus. Thus as our human nature, flesh and carnality have to be put to death; it is again no wonder then that the baker had to die!

To mark his birthday three days later, Pharaoh held a banquet for "all his servants," and as Joseph had predicted, he "lifted up the head of the chief butler and the chief baker among his servants" (Genesis 40:20). In effect, "He set the head cupbearer and the head baker in places of honour in the presence of all the guests," the Message translation says; while the BBE version says: "He gave honour to the chief wine servant and the chief bread–maker among the others." My first reaction to this fact is, why would Pharaoh honour them both at this banquet when he intended to execute the chief baker by hanging? I will address that question in a moment. But just as Joseph predicted (or more accurately prophesied), the chief butler was restored to his butlership. This word butlership also means a well-watered region and a fat pasture. He regained his cup-bearing status and activity to Pharaoh, and was restored to a well-watered region and a fat pasture. Likewise, Pharaoh hanged the chief baker just as Joseph had indicated.

As to why Pharaoh first honoured the butler and baker before executing the latter, Adam Clarke in his Commentary on the Bible suggests that "by lifting up the head, probably no more is meant than bringing them to trial, tantamount to what was done by Jezebel and the nobles of Israel to Naboth: "Set Naboth on high among the people; and set two men, sons of Belial, to bear witness against him" (I Kings 21:9). The issue of the trial was, that the baker alone was found guilty, and hanged; and the butler, being acquitted, was restored to his office." I am inclined to disagree with the phrase "no more is meant..." because a closer look at the phrase "lifted up" indicates that he meant much more. The phrase "lifted up" (nasa or nasah in the Hebrew) was carefully chosen by the wisdom of God because of its many connotations. Apart from its primary meaning to lift, exalt, accept, arise, magnify, advance and so on, the word also means "to forgive." Third, it means "to take away or take up." All three sets of meanings apply because the two courtiers are a picture of the One Christ who was "lifted up" on the cross. (See John 3:14; 8:28; 12:32-34.) Following this crucifixion which secured our forgiveness, He died, was buried and was taken up, and is now exalted above all.

Break The Bread, Drink The Wine

The butler and the baker point to bread and wine. Abram was the first person in the scriptures to appreciate the symbolic significance of bread and wine. In dealing with Abram and Melchizedek, you might recall that Abram is the first person to be called a Hebrew. (See Genesis 14:13.) This is from the root aver which means "to cross or pass over." This same word is used of the children of Israel crossing the Jordan to the Promised Land. (See Deuteronomy 27:3.) The apparent symbolism is confirmed when Paul calls Jesus our Passover. (See 1 Corinthians 5:7.) Thus this speaks of covenant as do the bread and wine. Abram gets this revelation from Melchizedek and uses it immediately upon leaving him and speaking to the other kings. This revelation also causes him and other neighbouring kings to give the God of Abram the tithes of the spoils of war. (See Genesis 14:17-24.)

Recall, if you will, that Abram embarked on that military campaign to rescue his nephew Lot among many others, who were prisoners of war. Upon his victorious return, he is met and blessed by Melchizedek, the priest of the Most High God, who being the King of Salem (Peace) and having no recorded antecedents was a type of Christ. Melchizedek's blessings are covenant blessings in which he on the basis of the wine, a type of the shed blood of the lamb, and bread, a type of his broken body, blesses Abram of the Most High God, possessor of heaven and earth, and the Most High God (of Abram) who had delivered his enemies into his hand.

A few thousand years later in the same vicinity, Jesus institutes the ordinance of communion at the last supper. As they ate, Jesus took bread, blessed it and (please note!) broke it. Then He gave it to the disciples, telling them "Take, eat; this is my body" (Matthew 26:26; Mark 14:22). Luke 22:19 adds some vital clues to help us understand the purpose of this statement regarding the bread. "This is my body which is given for you: this do in remembrance of me" (Luke 22:19). But it is Apostle Paul, who puts the final clue in place when he explains communion to the rowdy Corinthian believers who either never really understood the holy ordinance or had simply forgotten what it stood for. Paul, by inspiration, reports Jesus as saying, "Take eat; this is my body, which is broken for you, this do in remembrance of me." Jesus in effect was saying that as He was breaking the bread, so His body would be broken for the disciples (and indeed anyone who believes). But we will have to go back to the prophecies of Isaiah to understand what all that breaking was designed to do. Jesus, he informed us, bore our griefs and carried our sorrows. Yet in our arrogant ignorance we assumed He was being punished for His wrongdoing. However, it was for our transgressions that He was wounded, and for our iniquities that He was bruised; indeed His chastisement secured our peace and His wounds our healing. (See Isaiah 53:1-5.)

In the New Testament Paul declares that Jesus "was delivered for our offences and was raised again for our justification" (Romans 4:25), and again that "...Christ died for our sins according to the scriptures" (1 Corinthians 15:3). Similarly, when supper was ended, Jesus took the cup, gave thanks and gave it to the disciples, inviting them to partake of the cup of which He said: "For this is my blood of the New Testament which is shed for many for the remission of sins" (Matthew 26:27-28). This assertion is followed by one of the most significant yet overlooked scriptures, which reveals the further significance of the wine in the table of the Lord. "But I say unto you, I will not drink henceforth of this fruit of the vine, till that day when I drink it new with you in my Father's kingdom" (Matthew 26:29). This is a veiled reference to Jesus' resurrection and the dispensation of the Holy Spirit that was beginning, and how the resurrection would signify the coming of God's kingdom on earth. Putting it all together, we can see how the breaking of the bread points to the death aspect of Jesus' atonement and the wine, the resurrection aspect. From this we can conclude that the butler and the baker are types and shadows of bread and wine, of crucifixion and resurrection.

The King's Birthday

What feeds and fuels the faith of the believer is every "thus saith the Lord," for we know that God, has magnified His word above all His name, (Psalm 138:2), in other words if He said it, then it will come to pass. Thus, as Joseph had predicted, "It came to pass the third day, which was Pharaoh's birthday..." (Genesis 40:20).

The king's birthday by tradition was a time when all his servants were expected to especially honour and wait on him and his invited guests.

All hands were required to be on deck, and the absence of the butler and baker would have been quite obvious. This may have accounted for their cases being reviewed. This implies that our lives are inextricably woven into the fabric of our nations and their rulers. This is why the Psalmist tells us to "Pray for the peace of Jerusalem," because as he concludes: "They shall prosper that love" her. (Psalm 122:6). The Prophet Jeremiah on his part quotes, the Lord God as saying: "And seek the peace of the city wither I have caused you to be carried away captives, and pray unto the lord for it: for in the peace thereof shall ye have peace" (Jeremiah 29:7). Finally, in the New Testament, Apostle Paul admonishes his son, Timothy and the Church to make supplications, prayers and intercessions, and thanksgiving for all men, especially kings and all those in authority because they could determine whether we live quiet and peaceable lives characterised by all godliness and honesty. (See 1 Timothy 2:1-2.) Rulers also determine whether or not the environment is conducive for all to be saved and to come to the saving knowledge of the truth. (See 1 Timothy 2:4.) Thus Pharaoh's birthday proved to be the day of the baker's execution and the butler's elevation. In the New Testament, we see the celebrating of the birthday of another king being marked. The wicked, carnal king Herod on that day beheaded the righteous John the Baptist and promoted Herodias's daughter. (See Matthew 14:3-11.)

"This Day Have I Begotten Thee"

Our heavenly Pharaoh, our King of kings, is the great I Am. He is the One who is and is to come, and He does not have a birthday. Even His word that became flesh, who came forth unto God, to be a ruler

in Israel, had his "goings forth from of old, from everlasting" (Micah 5:2). Yet in the fullness of God's timing, Jesus came in the flesh. His birthday would not be accounted from the day of his birth, however, but from the day of his rebirth. On that day, the old man Adam, like the baker was put to death and the new creation, Christ, like the butler, was exalted. That day, the Lord said unto His precious only begotten Son: "Thou art my Son; this day have I begotten thee" (Psalm 2:7). On the birthday of the King of kings and Lord of lords, "The promise which was made unto the Fathers (that is Abraham, Isaac, Jacob, Joseph, etc.) God hath fulfilled the same unto us their children, in that He has raised up Jesus again; as it is also written in the second Psalm, thou art my Son, this day have I begotten thee" (Acts 13:32-33).

The birthday of our King was the day when He by Himself having "purged our sins, sat down on the right hand of the Majesty on high" (Hebrews 1:3). It was the day when His name was exalted above the angels as the butler was exalted above the baker; it was the day when the Almighty Father commanded: "And let all the angels of God worship Him" (Hebrews 1:6). It was the day when the Father declared unto the Son: "Thy throne, O God, is forever and ever: a sceptre of righteousness is the sceptre of thy Kingdom. Thou hast loved righteousness, and hated iniquity; therefore God, even thy God, hath anointed thee with the oil of gladness above thy fellows" (Hebrews 1:8-9). And as the king's birthday marked a new dawn, a new birth for the butler, our King's birthday also marks a new dawn for the believer. He is the first begotten of the dead (Revelation 1:5), and has become the "first fruits of them that slept" (1 Corinthians 15:20). With that confident assurance the butler can face a new day but then again, so ultimately can the baker because "as we have borne the image of the earthy, we shall also bear the image of the heavenly" (1 Corinthians 15:49). On the king's birthday, "He made a feast unto all his servants" (Genesis 40:20). This is a picture of the Lord's Table, a feast prepared for all servants who by partaking of it have become sons. It is the table prepared for us in the presence of our enemies. (See Psalm 23:5.) On our King's birthday, everything we lost in Adam was restored to us. We are restored to our butlership, fat pasture and our well-watered region. Like the Psalmist, we have been proved and tried as silver is tried, gone through sundry afflictions, and had men "ride over our heads, passing through fire and floods, but God has ultimately brought us to a wealthy place, a place of satisfaction and overflowing with blessings. (See Psalm 66:10-12.)

The chapter ends with the sad fact that the chief butler did not remember Joseph. This means as the Hebrew word shakach or shakeach implies that the butler was neither mindful of him, nor made mention of him. Rather, he promptly forgot him, was oblivious of him and mislaid him from his memory and attention. Perhaps this is what in Amos 6:6, the Prophet was seeing in the spirit when he complained about those "that drink wine in bowls" (the butler?) and are "not grieved for the affliction of Joseph," (who was still in prison). Many of us are in this same place, where Joseph was, aware of God's promises, confident of an imminent change and relaxing in the "comfy" bosom of expectation, born of obedience. Yet those we have sacrificed for have promptly forgotten and abandoned us. But we must remember that this is the Lord's doing. Primarily, God is weaning us from trusting in man or in the arm of flesh, which will always fail, while God never fails. Moreover, God is so jealous of His Benefactor status over our lives, that, He will not permit anyone to share in that glory or limelight. Had the butler engineered Joseph's liberty, he would have also sought to control his destiny.

Secondarily, It is vital to realise that it is only God who "changeth the times and the seasons: He removeth kings, and setteth up kings: he giveth wisdom unto the wise, and knowledge to them that know understanding: he revealeth the deep and secret things: He knoweth what is in the darkness, and the light dwelleth with Him" (Daniel 2:21-23). Ecclesiastes 3:2 tells us: "To everything there is a season, and a time to every purpose under the heaven." Just as God did not send his Son "till the fullness of time was come" (Galatians 4:4), so your situation will not change till God's set time has come. In the meantime, like Job, we also declare: "All the days of my appointed time will I wait, till my change come" (Job14:14). A change that is engineered by men is fragile, fractious, amorphous and transitory. A God-ordained change on the other hand, is stable, solid, durable and destiny-enhancing. Joseph rested in the knowledge that the butler may have forgotten him, but the King of glory had not, could not, would never forget him. Dearly beloved, hang on with the blessed assurance that the Almighty, the Lord of hosts is not only mindful of you and of His covenant towards you, but will visit and bless you and by His thoughts of peace bring you to an expected end, a future and a hope. (See Psalm 8:4; Psalm 111:5; Jeremiah 29:11.)

Pharaoh's Dream:

Joseph woke with a start, drenched in sweat, and his heart was pounding for reasons he could not fathom. Normally, he mused, these kind of palpitations accompanied nightmares wherein armed brigands in hot pursuit seeking his harm, were gaining on him; or some wild animal was about to pounce and make a meal of him. At that point he usually woke up with a pulsating heart threatening to leap out of his chest. But it couldn't have been that because he had just slept like a baby and enjoyed a deep, dreamless sleep. For one (in)famous for his dreams, that was ironic. However, this time the feeling was one of eager anticipation, a strange kind of excitement rather reminiscent of the night before a long-awaited excursion. He could not articulate it but felt strongly that something was about to happen. Could it be? Did he dare dream (oh, that word again!) that today would be the day when he was freed from prison? Did he dare hope for release after so many years, unlawfully incarcerated for standing by his convictions? Ironically the loud, accusing voice of regret mocked him for being 'slow,' uninformed about how the 'real' world operates and for being the architect of his own doom. Yet he heard a still small voice of calm and peace, with a whisper so loud that it warmed his heart, reminding him of eternal truths: he knew that doing the right thing was always the right thing to do (even when no one was looking). He mused that while others may not necessarily approve, it always got you the right results in the end. Was he about to be vindicated? Was truth about to prevail? Or was he being daft to dwell on such possibilities? Could he afford to hope for things he could not see, believing God was still in control and would ultimately reward him? Ironically during that very night of dreamless sleep Pharaoh would dream two troubling and cryptic dreams of his own.

CHAPTER FIVE

MY TIME HAS COME

"And it came to pass at the end of two full years that Pharaoh dreamed: and, behold, he stood by the river" (Genesis 41:1).

It is interesting to note that two full years pass with no change after Joseph's encounter with the butler. At that point he must have sensed that the dream meant something was about to change. He knew that: "A man's gift makes room for him, and brings him before great men" (Proverbs 18:6, KJV). Somehow he knew that for him to get justice, a power higher than Potiphar's would have to intervene. Remember he had told the butler: "Make mention of me unto Pharaoh, and bring me out of this house" (Genesis 40:14). He also knew by inspiration that his ability to dream and interpret dreams would guarantee his elevation. Keep in focus that your power to dream will set you among the stars. Furthermore, it is crucial to note also that the passage of time does not diminish the potency of your dream. Indeed, we have need of patience, because after having done that which is right and in line with God's will, we will receive the promise. (See Hebrews 10:36.) Joseph remained incarcerated till the time that his word came. (See Psalm 105:19.) A vision is truly for an appointed time and even though it appears delayed, the prophet Habakkuk assures us that it will come to pass. (See Habakkuk 2:3.)

To get back to our story Pharaoh dreamed that he stood by the river (doubtlessly, the Nile), where he sees seven beautiful, well-fed cows come out of the river and begin to graze in a meadow directly behind them. Out of the same river came, seven other cows, which then stood beside the fat cows, on the river banks. In a perversely ironic way this serves to highlight the dramatic contrast between the two sets of cattle. The second set is as gaunt as the first set is robust, as sickly as the others were healthy. Without warning the lean cows ate the fat cows. At that point Pharaoh woke up. Pharaoh then went back to sleep and had a second dream. This time he saw seven ears of grain, full-bodied and lush, growing out of a single stalk. Then seven more ears sprang forth, but they were small and shrivelled. Please observe that the same adjective for the fat cattle is used to describe the good ears of corn, i.e., both the words "fat-fleshed" and "fat" originate from the Hebrew word barky, while the phrases "well-favoured" and "good" are synonyms for pleasant and prosperous in appearance.

Similarly, the Hebrew word "daq" is translated "lean-fleshed" for the gaunt cattle and "thin" for the ears of grain. In this dream the thin ears ate up the full ears and suddenly Pharaoh awoke. "And behold, it was a dream" (Genesis 41:7). This last phrase is added (The Contemporary English Version says "It had only been a dream") because the dream was so vivid and real that Pharaoh was awestruck. There was something about this dream that made Pharaoh realise that it was not just "divers vanities" as suggested by the preacher in Ecclesiastes 5:7. This explains why his spirit was troubled when he awoke in the morning. Pharaoh knew deep inside that these dreams required interpretation. In effect, he discerned that it was a divine, coded message that required wise men to decipher it. Happily, "The secret things belong unto the Lord our God; but those things which are revealed belong unto us and to our children forever, that we may do all the words of this law" (Deuteronomy 29:29, KJV).

God was the source of the dreams and he had cleverly concealed their interpretation from the magicians and wise men so that Joseph would be remembered and brought on the scene. If as Shakespeare wisely opined, "All the world's a stage..." (William Shakespeare: As you like It- Monologue by melancholy Jacques),--then it was time for Joseph to make his dramatic entrance! At this point, the chief butler recalled Joseph's request to be remembered to the king. He explained to Pharaoh how he and the chief baker had both dreamt and how

Joseph had accurately interpreted the dreams. Many times, we get offended and upset when people who can help us fail or refuse to do so. But like Joseph, we must realise that God is in control and has a timetable. In the fullness of God's time, you will not stay a day, or even a moment longer in captivity than God has ordained or permitted! Imagine how it would have turned out if the butler had spoken to Pharaoh earlier (prematurely surely!). How would the butler have explained Joseph's incarceration? It might have ended up in a messy investigation that could have cast Joseph in a bad light.

Might the butler's premature intervention not have caused more problems for Joseph? The butler explained the details of their interaction. "And it came to pass, as he interpreted to us, so it was; me he restored unto mine office, and him he hanged" (Genesis 41:13).

This verse is both intriguing and exciting, not just for what it says but also for what it implies. The butler is not only recommending Joseph for his interpretation of dreams but also for his gift of discerning their meaning. He seems to suggest that it was Joseph who restored him to his position and executed his contemporary, the baker. This is a powerful lesson for dreamers, seers, visionaries and sages both now and in the future. An unimplemented dream is nothing short of a juvenile fantasy. An unfulfilled vision is like an exciting but pointless fairy tale, like planting a crop without harvest. The significance of this will be seen after Joseph successfully interprets Pharaoh's dream. After the butler's glowing recommendation and the fact that the king was desperate for interpretation Pharaoh sent for Joseph, who was quickly brought out of the dungeon. Just as in Joseph's case, at the appointed time, your former accusers, captors, jailers, "nay-Sayers"--that is skeptics and unjust critics, will expedite your release.

Note that it was the same people who told blind Bartimaeus to hold his peace that shortly told him to be of good cheer because the Master had sent for him. (See Mark 10:49.) In the next forty-eight hours, God is going to cause you who are reading this to be elevated and blessed by someone who has antagonised you over the years.

Now, consider this: Pharaoh was in a hurry to see Joseph, but Joseph took his time getting ready. The text says, "He shaved himself and changed his raiment, and came unto Pharaoh." Many of us have wonderful messages but poor presentation skills; others have wonderful products but atrocious packaging; yet others have uncommon skills but commoners' manners.

Scores of us fail at interviews not because we lack the qualification or experience required, but because our appearance doesn't live up to the positions we aspire to. Rather than speaking softly and wearing the appropriate garb, our appearance reveals our past stations in life.

While in captivity Joseph had schooled himself on the customs of the Egyptians at all levels. He was acquainted with both the etiquette of the court and the workings of ordinary society. As a Hebrew, Joseph was inclined to grow a beard, which would have been a much more practical option while imprisoned. In fact, a cursory journey through Jewish history shows that a beard was a symbol of age, status, authority and respect. David and his men sported beards. (See 1 Samuel 21:13; 2 Samuel 10:4-5); as did Mephibosheth and Amasa (see 2 Samuel 19:24; 20:9); Ezra and Ezekiel, (see Ezra 9:3; Ezekiel 5:1); the men of Shechem (see Jeremiah 41:5); and of course the high priest, Aaron, whose beard is the centre of focus in that great psalm of brotherly unity. (See Psalm 133:2.)

However, Joseph realised that a man only gets one chance to make a lasting and salutary first impression. He also understood that no matter how gifted, anointed, knowledgeable, talented, or skilled a man is, his appearance can hinder his career aspirations.

One final note--when you dress for where you are, you are doomed to remain there. When you dress for where you are going you will inevitably be catapulted there in due season. Notice that Joseph shaved then changed his raiment. There are certain things we must shave off and certain others we must put on before we can stand before great men. In fact, it is wise for anyone with dreams to dress for success.

When Joseph came in to Pharaoh, Pharaoh wasted no time but got right to the point. He wanted to know the meaning of his dreams, and was already aware that they were somehow related. He said, "I have dreamed a dream. Then he added, "Thou canst understand a dream to interpret it" (Genesis 41:15).

Life constantly throws challenges at us and we have the choice to compromise or to do what is right. It is here that Joseph's habit of doing the right thing, finally paid off by giving him audience before a great man.

Joseph's response demonstrates the reason for his promotion.

"It is not in me: God shall give Pharaoh an answer of peace" (Genesis 41:16). This is symptomatic of the kind of humility that precedes promotion. John the Baptist said it most succinctly when he surrendered lordship to Jesus declaring, "A man can receive nothing except it be given him from heaven" (John 3:27).

With the threat of death hanging over his head Daniel declared: "But there is a God in heaven that revealeth secrets, and maketh known to the King Nebuchadnezzar what shall be in the latter days. Thy dream and the visions of thy head upon thy bed are these..." (Daniel 2:28), so he then proceeded to interpret by divine inspiration the king's dream. Jesus himself said, "For without me ye can do nothing" (John 15:5).

It is important to note also, in keeping with the confidence the butler placed in Joseph, that Joseph assured Pharaoh that God would give him an answer of peace. The word peace--shalom--means health, security, tranquility, welfare, good condition, success and comfort. The message here is that no matter what situation we face, whether pleasant or difficult, God will always answer with His peace. In effect, He works all things together for our good if we love him and are the called according to his purpose" (Romans 8:28). A veiled condition is to be found in the word "answer." Keeping in mind that an answer is always the response to a question, we can conclude that Pharaoh was not satisfied to let his dreams remain a mystery. Something inside told him there was more to the dreams than met the eye so he pursued an answer.

In the New Testament Jesus said we should ask, seek and knock with the assurance that if we ask in faith we will receive. James 4:2 confirms that: "...Ye have not, because ye ask not." Unlike King Nebuchadnezzar who dreamed dreams but failed to recall them, Pharaoh remembered, but did not understand them.

When Pharaoh explained his dream we see a remarkable reversal of roles: a sovereign seeking the wisdom of a young foreign slave.

As noted earlier, it is clear that Pharaoh knew that both his dreams were one and the same; they are like the root and shoot of a plant, which though distinctive, are part of the same plant, which is why he does not speak of them as two dreams but as one. "In my dream..." and verse 22: "I saw in my dream..." (Genesis 41:17-22). Joseph confirmed what Pharaoh knew but did not understand, what he saw but could not decipher or decode. "The dream of Pharaoh is one" (Genesis 41:25). Joseph quickly revealed the meaning of the dream. "God hath showed Pharaoh what he is about to do" (Genesis 41:25). This incident demonstrates that God is willing and eager to reach out to communicate with those He loves. He still wants to speak with us directly, without human mediators or middle men. He wants intimacy that cannot be attained by any other means than talking. The problem is that we fail to listen and obey God, which blocks our fellowship and leaves us alone to fend for ourselves.

If we say we love God we are to stop asking everyone's opinion but His, and go straight to the source, so He can speak to us.

Joseph then proceeds to tell Pharaoh that the seven good oxen and the seven good ears both represent seven good years, as indeed the seven skinny oxen and the seven empty ears represent seven years of famine. Again Joseph reiterates that God is warning Pharaoh about the future, in order to give him wisdom and show him how to prepare for this situation.

From this point, however, Joseph goes from explaining the dream to interpreting it. In the process he has graduated from knowing to under-standing. Here it is important to understand that those with knowledge will exercise power over ignorant men. But men of understanding will stand above them both. Joseph explains that Egypt was about to enjoy an incredible economic boom that would span a period of seven years. This would be followed by seven years of depression and famine that would obliterate any memory of the past good years. Again, Joseph reiterates the point he had made earlier: "And the plenty shall not be known in the land by reason of that famine following; for it shall be very grievous" (Genesis 41:31). Anyone with even minor powers of perception would have noticed that in the very short space of about seven verses Joseph employs the tool of repetition as a matter of course. And he does not do it for literary emphasis or dramatic effect.

...Every Word Is Established

Joseph's first encounter with God was by the two dreams he received by inspiration. Interestingly, both dreams prophesied his dominion and rule over his brothers and his parents. From those two dreams with one meaning and also obviously from his father's counsel, he discovered a potent vital and indispensable principle--that of how God's counsel is established. He tells Pharaoh therefore--"...and for that the dream was doubled unto Pharaoh twice, it is because the thing is established by God, and God will shortly bring it to pass" (Genesis 41:32). In other words, Joseph teaches Pharaoh something he has learned about how God establishes things He intends to bring to pass; He doubles them or repeats them. To understand this concept, we will need to go to Mosaic Law to see how it was initiated. The Law states that anyone who was found to have committed idolatry was to be stoned to death. However, there was a rigorous process that preceded the capital punishment. Hearsay alone was not sufficient to act on; you also had to carefully and diligently inquire ("look at the evidence and investigate carefully" (Deuteronomy 17:2-6, MSG). Capital punishment was only used if there was absolutely no doubt about the person's guilt. Moses thus clearly explains the principle Joseph was expounding: "At the mouth of two witnesses or three witnesses, shall he that is worthy of death be put to death; but at the mouth of one witness he shall not be put to death" (Deuteronomy 17:6). Let us immediately put this newly learned principle to the test. Does it occur anywhere else, at the mouth of another one or two witnesses? "One witness shall not rise up against a man for any iniquity, or for any sin, in any sin that he sinneth: at the mouth of two witnesses, or at the mouth of three witnesses, shall the matter be established" (Deuteronomy 19:15).

So here we have a second witness to this wisdom key to which Joseph introduces us. Finally we read: "Whoso killeth any person, the murderer shall be put to death by the mouth of witnesses: but one witness shall not testify against any person to cause him to die" (Numbers 35:30). Thus we see that even the law that requires multiple witnesses to establish the truth of a matter must and has itself been subject to its own dictates. It is interesting to note that this law is the basis of modern jurisprudence. Even today, a person cannot be convicted by one source or one person's evidence. Even with advanced forensic science and technology there must be corroborating evidence that actually, for example, puts the suspect on the scene, or ties him to the crime. Many will immediately argue that this is under the law and so has no relevance to the life and demeanour of the New Testament saint. So let's see how it stands up under the new covenant. Jesus, in teaching the disciples how to deal with offences in general, introduced them to what to them looked like a new principle. "If your brother sins against you," Jesus told his disciples, "go to him and show him his fault. But do it privately, just between yourselves. If he listens to you, you have won your brother back."(Matthew 18:15 GNB). I strongly believe that if everyone, whether Christian or non-Christian, adopted just this first step in the divine conflict resolution strategy, the majority of conflicts would be instantly resolved.

In part two of this lesson Jesus went on to explain that if your offended brother was not willing to make peace you were to take one or two other people of mutual acquaintance to serve as arbitrators. He declared that the purpose of this step is so that: "In the mouth of two or three witnesses every word may be established" (Matthew 18:16). Here we immediately see the Lord Himself taking an Old Testament law, relating to capital offences and applying it to a conflict resolution situation. Thus from being a law in the Old Testament it becomes a principle for victorious living in the New Testament. As we did in the Old Testament, we will subject this principle to its own dictates and see if it occurs at the mouth of other witnesses. In the gospel of John, Jesus, among other things, asserted that He is the light of the world. The Pharisees immediately tried to use this law of witnesses against Him, declaring that since He was the only person testifying by Himself of Himself, His witness could not be true. Jesus in turn did not dispute the righteous dictates of that (or any other) law but systematically began to apply it and to show them how He not only fulfilled it, but was actually the fulfilment of it.

Jesus began by giving his credentials, right, and authority for bearing record of Himself–unlike the Pharisees He knew where He was coming from and where He was going. Further declaring His unity with His heavenly Father, Jesus alludes to a statement He made earlier. The Pharisees, who had no right to judge, were too quick to do so, and did so in the flesh. He, to whom judgment was committed, however, judged no man. If, however, Jesus decided to exercise His mandate to judge, He would do so in truth. (See John 8:12-16.) He said this was because, "The Father judgeth no man, but hath committed all judgment unto the Son" (John 5:22). "For I am not alone, but I and the Father that sent me" (John 8:16). Jesus, who realised that the hard-hearted Pharisees were deliberately missing the inference, then pointed to the law of witnesses. "It is also written in your law," He postulated, "that the testimony of two men is true" (John 8:17). He was one witness and His Father who sent Him was another witness. The disciples themselves were also to be witnesses. The born-again believer (see Acts 1:8) was to also be a witness. The works that Jesus did (see John 5:36) were also witnesses, as was John the Baptist. The important fact to extrapolate in this whole story is that truth or testimony is established at the mouth of two or three witnesses. At this juncture, we have seen this principle being subjected to its own dictates. But some may argue that the two witnesses of the New Testament are one and the same person. They may surmise: "If we get another person saying the same thing then we will accept it." So may I invite the Apostle Paul to lend credence to what we have discovered so far? In 2 Corinthians 13:1 Apostle Paul says, "This is the third time I am coming to you. In the mouth of two or three witnesses shall every word be established." This is probably the clearest outline and application of this principle that there is in the

New Testament. Apostle Paul applies this principle so consistently in all his epistles that such doctrines, instructions, principles and so on are not only repeated in one epistle but are common to two, three or more, and in some cases all the epistles. He outlines his motive for repetition: "To write the same things to you, to me indeed is not grievous, but for you it is safe" (Philippians 3:1b).

1 John 5:8 tells us: "There are three that bear witness in earth, the spirit, and the water and the blood: and these three agree in one." Finally, when He wanted to show the immutability of His counsel, God the Father confirmed it by an oath so that the dual witness would be a strong encouragement to us as heirs of the promise. (See Hebrews 6:18.)

However, let us get back to Joseph, as he outlines the principle of witnesses, and its purpose: "And for that the dream was doubled unto Pharaoh twice; it is because the thing is established by God, and God will shortly bring it to pass" (Genesis 41:32). If Joseph had stopped here, Pharaoh would have been satisfied and would have rewarded Joseph and probably granted him his freedom and sent him on his way back to his family from whom he had been separated those many years. But from this point on, Joseph moved from knowledge (being aware of the facts) and understanding (knowing how the facts work) to wisdom, prudence and discernment. He told Pharaoh how the wealth of the seven years of abundance was to be stored in granaries and silos in several cities under the supervision of a man of discretion (biyn--mentally separate or distinguished, diligent, discerning, informed, prudent, cunning, understanding,) and wise (intelligent, skilful and artful, wise-hearted). This would ensure that the years of famine would not be felt. (See Genesis 41:33-36.) Note that Joseph had no agenda. A man of prudence has no agenda but the advancement of God's kingdom. It is ironic that in suggesting that Pharaoh seek out such a man, Joseph was preparing for his own appointment. Wisdom is the application of knowledge and understanding for the advancement of the kingdom and the benefit of God's people. Also note that in between all this, he introduces the principle of the fifth, which we will look at in detail a little later. (See Genesis 41:34.) Joseph's idea should be the principle of national, state, family and personal financial prudence. In the good cycles, we must diligently invest and not spend all we have on pleasurable living. A good farmer knows that a part of any and every harvest is for re-investing. Because the counsel was God-given and was obviously (with the gift of foreknowledge and hindsight!) common sense, Pharaoh and his court accepted it. The only challenge was looking for a man who would execute this prudent plan, one in whom as Pharaoh said to his servants, the breath, the life and the spirit of God resides. This is a clear picture of the New Testament believer who is the sanctuary and dwelling place of the Holy Spirit. (See 1 Corinthians 6:19.)

At this point, Pharaoh could have become rationalistic and nationalistic. He, like many of us, might have reasoned that now that the dream was clear it would be wise to have an Egyptian and preferably one of his sons or relatives to administer this great revealed plan. But this Pharaoh was wise, hence his success. He was good, hence God's commitment to bless him. Pharaoh rightly reasoned that Joseph had taught them all they knew about the situation but may not have told them all he knew! Moreover, if complications arose, as they inevitably always do, in the administration of the solution, Pharaoh reasoned that since Joseph was connected to the Source, he would always have the right answers. If God showed you all this, Pharaoh conjectured, then there is no one as discreet and wise as you are. Since this Pharaoh was benevolent, God decided to use him to typify Himself even as Joseph typified the Christ. Pharaoh's response could well have been God speaking to Jesus and giving him authority over all the works of his hands: "Thou shall be over my house" (Genesis 41:40). Pharaoh tells Joseph. The writer of Hebrews lets us know that we are the house and that Christ is the builder and is a Son over His own house. (See Hebrews 3:1-6; 10:21.) Jesus was thus given authority over God's house, in the same way Joseph was given authority over Pharaoh's. Pharaoh continues by saying "...and according to thy word shall all my people be ruled" (Paul tells the Philippians that God has highly exalted Jesus and given Him a name, which carries fame, reputation and implies authority and dignity, above every other name, on earth and under the earth.) (See Philippians 2:9-11.) Pharaoh concludes by telling Joseph "...Only in the throne will I be greater than thou." Paul in turn explains that the Father has put all things under Jesus, but the Father is "excepted" and is superior only on the throne. (See 1 Corinthians 15:27-28.)

The beauty of all this authority is not that it is given to Jesus but that He declares that as the Father has sent Him so He is sending us; that as the Father has given Him the authority of His name, so Jesus is giving us the authority of His! This, Jesus assures us, guarantees us that whatever we ask in His name, the Father will do for us. He also assures us of greater works than He did because He was departing to the Father but leaving us the authority of sons. (See John 14:12-14; 15:16; 16:23-27.) So as Pharaoh set Joseph over all the land of Egypt, God set Jesus over the whole earth. Pharaoh took off his ring (a seal, a signet) from his hand and put it on Joseph's hand. The parallel account in the Gospel of John tells us: "For God sent not his Son into the world to condemn the world; but that the world through him might be saved" (John 3:17). Similarly, Jesus assures believers: "In my name shall they cast out devils..." (Matthew 16:17), thereby passing on to believers the authority bequeathed to Him by His heavenly Father. Alleluia!

Furthermore, Joseph was arrayed in vestures of fine (silk) linen and a gold chain was put about his neck. Isaiah 45:23 shows us the correlation between righteousness and authority. It is absolute unadulterated righteousness that commands absolute yet incorruptible authority. The righteousness that comes by works, the law and religion, can of course never be absolute or unadulterated. He is therefore referring to the true righteousness that comes through faith in the sacrificial death of the Lamb of God, Jesus the Christ. "I have sworn by myself, the word is gone out of my mouth in righteousness, and shall not return, that unto me every knee shall bow, every tongue shall swear" (Isaiah: 45:23).

As a child of God, you cannot walk in the full authority of the finished work of Christ if you do not absolutely believe you have been made right with God by His own standards of righteousness. Many of us cannot live victoriously and exercise dominion over life's challenges. This is because of the condemnation of past sins, and a feeling of inadequacy birthed by our inability to earn our righteousness, even after our sins are washed away. Pharaoh then made Joseph to ride in his second chariot and they cried before him: "Bow the knee," and Joseph was made ruler of all Egypt. Pharaoh further gave Joseph absolute sovereignty, second only to himself. No one could do anything in the realm without Joseph's approval. Wow! In the short time that Pharaoh has talked with him, and obviously because of both the butler's and Potiphar's commendations and references, Pharaoh had learnt enough about Joseph to know he could be trusted with such absolute power. Remember that John Emerich Edward Dalberg in a letter to Bishop Mandell Crieghton in 1887 postulated that "Power tends to corrupt and absolute power corrupts absolutely". Joseph, however, was incorruptible and would later amply justify the trust placed in him. Pharaoh gave Joseph a significant name, which could only have been inspired by Father Jehovah God, Himself. The name was Zaphnath-Paaneah. This name signifies in the Coptic a revealer of secrets or one to whom secrets are revealed. However, it literally means Prince of the Life of the Age. These are divine titles that no man can lay claim to. Without doubt, the Christ is the only one who reveals secrets because all secrets are revealed to Him by His Father.

(See John 3:35 & 5:20.) More importantly, who other than Christ could rightly be called, "The Prince of the Life of the Age"? No wonder John the Beloved said, "All things were made by Him; and without Him was not anything made that was made. In Him was life; and the life was the light of men" (John 1:3-4).

For us, if our Saviour and Christ, who is Lord and God, has the key to all secrets, it is obvious that this Lord will reveal them to us who are His beloved. More so, because He said we should ask and then we will receive, that our joy may be full. (See John 16:24.) Furthermore, He admonishes us to call unto Him, and He will answer us and show us great and mighty things, which we do not know. (See Jeremiah 33:3.) We never have to be in the dark, for the revealer of secrets is our God and Father. Alleluia!

On the issue of life, Isaiah 9:6 tells us that the Messiah is the "Prince of Peace." The word "Prince" implies dominion, headship and rulership. The Apostle Peter, on his part, in his sermon on Mars Hill, declared that, "In Him we live and move and have our being" (Acts 17:28). Having given Joseph the messianic name, Pharaoh then gives Joseph a wife, Asenath, the daughter of Poti-pherah, priest or prince of On. One cannot help but notice the subtle irony: Joseph refused the illicit relationship with the wife of Potiphar and won a legitimate relationship with the daughter of Poti-pherah. The message: Whatever you compromise to get, you ultimately lose. If you will not compromise, however, you will get more than you imagined or even dared to ask--Poti-pherah instead of Potiphar. This name means "belonging to the sun." Joseph belonged to the Sun of Righteousness rising with healing in His wings. (See Malachi 4:2.) At this point, Joseph was thirty years old and his dreams were beginning to come to pass as he "went out over all the land of Egypt" (Genesis 41:46). Thirty is the number that signifies the blood. In effect, it is only by the power of the blood that Joseph could boldly and with favour, stand before Pharaoh the King of Egypt, depart from his presence and exercise dominion in all Egypt. "And in the seven plenteous years the earth brought forth by handfuls" (Genesis 41:47). When the children of Israel asked how to discern a true prophet, Moses answered: "When a prophet speaketh in the name of the Lord, if the thing follow not, nor come to pass, that is the thing which the Lord hath not spoken, but the prophet hath spoken it presumptuously: thou shalt not be afraid of him." (Deuteronomy 18:22). In effect the Message version says, "If what the prophet spoke in God's name doesn't happen, then obviously God wasn't behind it; the prophet made it up. Forget about him." Because Joseph's interpretations and prophecy were very specific and complex the very imminent passage of time would quickly expose him as an oracle of the living God or as a presumptuous charlatan.

Indeed the seven bountiful years caused the earth to bring forth in unprecedented abundance. God had vindicated Joseph and His divine plan, which had been in place all the time now became more apparent, though the best was yet to come. Joseph built granaries and silos in every major Egyptian city where he stockpiled the surplus food from their neighbouring farmlands. So much was the store of grain, that it was likened to the sand of the sea, so that effective record-keeping became not just futile, but truly impossible. During this period of abundance, Joseph's wife Asenath bore him two children whom Joseph symbolically and prophetically named Manasseh and Ephraim. Manasseh means forgetting. Joseph's rationale for naming his first-born as such was, because God had helped him to forget all his hardships and trouble, and his family back in Canaan. Ephraim, on the other hand means fruitful, for as Joseph realised, God had caused him to be fruitful in the land of his affliction. The prophetic significance of these two sons will unfold as Joseph's story progresses towards its exciting climax.

As Joseph predicted, like an Olympic relay runner the lean years took the baton from the prosperous years and a season of severe dearth followed. This acute famine, which was comparable to the Great Depression of the 1930's, affected all countries except Egypt where Joseph's foresight had guaranteed an abundant supply of food. Soon however, even Egypt began to feel the effect of the famine, and the people cried out to Pharaoh for bread. Pharaoh's instruction to all the Egyptians was that they should go to Joseph and: "What he saith to you, do." (Genesis 41:55). Immediately, a parallel between this incident and Jesus at the wedding of Cana of Galilee springs to mind. At that wedding, the wine had run out and Jesus' mother, Mary, enlisted his help. She then turned to the servants and gave them instructions identical to Pharaoh's: "Whatsoever He saith unto you, do it" (John 2:5). Pharaoh gave that instruction because he as the Supreme ruler of Egypt had delegated all power and authority to Joseph in his capacity as the favoured second-in-command. Mary instructed the servants, knowing that Jesus was the Messiah and all power and authority in heaven, on earth and under the earth were given to Him. She recalled all the things she had kept in her heart from the angelic annunciation of His birth, to the visits of the shepherds and angels, to the prophecies of Zacharias and Elizabeth; to their Jerusalem visit when He was twelve, to His baptism by John in the Jordan, and the call of the disciples. But more importantly, she realised that He was the fulfilment of all the Old Testament prophecies.

Pharaoh and Mary teach us the invaluable lesson that it is not enough to know and understand the Word of God, but we must also know when to apply it to His glory, the advancement of the Kingdom and the benefit of mankind. We must also come to grips with the fact that: "To obey is better than sacrifice, and to hearken than the fat of rams" (1 Samuel 15:22). In fact to know the truth and not to do it is pharisaic and despicable in the sight of God. If all Christians made it a priority to obey and live the truth they know, what a great difference we would make in our world! Who is worthy of absolute obedience if not the One whom the Heavenly Pharaoh has exalted and given a name above every other name! Meanwhile, the famine raged and progressively ravaged Egypt and all other nations. What we have been experiencing in the past few years, the global economic downturn with severe food shortage implications and, an attendant financial and banking crisis is a mild picture of what ancient Egypt went through. It was time for Joseph to open all the storehouses and to begin to sell food to the Egyptians. Soon, people from other countries also arrived in Egypt seeking to buy corn, under the supervision of Joseph.

CHAPTER SIX

CHICKENS COME HOME TO ROOST

The most riveting novels have intricate plots that run parallel, till with some amazing craftsmanship, and to the delight of unsuspecting readers and the amazement of the characters themselves, a connection is made between them. When Joseph's brothers sold him into slavery, they never expected to see him again. On his part Joseph knew that at some point, his God-given vision would come to pass; but as to when and how, he was completely in the dark. The Master Craftsman, that great Author of our life scripts, the One who causes all things to work together for our good, was about to slot the last jigsaw piece in place. The global famine would be the catalyst for a shocking family reunion. The famine in the land of Canaan became so grievous that Jacob decided to send his sons to Egypt to purchase food. Jacob was however up to his old tricks and openly revealed that Rachel was his favourite wife, and her offspring his preferred children. In the end, he sent Joseph's ten older brothers but refused to release Benjamin, Joseph's only full-blood brother, using the excuse: "lest peradventure mischief befall him" (Genesis 42:4).

Well over twenty years had passed since Joseph's mysterious disappearance and presumed death, and Jacob still showed the same favouritism to his younger brother. He was totally indifferent to the feelings of the other ten sons. In this, Jacob was totally unrepresentative of God with whom there is no "respect of persons" (Romans 2:11). James 2:1-4 speaks strongly against, favouring one person over another in our churches because of their wealth or social status. God goes further, warning us not to even favour the poor because of their poverty or to discriminate against the wealthy simply because of their wealth. So the sons of Israel went to Egypt to buy corn. It is of course significant that Jacob heard there was corn in Egypt and Joseph would later execute a symbolic action that explains the significance of this said corn, in a befuddling story about stolen money and silver cups in a knapsack.

We are told that Joseph was the governor over the land. Now remember, Pharaoh had appointed him the ruler with absolute control and authority, and in that position he supervised the sale of grain to citizens and strangers alike. So when his brothers arrived, they "bowed down themselves before him with their faces to the earth" (Genesis 42:6). Wow!

So at least fifteen years after he first had his dream, his word from God, his glimpse into a glorious destiny, was now coming to pass! Indeed, for every "thus saith the Lord…" there is a corresponding, "And it came to pass." In between however, there is also the phrase: "You have need of patience that after you have done the will of God, you may receive the promise" (Hebrews 10:36). It is not enough to have faith, for it is written that you must be followers of those who through faith and patience inherit the promise. (See Hebrew 6:12.) Joseph's great-grandfather waited twenty-five years for the promise; his grandfather Isaac waited twenty years before his wife Rebekah gave birth to twins, Jacob and Esau. Everyone knew that it took time before his mother Rachel, finally gave birth to Joseph, and later on to his brother Benjamin, a birth, which cost her, her life. So Joseph was in good company in the waiting phase.

Whatever God has promised you, He will bring it to pass in the fullness of His time. His thoughts are not carnal men's thoughts, nor are His ways carnal men's ways. A day with God is as a thousand years and a thousand years are as a day. While God works with time He is not bound by time. He inhabits eternity and eternity dwells within Him. If God said it, then He has obliged Himself to do it. If He did not intend to do it, He would never have said it. His word is His bond.

When Joseph saw his brothers, he immediately recognised them, though they, of course, did not recognise him. This is not surprising as over fifteen years have passed since they last saw each other. Moreover he was probably then still a gangling teenager whose voice had not yet broken. Now, here he was. mature and royal, and as an Egyptian ruler he would no doubt be clean-shaven, well-dressed and dignified. With a much deeper voice, which he would also disguise somewhat, and speaking through an interpreter, there was no way they could recognise him. Bear in mind also that they were racked with guilt, exacerbated by the unending lamentation of their father over 'his' son--as though the others were not his sons! They would therefore have tried to banish all thoughts of Joseph to the dunghill of history. They never, in their wildest dreams, imagined that this high-ranking, influential "Egyptian" official could be their brother.

This is a perfect picture of Jesus when He met with the disciples on the road to Emmaus. He talked to them, questioned them and even taught them, yet they did not recognise Him. (See Luke 24:13-31.)

Joseph pretended not to know his brothers but instead spoke harshly to them in order to discover the current state of his brothers' hearts. Were they still the same scheming, conniving, murderous villains, or had the passage of time brought repentance, rehabilitation and even regeneration? Joseph's Christ-like nature immediately shows through. His brothers were now completely at his mercy, and he could have trumped up treason charges (which he referred to) and had them summarily executed and not an eyebrow would have been raised.

Note that King David had this same mind of Christ and on two occasions when he could have killed Saul, he refused to succumb to the spirit of vengeance.

In a harsh tone Joseph demanded, "Where do you come from?" (Genesis 42:7) They answered that they were from Canaan and had come to buy food. At this juncture, nostalgic thoughts flood Joseph's mind. He is seventeen once again and the dream of his brother's sheaves bowing before his sheaf replays in his mind in vivid Technicolor. This brings a sly smile to his face, which the memory of their response quickly converts to a grimace, as he spits out the accusation. "You are spies! You've come here to find out where our country is weak" (Gen 42:9 CEV). Trembling, they hastily replied, "No sir... We're your servants, and we have only come to buy grain" (Genesis 42:10). Joseph repeats his accusation and to convince him they are not spies, Joseph's brothers tell him their family history, recalling that they came from a family of twelve brothers, the youngest being at home with their father and one that was dead. Joseph now had them exactly where he wanted them. He had forced them to admit to his death for which they would naturally feel responsible, and at the same time to inform him of the welfare of his father, Jacob, and his brother Benjamin. But he presses on as he executes a plan known only to him, "It is as I said; you have come with some secret purpose" (Genesis 42:14). Now the only way they could prove they were not spies would be to bring back their youngest brother. In fact, he planned to lock all but one of them in prison till the chosen one went home and brought back their youngest brother. Notice how Joseph keeps swearing by the life of Pharaoh. I suspect this was to further throw them off the scent just in case, by any remote chance, they recognised some of his mannerisms or detected something vaguely familiar about him. But there was no fear of that, as they had absolutely no inkling of the identity of the one who spoke to them.

Joseph then locked all of them up in prison for--you guessed it-- three days. Again these three days represent the three days of Jonah in the belly of the whale, the three days of the butler and the baker which all point to the three days Jesus spent in the belly of the earth after His crucifixion, death and burial. Like Jesus, Joseph had gone through much more than he could have imagined. However, for his brothers to be "redeemed" they would have to identify with his finished work. What a glorious picture of salvation! Our heavenly Joseph paid the price and was held captive in the depths of the earth for three days and three nights. We accept the principle of His substitutionary death as the Lamb of God, and believe with our hearts that He is the Son of God sent to die as the propitiation for our sins. We believe that on the third day, He was raised from the dead for our justification. We confess with our mouths our sins and confess this same Jesus as our Lord and personal Saviour. Simply by identifying with His finished work on the cross, we are saved. How awesome!

Joseph planned to make his brothers admit that they had sinned and make them confess with their mouths (that sin). On that most significant of days, the third day, Joseph appeared to change his mind and said, "This do and live; for I fear God..." Instead of keeping them all in prison and sending one to fetch Benjamin, he would keep one and send home the other nine. The word "live" is Chaka in the Hebrew and it means to live, revive, make alive, quicken, restore to life and to be whole. This is the very same word used in Habakkuk 2:4: "The just shall live by his faith." Thus we see the divine hand drawing the parallel between three days in prison and being quickened or made alive.

Joseph then told them that he was giving them this new option because he had a moral and reverential fear of God. If they were just men, then they would not mind leaving one of their company in prison as surety while they took grain home for their famine-afflicted families, and then came back with their youngest brother to verify their story. Joseph referred to his fear of God to provoke their collective consciences, while questioning their uprightness. It is the realisation that we have all sinned and come short of the righteousness of God that finally brings us to repentance. Joseph's ploy worked, for immediately, the brothers began to talk among themselves. "We are very guilty concerning our brother, in that we saw the anguish of his soul, when he besought us, and we would not hear; therefore is this distress come upon us" (Genesis 42:21). They use the word "guilty" (Hebrew – ashem), which suggests presenting a sin offering because one is at fault. Next, they regretted their hard-heartedness when confronted with the young Joseph's anguish of soul. This immediately points to the Garden of Gethsemane where Jesus went with all the disciples the night before His death. Taking Peter, James and John, He went further to a place of solitary prayer uttering words, which showed His anguish of soul: "My soul is exceeding sorrowful even unto death..." (Matthew 26:38). This incident was foreseen by the prophet Isaiah who explains its purpose. "He shall see of the travail of his soul, and shall be satisfied: by His knowledge shall my righteous servant justify many; for He shall bear their iniquities" (Isaiah 53:11, KJ).

Of Soul Ties and Sundry Matters

Paul's epistles give us insight into things that are often glossed over in other parts of the Bible. He unravels the triune nature of man: man is a spirit, he lives in a body and he has a soul. Man's spirit is God-conscious and referred to as "the candle of the Lord" (Proverbs 20:27), KJV). It is there that man communicates with God and receives inspiration and spiritual illumination. Man's soul, which includes his will, his intellect and his emotions, is self-conscious; while man's body, because it includes his five-senses is sense-conscious. Man's spirit was created or more accurately, released when God spoke saying, "Let us make man in our image and after our likeness..." (Genesis 1:26, KJV). The body of man, on the other hand, was formed from the dust of the earth. Man's soul was made when God "breathed into his nostrils the breath of life; and man became a living soul"

(Genesis 2:7, KJV). It was at this point that blood entered into man's body. How do we know this? Moses quotes God in Leviticus declaring, "For the life of the flesh is in the blood... it is the blood that maketh an atonement for the soul" (Leviticus 17:11). The same word nephesh in the Hebrew is used for life and soul. So the life (nephesh) or soul of the flesh is in the blood. This is why blood makes atonement for the soul. In effect, the lifeline of the flesh is in the blood and the blood represents a living soul. This is why you literally bleed to death if your blood is drained. What, you may ask, is the significance of all this in relation to Joseph as a type of Jesus?

When Adam and Eve fell in the Garden of Eden their spirits died and communication with God was severed. This explains why they went into hiding when God subsequent to the fall, sought their company as He had erstwhile done on a regular basis. Their souls also fell and with that fall they lost their sense of security, significance and self-worth, which had been deeply embedded in the core of their being at creation. Instead they found themselves feeling insecure, insignificant and inferior. Suddenly they felt guilt, recrimination, accusation, alienation, and separation, patterns of rationalisation and the bondage of expectation that now became the order of the day. Their bodies also began the slow degenerative spiral that culminated in Adam's physical death at the age of 930. As an aside, observe from biblical and natural history that since the fall no one has ever lived up to, let alone beyond a thousand years. This is because God had warned Adam that in the day he ate of the fruit of the tree of the knowledge of good and evil, he would surely die. (See Genesis 2:17.) His spirit died immediately in the physical, twenty-four-hour day while his body died in the day that is like a thousand years with the Lord (which in his case was seventy years short of 1000). How consistent and trustworthy is the Word of God! To reconcile man's spirit to God, Jesus had to be separated from His father and then go down to the pit. To redeem man's flesh, Jesus was stricken, smitten, afflicted, wounded, bruised, punished, chastised and beaten with stripes all in his flesh so that we would be healed and made whole.

This leaves the redemption of the soul. Jesus explains to the disciples during their famous power tussle that, "the Son of man came...to give His life a ransom for many" (Matthew 20:28). The word "life" is Psuchc the Greek equivalent of the Hebrew word, nephesh. So what happened in this Garden of Gethsemane, which literally translates as an oil press? Jesus began to be squeezed as seeds, like olives or nuts, are squeezed to extract their virgin oil. As Jesus was squeezed, He began to sweat blood, which represents His soul. This explains His earlier comment: "My soul is exceeding sorrowful, even unto death" (Matthew 26:38). Jesus was thus releasing His soul in exchange for the purchase, redemption, sanctification of ours, in fulfilment of the prophecy: "When thou shall make His soul an offering for sin, He shall see His seed..." (Isaiah 53:10). It was this travail, anguish of Jesus' soul that the Father saw and was satisfied. This is why, despite His pleas, the cup could not pass over Him. (See Matthew 26:42.) Joseph's separation from his father and brethren, and his being thrown into the pit without water, typify the Lord Jesus' separation and descent into Hades for the redemption of mankind's spirit. Joseph's journey as a slave through the desert and his tenure in prison serve as symbols of the redemption of the body. His anguish of soul and the refusal of his brothers to hearken to his cries and petitions typify the Gethsemane experience that paid the price for the restoration of our souls. For believers the implications of these facts are profound. Whatever our past experiences and current situations, we can be fully assured that it is well with our souls and that since God has gone to such lengths in Christ to pay our ransom, He will complete it by causing our deliverance to become manifest. In fact, the prophet Nahum warns those who are our adversaries asking them: "What do you imagine against the Lord? He will make an utter end: affliction shall not arise a second time." The Message puts it like this: "Why waste time conniving against God? He is putting an end to all such scheming. For troublemakers no second chances. Glory, alleluia! Affliction shall not rise up the second time" (Nahum 1:9). Our Saviour is risen, but affliction shall not rise up again. Even the laws of men state that a man cannot be tried twice for the same offence--the law against double jeopardy prevents this. Be fully assured that you will not end up in hell, because Jesus already did that; you will not stay down, because death could not hold Him captive; you will not remain in anguish, because God saw the travail of His soul; you are coming out of that situation to rule and reign with the King of glory, the One who is Alpha and Omega, the First and the Last.

Meanwhile, back to Joseph and his brothers; Reuben spoke up, reminding his brothers that he warned them to no avail, to do the lad no harm, and his blood was now being required at their hands. All this while, Joseph was listening in on their conversation, maintaining his anonymity by speaking through an interpreter. At this point, Joseph's tender heart was overwhelmed and he turned away from his brothers and wept as Jesus did over Jerusalem and at Lazarus' tomb. When he was composed enough to speak again, Joseph turned to his brothers and in a mock show of anger took Simeon from their midst and had him bound as they all watched, obviously in horror. So why was Simeon, chosen to be bound? Reuben who was the firstborn would have been selected, but Joseph realises that he made every effort to prevent his death, which is exactly what would have happened but for Reuben's intervention. He was also not present when Joseph was finally sold. And if Joseph had any reasonable doubts about Reuben's involvement, he had just heard him vindicate himself without any contradiction from his siblings. Because Simeon was next in line, the dubious honour fell to him. The spiritual lesson here is that with increased power and blessings come increased responsibility. "To whom much is given", the Word warns, " much is also expected." (See Luke 12:48.) We hanker for, pray for and strive for thirtyfold, sixtyfold and a hundredfold blessings from God, not realising that the degree of our fruitfulness will be consistent with spiritual and natural things and more significantly, with negative and positive things also. This means that when we sin the consequences of our actions will come back to us thirty, sixty, or a hundredfold, depending on the level at which we are then being blessed.

Next we see a picture of grace at work. Having plotted his death, the brothers deserved nothing but death, or at best, incarceration. Instead, Joseph commanded that their sacks be filled with corn; (Strong describes corn as grain of any kind, also wheat) that everyone was to have the money he paid for the grain returned to his sack; and that provision for their journey home was to be made available to them. This is the crux of the New Testament message. It is only because of God's amazing grace that He demonstrated His love for us so that even while we were still sinful, Christ would die for us. We deserved death but got life. The just paid the price for the unjust. Money is not a factor in this great work that God is doing. He admonishes us to come with our spiritual hunger and our spiritual thirst and we shall be filled. (See Matthew 5:6, KJV.)

In fact the prophet Isaiah sounds God's clarion call: "Ho everyone that thirsteth, come ye, buy, and eat; yea, come, buy wine and milk without money and without price" (Isaiah 55:1, KJV). In his message on the first New Testament Pentecost Peter would liken the Holy Spirit to new wine (See Acts 2:13-16), and in his first epistle, the Word of God to "sincere milk." (See 1 Peter 2:2, KJV.)

On his part Moses would inform us that the Promised Land is a land of wheat and barley amongst other great provisions. The message Joseph was typifying, in putting their money back in their sacks among the grain, is that salvation was inestimably costly to Jesus but is made freely available to us. Therefore, anyone who has a desire can come to buy this spiritual nourishment, without money. (See Isaiah 55:1.) In the next couple of chapters, we shall explore the ramifications of the corn, the sack and related issues in more detail. And so the brothers loaded their donkeys with the grain and left for home. On the way, when they stopped for the night, one of them opened his sack to extract grain with which to feed his donkey and discovered to his utter consternation that his money was in the mouth of his sack. The news of this brought amazement and dread to the camp as each of them clearly understood the implications of not having paid for some of the grain, in the light of the accusations and inquisition they had earlier faced as spies.

The restoration of one of the brothers' money here, is referred to by them as "What...hath God done unto us?" Though they said these things in fear, clearly misunderstanding God's motive, in fact misrepresenting Him, they are aware that this is God's doing, and they fear His punishment. So, like Caiaphas who being the high priest in Jesus' day prophesied that it was expedient that Jesus die for the people and prevent the nation from perishing, they prophesied in ignorance. Most times, God is doing one thing while we are seeing another. May God truly enlighten the eyes of our understanding. For us who have understanding, their cry of "What is this that God hath done unto us?" (Genesis 42:28, KJV) points forward to the cry of the children of Israel when God first rained manna from heaven; and periscopes further, forward to Calvary as we marvel with the selfsame words at the wonder of the cross. When the brothers get home, they relay their experiences and encounter with "the lord of the land"--his harsh treatment of them, his accusations of espionage and his request that they bring back Benjamin to prove the veracity of their story. This would also prove they were "just" men, (that word again!) secure the release of Simeon and grant them the freedom to freely trade in all of Egypt. It had been a most harrowing experience and relating it to their father was almost like reliving the nightmare, which was by no means over. In fact, the worst was yet to come; as they all began to empty their sacks, they discovered that each one's bundle of money was in his sack. This time, Jacob grew upset, only adding to their distress.

Jacob immediately raises a lamentation. He accuses the 'remnant' of taking his children from him; though he did not know how true his words were, these words must have cut his sons to the very depths of their hearts. Having taken Joseph and Simeon, he bemoans, they now intend to take Benjamin away too. He concludes that: "All these things are against me" (Genesis 42:36). It is amazing how quickly prevailing circumstances can make us forget the Word of God. This is the patriarch Jacob, the one chosen above his senior twin; the one God had spoken to at Bethel, assuring him of His protection and guaranteeing him increase and children as the dust of the earth; the one God had promised He would never leave till he had fulfilled his destiny. How could Jacob have forgotten that if God is for us, no one and nothing can be against us? How could he not know that all things work together for good to them that are God-lovers and the purpose-called, fulfillers of divine calling and destiny? But before we judge Jacob too harshly and feel too smug, how many of us even with the gift of prophecy, the Word of God, the experiences of our Bible forbears and even our own encounters with God, still think that: "All these things are against me"?

What would it take for us to know that as with Joseph, our heavenly Joseph, Jesus, is behind the scenes working it all out, to our advantage. Joseph had a plan that would ultimately result in not just his brothers' deliverance, but many other people's besides. Joseph was an incredibly prudent man. He knew about his father's obsessive love for Rachel, himself and now Benjamin. No doubt he knew that Jacob would not release Benjamin without some unusual persuasive and bargaining skills on his brothers' part. Would they be willing to do what was necessary, to pay whatever price, to make whatever sacrifices required? Or would they simply "sacrifice" Simeon as they had done him, a couple of decades earlier?

It is vital to note that Joseph prepares tests, and not temptations for his brothers. Tests are redemptive by nature and are designed to highlight your vulnerabilities and weaknesses so that you can overcome them. Temptations on the other hand are destructive and designed to trip you up, pull you down, disgrace and expose you. After Jacob's grief-stricken outburst, Reuben steps forward and takes responsibility in the way he should have over the Joseph affair. "...Father, if I don't bring Benjamin back, you can kill both of my sons. Trust me with him, and I will bring him back" (Genesis 42:37, CEV). This was a strong assertion and a bold claim. Joseph's aim was being fulfilled. As much as he wanted to locate the current state of his brothers' hearts, he also wanted them to come to the place of repentance while taking responsibility for their future actions. Perhaps the most significant and subtle test Joseph designed was to test whether they were still indifferent to their father's feelings, knowing what torment the "death" of Joseph would have caused him. As mentioned earlier in passing, Reuben was first to step up to the plate and his comment is quite instructive. He gives his father the strongest possible assurance and apart from taking personal responsibility, he even offers to leave his two sons as hostages should he fail to deliver on his promise of safely returning Benjamin. Wow! Reuben was ready to lose both his sons and experience the pain his father had felt upon receiving the news of Joseph's death. There was no guarantee that this strange Egyptian official would not revert to his former erratic behaviour, but he was not going to put Benjamin in any danger and would do whatever it took to bring him back home. But Jacob remained unimpressed and said, "I won't let my son Benjamin go down to Egypt with the rest of you. His brother is already dead, and he is the only son I have left. I am an old man, and if anything happens to him on the way I'll die from sorrow, and all of you will be to blame" (Genesis 42:38 CEV).

Jacob is evidence that you can be unwise though you are anointed, chosen, appointed, and called. He is displaying the very attitude that led to Joseph's predicament. He refers to Benjamin as "my son" and refers to him as the only son he has left. How on earth did he expect his other sons to react to this brazen favouritism and the feelings of rejection it doubtlessly birthed? But for the grace of God and the unrelenting and unresolved guilt of Joseph's issue, it was enough for them to dispose of Benjamin in a similar manner. As parents, we must realise the effect our words have on our children, either to propel them to the lofty heights of a glorious destiny or to the dung heaps of rejection, frustration and failure. We must also recognise the potential they have for fuelling sibling rivalry and even family problems long after we are gone. Consider that it was Laban's chicanery that caused Jacob to end up with a woman he didn't love and whose children therefore had to live with the painful pangs of ignominy and rejection all their lives. The sad truth is: Jacob's blatant favouritism sparked off Joseph's travails. It is ironic to note that if Jacob had had his way, Joseph would never have ventured beyond the immediate environs of his hometown in the Canaan region. Jacob would have smothered Joseph's destiny with his protective mollycoddling. Every parent must realise that true love must take risks. There must come a time when the most loving thing a parent can do is not to lock the child in from the dangers of the big bad world, but release them by faith to overcome, prosper and be victorious. After all, God the Father took the risk of sending His Son down to earth, to embark on that most risky of projects because He is the author, modeller and finisher of the same faith by which He encourages the just to live.

CHAPTER SEVEN

"...AND IF I PERISH, I PERISH"

The previous chapter ends with a stalemate as Reuben fails to convince Jacob to release "his son" Benjamin to meet the conditions of their return to Egypt to purchase more food. Apart from the obvious reason Jacob gives for not releasing Benjamin, there are possibly two other reasons for the stalemate. The first possible reason is that, Reuben had lost his moral authority and credibility with his father in regard to an issue of some sensitivity. Secondly, having just returned with plenty of food, Jacob felt he had a bit of time before he needed to revisit the issue. In the meantime, the famine in the land of Canaan grew worse and the food eventually ran out. Jacob then asked his sons to go back to Egypt to buy food. This time, because Reuben failed to convince his father to release Benjamin, he handed the baton over to Judah. Judah corroborated Reuben's account, reminding Jacob that the Egyptian lord gave a stern warning to them, backed by an oath that they were not to appear before him unless they brought their youngest brother with them.

So, Judah concluded, if Jacob released Benjamin, they would go with him to buy grain, if he did not, then they would simply not go. Jacob soon found himself in a tight corner and unreasonably began to play the blame game; "...Why were you so cruel to me as to say to him that you have a brother?" (Genesis 43:6, BBE). Jacob's anguish caused him to think irrationally. Yet he seemed quite strident in insisting that there was some foul play on the older sons' part in relation to first Joseph and then Benjamin. Maybe, he sensed the envy of the older siblings from the time Joseph began to share his dreams. Perhaps, even after doing their best to conceal their jealous feelings against Rachel's children, their father finally grasped the truth.

Judah's response to Jacob's accusation shows that Joseph had very carefully engineered this dilemma so that it would serve as a "discerner of the thoughts and intents of the heart" (see Hebrew 4:12) of all concerned. Judah made it clear that once they revealed his existence Joseph asked pointed questions about whether their father was still alive, and also whether they had another brother. There was no way, he rightly conjectured, they could have known that this ruler would ask them to bring their brother.

At that point Judah did something awesome that proved how far he and his brothers had come. He made it clear to Jacob that failure to send Benjamin would result in the death by starvation of all the brothers, their children and even Jacob himself. Since this was a fait accompli, (a done deal) Judah, as Reuben had done, offered to stand as surety for Benjamin. "I'll take full responsibility for his safety, it's my life on the line for his. If I do not bring him back safe and sound, I'm the guilty one; I'll take all the blame" (Genesis 43:8 MSG).

Judah ended his argument by saying that they could have been there and back apart from the delay. This indicates that the debate went on for some weeks and maybe even months.

Many spiritual lessons are buried in this episode. Primarily, it is clear that the brothers' consciences troubled them from the moment they sold Joseph. It is apparent that there was collective guilt, recrimination and finger-pointing. There was even remorse, much like that which Judas felt. It took clever engineering on the part of Joseph, to get them, not only to accept their wrongdoing but, to confess it and later turn away from it. Thus our heavenly Joseph, the Lord Jesus Christ, engineers circumstances that force us to confront our sins and to accept that they have separated us from a just and holy God who cannot look on iniquity. (See Habakkuk 1:13.) But we must not stop there, however; we are to move on to confess these sins, calling them what God calls them and not trying to sugar-coat or excuse them.

Having extra-marital relationships for example, should be recognised as adultery and fornication and not just as "having an affair." If we agree with God we should not colour the truth—a lie would be a lie and not terminological inexactitude! And once at the point of confession, repentance follows as we proceed in a completely new direction, a 180-degree turn.

Note, however, that no repentance is complete without recognition of the substitutionary death of the Lamb of God to take away our sin-nature. This was the point Reuben had reached when he was ready to lay down the lives of his two sons in exchange for Benjamin's life. Judah had also reached this point when he offered himself as substitute for Benjamin and was willing to bear the blame forever if any harm were to befall the beloved son. It is also noteworthy that Benjamin was so precious to his father that lives had to be given in exchange for his life. In Isaiah 43:4, (KJV) we see the prophet refer to Jacob as an individual but also to the nation of Israel in type, and thus it becomes applicable to Benjamin–"Since thou wast precious in my sight, thou hast been honourable, and I have loved thee: therefore will I give men for thee, and people for thy life."

One cannot help but feel for Simeon who was chosen to be incarcerated and whose loss did not cause Jacob to lose much sleep. Maybe, like Simeon you are the son of the unfavoured wife and you seem to be languishing forgotten in prison. Take heart, God is on your side and will cause things to balance out to your advantage. After all, was it not because the Lord saw that your mother Leah was hated, that he opened her womb and you were one of the fruits of her divine favour? (See Genesis 29:31.) Is it not also written, "When my father and my mother forsake me then the Lord will take me up" (Psalm 27:10). Though it did not appear to be the case, Simeon was not forsaken. In fact, he was favoured to be a partaker of what his brother had experienced. In knowing our heavenly Joseph and the power of His resurrection, Paul suggests to us that we must partake of the fellowship of His sufferings i.e., share in His pains while becoming like Him in His death. (See Philippians 3:10.)

When Israel realised he had no other option, he finally gave in. He decided not to worry about things over which he had no control, but to take charge of those things that he could influence. Knowing the power of a gift, for it is written that, "A man's gift makes room for him and brings him before great men" (Proverbs 18:16, NKJV), Israel sent his sons with some of the best products of the land, some balm and honey, spices and perfumes, myrrh, pistachio nuts and almonds. Israel was aware also that, "A gift in secret pacifieth anger: and a reward in the bosom strong wrath" (Proverbs 21:14). After all, when he was to meet his brother, Esau for the first time after having deceived him out of his blessings many years before, he employed the ministry of gifts to intercede on his behalf, (see Genesis 32:18.)

His sons were also to take back twice the amount of money for the grain because he felt there must have been some mistake, when their money was put back in their sacks. And, yes, he was also releasing Benjamin to go with them unto the man in question. His prayer was that God Almighty would grant them mercy before the man and that he would send away, "your other brother, and Benjamin." Israel would never change in this his attitude and though his is negative, he is a type of the Lord who does not change. (Malachi 3:6) He is a type of Christ, who is the same yesterday, today and forever. (Hebrews 13:8.)

Israel's last statement before his sons' departure is instructive: "If I be bereaved of my children, I am bereaved." Every time we as believers make a decision, God expects it to be based on faith. This is first because: the just shall live by faith and second because: without faith it is impossible to please God. (See Hebrews 10:38 & 11:6.) In fact, according to Romans 14:23, anything that is not faith-motivated, faith-originated, or faith-executed is sin. Since faith is the substance of hope and the evidence of spiritual but unseen natural things, it involves an element of risk. God usually boxes us in till we have no option but to trust wholly in Him even when it seems to be a "death sentence."

Esther's act of faith could have spelt death for her if it went wrong hence her faithful cry of resignation: "And if I perish, I perish" (Esther 4:16). In the same way, God had boxed Israel in and brought him to that point where he is ready to pay the price of faith. Abraham, his grandfather before him, faced that same predicament when God instructed him to offer up Isaac as a sacrifice.

The beautiful irony for the truly discerning believer is that it really is not a risk for there is no risk-taking or volatility in our God or His Word. Alleluia! This is what it means when He says, "Every good gift and every perfect gift is from above, and cometh down from the Father of lights, with whom is no variableness, neither shadow of turning." The Message puts it this way: "Every desirable and beneficial gift comes out of heaven. The gifts are rivers of light cascading down from the Father of Light. There is nothing deceitful in God, nothing two-faced, nothing fickle" (James 1:7).

At last, the brothers hastily set off on their second journey to Egypt armed with not only gifts but also with twice as much money, and of course, their most precious "cargo," Benjamin. In due time, they stand before Joseph.

Upon seeing Benjamin with them, Joseph tells the ruler of his house to bring them all to his home, slaughter an animal and cook it so that they can dine with him at noon. This is a good place to review the four principles of stewardship and how Joseph's faithfulness with small things now ensured that he was in charge of great things. His faithfulness with "unrighteous mammon" now saw him in charge of true riches. But the third principle is most obvious--his faithfulness as ruler over Potiphar's house had now ensured that he, in turn had a ruler over his own house. What a long way the slave from Canaan had come! We shall soon see the fourth principle in play. As the ruler of Joseph's house carried out his commands and brought the brothers to the palatial dwelling, they were too terrified to take in the glorious sights and the splendour along the way. All they could think of was that this was some sort of trap. The man obviously intended to arrest them, make them his slaves and confiscate their donkeys because he believed they made off with the money that was found in their sacks on the first trip. At the door of Joseph's house, they decide to state their case to Joseph's chief servant. If they were going to go into captivity they would at least put up a creditable defence.

"Oh Sir," they began, "we came indeed down at the first time to buy food: And it came to pass, when we came to the inn, that we opened our sacks, and, behold, every man's money was in the mouth of his sack, our money in full weight: and we have brought it again on our hands to buy food: we cannot tell who put our money in our sacks" (Genesis 43:20-22). It is interesting and ironic that God has exalted Joseph so highly that his brothers are literally bowing before not just him but even before his chief servant.

Concerning their apprehension, the chief servant spoke exactly as many angels and heavenly heralds had spoken to men of God in times past, "Peace be to you, fear not...." Then he speaks in addition a message of grace, "Your God, and the God of your fathers hath given you treasure in your sacks: I had your money" (Genesis 43:23). What he is saying is best captured in the Contemporary English Version of the Bible which says, "It's alright," the servant replied. "Don't worry. The God you and your father worship must have put the money there, because I received your payment in full" (Genesis 43:23 CEV).

The servant knew about the peace of God (shalom); the "fear-nots" of God; the intergenerational nature of God; the hidden treasures of God and the grace of God. He could only have learned that from his master Joseph. The major reason God gives us such revelation is so that, once we are blessed by them we can become a blessing by sharing them. Once the chief servant gives these words of comfort, he brings Simeon out to them. And now that they are in Joseph's house, he gives them water to wash their feet while he also tends their donkeys. The brothers on their part prepare their gifts for Joseph's arrival at noon, once they know that they are having lunch with him. This is decidedly reminiscent of Jesus when He had lunch with a publican named Zaccheus who clambered up a tree to see Jesus one day as he passed through Jericho. When Joseph came home, the brothers duly presented their gifts and "bowed themselves to him to the earth." Needless to say the word used for "bowed themselves" here is the very same word Joseph used when he related his dream of "bowing sheaves" to his brothers. This is the second time his brothers bowed before him in fulfilment of his dream.

Joseph enquires of their welfare and especially whether their father was still alive. After replying that Joseph's "servant," their father was still alive and in good health, they thought it appropriate to again bow down their heads and prostrate reflexively in homage to this royal official making it the third time they had fulfilled scripture, which cannot lie. At this juncture Joseph looked around to identify the only brother that shared the same mother with him, Benjamin. Upon identifying him, he continued his pretext of ignorance, "Is this your younger brother, of whom ye spoke unto me?" He then proceeds to bless him. "God be gracious unto thee, my son" (Genesis 43:29), Joseph declares in patrimonial beneficence. It was absolutely vital that the charade be maintained, for Joseph was planning one final and crucial test.

At this point, Joseph was overwhelmed by a flood of deep yearning for his brother Benjamin, and he rushed off to his room to weep. After washing his face and regaining control of his emotions, he reappeared and commanded his servants to serve the meal. Joseph was served at his private table; the brothers were set apart as were the Egyptians. It is ironic that the Egyptians would not eat with the Hebrews because it was morally abhorrent to them, causing them, as they supposed, to become unclean. Indeed, it was tantamount to idolatry! How strange it is that most unbelievers, however misguidedly, understand the principle of unequal yoking and strongly shy away from it while many believers see nothing wrong with joining with unbelievers with much greater stakes. These include such things as: marriage, close friendship, intimate relationships, and unwholesome business partnerships to name just a few.

The next piece in this enigmatic saga is the seating arrangement: they all sat facing Joseph, arranged in descending order of age, from the first born to the youngest. This truly perplexed them as they wondered what would happen next. How on earth could this strange man know the order of their birth? Why was he so unpredictable and volatile, one minute genuinely and tenderly inquiring about their welfare and the next moment harshly accusing them of all kinds of crimes; the very next inviting them to lunch; one moment locking up their brother, the next, showering them with gifts!

Many times, we have the same ambivalent feelings towards God because we are ignorant of the nature of His greater purposes in His dealings with us. As their food was served, Joseph sent "messes" of food from his table to each of his brothers but sent five times as much to Benjamin. While it could have been just portions of food that Joseph sent to his brothers, the word "mess" also means a raising (as of the hands in prayer), an utterance, a beacon, a gift, an oblation or a reward.

I suspect that he gave them presents probably as a simple courtesy in response to the gifts they gave to him at the start of the meal. Our heavenly Joseph ever lives to make intercession for us, offering daily oblations as it were on our behalf. If men enjoy the rain and every good thing from the good God, we His children get five times as much as any others; we enjoy His grace which the number five represents. Thus Joseph's brothers drank with him and had a very good time. Giving Benjamin five times more than the others was the penultimate aspect of a well-devised plan designed to continue the test on the state of Joseph's brothers' hearts.

CHAPTER EIGHT

THE EMPTY SILVER CUP

Later, Joseph instructed the steward of his house to fill the men's sacks with as much food as they could carry and to return every man's money, putting it in the mouth of his sack. Finally, in addition to returning his money in like manner, he was to put Joseph's silver cup in the top of Benjamin's sack alongside the money. As strange and inexplicable as this request sounds, the chief steward did not question Joseph but simply did as his master ordered. In this way, this steward is comparable to Eleazer who did the same in service to Abraham, Joseph's great-grandfather, when he was sent to get a wife for Isaac. Together, they are a type of the Holy Spirit who "shall not speak of Himself; but whatsoever He shall hear, that shall He speak...." (John 16:13). The steward's job is to glorify his master in much the same way the Holy Spirit takes of what is God's and announces it, makes it clear and delivers it to us (see John 16:14) so that God may be glorified in us. In like manner, Jesus calls on us to be faithful. Joseph knew in his heart why he gave the instructions. He also reserved and exercised the right to withhold the explanation, which the passage and the fullness of time eventually brought to light. The next time therefore that God gives you an incomprehensible, inexplicable, "unreasonable" instruction, just go ahead and obey it, for the foolishness of God is infinitely always invariably wiser than you are. (See 1 Corinthians 1:25.)

At the break of day, the men and their donkeys were sent on their way. They were scarcely out of town when Joseph sent his servant to accost them. He asked them why they repaid his master's good to them with evil by purloining his silver chalice from which he not only drank but also predicted the future through divination. Now we know that Joseph was privileged to receive information about the future from God and did not engage in the common idolatrous Egyptian practices of fortune-telling by divination. Again this was designed to portray him as an Egyptian and to strike the fear of God into his brothers' hearts. "Truly, you have done evil," the steward concluded with his accusations. Their response was quick, categorical and almost self-righteous, "Why does my lord say such words as these? Far be it from your servants to do such a thing..." (Genesis 44:7, BBE). After all, they argue confidently, they came all the way from Canaan to return the money they found in their sacks.. Why then would they steal silver or gold from the steward's master's house, they reasoned. They should have stopped there but to strengthen their case they decide to add a deadly stipulation –"If you find that one of us has the cup, then kill him, and the rest of us will become your slaves" (Genesis 44:9 CEV). If the brothers were well-acquainted with God's Word they would have realised that there is an injunction against rash declarations and promises: "Be not rash with thy mouth, and let not thine heart be hasty to utter anything... therefore let thy words be few.... Better it is that thou shouldest not vow, than that thou shouldest vow and not pay.... Suffer not thy mouth to cause thy flesh to sin; neither say thou before the angel, that it was an error..." (Ecclesiastes 5:6). This hastiness to make rash oaths seems to be a family trait.

Recall that when their father, Jacob, tried to escape from his uncle and father-in-law, Laban, for reasons we do not grasp, and unbeknown to Jacob, Rachel stole the family idols. When Laban accused Jacob, he forgot he was a prophet and because he was so sure that neither he nor his, had taken the idols, he declared, "With whomsoever thou findest thy gods let him not live... for Jacob knew not that Rachel had stolen them" (Genesis 31:32). From this moment, Rachel was as good as dead. It is my conjecture that what saved her from dropping dead instantly, was the prophecy she uttered at the birth of her first child

Joseph. While celebrating the fact that God had taken away the reproach of her barrenness, she called her son Joseph and said: "The Lord shall add to me another son" (Genesis 30:24).

And just as Simeon could not die because there was a prophecy over his life-that he would not die till he saw the Lord's Christ- so Rachel was preserved till Benjamin's birth at which point she promptly passed away. Oh that we would realise of a truth, that death and life are in the power of our tongue and we will eat everything we say. (See Proverbs 18:21.) No wonder one wise man once said, he makes sure that all his utterances are savoury just in case he has to eat his words! Joseph's servant must have had a glint in his eyes knowing what he did: "Good!" the man replied, "I'll do what you have said. But only the one who has the cup will become my slave. The rest of you can go free" (Genesis 44:10, CEV). Very quickly, they all took down their sacks and opened them and the steward began his search with the eldest and worked his way down. The sense of relief and justification would have grown with the clearing of each of the ten elder brothers and by the time it got to Benjamin, everyone would have been packing, waiting to be dismissed when, horror of horrors, the cup was found in Benjamin's sack! What would the old brothers who had sold Joseph have done in these circumstances? They would have callously gone back to their father and reported the situation gleefully, observing that Benjamin only got what he deserved. After all why on earth would he be so foolish as to expropriate the chalice of a noble who had been nothing but good to them? Remember that it was out of jealousy that they had treated Joseph the way they did. That Israel had in many respects made Benjamin the object of his redoubled affection is quite incontestable. Joseph was therefore eagerly and diligently watching their reactions to see for himself how far forward his brothers had really come.

In abject distress, the brothers ripped their clothes, loaded up their donkeys and went back to the city with the chief steward. The text says when Judah and his brethren came to Joseph's house, he was still at home and for the fourth time they cast themselves face down on the ground before Joseph. Obviously, he had waited at home hoping they would soon return- "or would they?" he wondered. "And Joseph said, "What is this thing which you have done? Had you no thought that such a man as I would have power to see what is secret?" (Genesis 44:15, BBE) Joseph claimed the power of prognostication so that they would not try to pull the wool over his eyes. He wanted them to come clean. Here Joseph was clearly exemplifying the attributes of Jesus Christ, the Living Word who is described in Hebrew as alive and powerful, active and sharper than any two-edged sword, "cutting through and making a division even of the soul and the spirit, the bones and the muscles, and quick to see the thoughts and purposes of the heart" (Hebrews 4:12, BBE). The thought continues saying "nothing is hidden from God! He sees through everything and we will have to tell him the truth." (CEV) The King James Version says: "Neither is there any creature that is not manifest in His sight: but all things are naked and opened unto the eyes of Him with whom we have to do" (Hebrews 4:13). The narrative shifts from referring to the brothers in general to saying "Judah and his brethren." (See Genesis 44:14.) This means that Judah who had previously been only one of the group, suddenly came to the forefront in fulfilment of his pledge to his father and in fulfilment of his prophetic destiny later outlined by his father in Gen.49:10.

Although Reuben had initially pledged to give his sons as hostages, their father had not taken him up on his offer. Judah's proposal had however been accepted. Judah therefore did not hesitate to be the spokesman. "What can we say master? What is there to say? How can we prove our innocence? God is behind this, exposing how bad we are. We stand guilty before you and are ready to be your slaves— we're all in this together, the rest of us as guilty as the one with the chalice" (Genesis 44:16, MSG). Upon hearing this, Joseph's heart no doubt was greatly delighted. The brothers had overcome their divisions and jealousies, and now understood identification and the principle of substitution. They were also united in one accord. Indeed, as the psalmist declares, it is good and pleasant for brethren to dwell together in unity: (See Psalm 133:1). Once that point was proven, Joseph would now want to know whether their father's feelings now figured in their plans. After all, they were totally indifferent to this when they sold Joseph. God forbid, Joseph told them, that he would lock up the innocent with the guilty. He would retain the guilty one and the rest could return in peace to their father. This was a classic open door and the faint-hearted, insincere and double-minded would have jumped at this opportunity reasoning that they had at least done all they could do to save Benjamin. This temptation and pressure brought out the leader in Judah.

Like Esther when she appeared before the king, he was aware that it was a gamble that could cost him his life. Judah came near to this chamberlain to the Prime Minister and reverently asked to speak a word in his ears. He acknowledged that Joseph had as much power as Pharaoh himself and that he, Judah, would qualify to be nothing more than a slave. Yet he had to risk the possibility of Joseph's anger in order to state his case. He recalled (as though Joseph could forget) how Joseph had asked them at the onset if they had a father and a brother; their answer had been that their aged father was back home, with a young child of his old age. His one brother was dead and Benjamin, the only son of his mother, was very dear to his father.

He further explained how Joseph said to bring back the boy so that he could see him and how they objected, claiming that if the child left his father, the old man would die. Yet when Joseph insisted, claiming that they could not return unless the boy accompanied them, they argued with their father that the man's demands must be met in order for them to return. Their father reminded them that if he lost Benjamin after already losing Joseph, he would die a heartbroken man. Imagine,

Judah began to conclude, if we were to return without the lad, whose life is intertwined inexorably with our father's, then we will no doubt be responsible for the old man's instant death by grief. Judah then finished his story, saying that he had personally guaranteed the safe return of his brother, and if he, Judah, did not bring the boy safely back home, he would stand condemned before his father for the rest of his life.

If Judah had stopped there, Joseph would have been sufficiently impressed and would probably have revealed himself to his brothers at this time. But Judah said, "Now therefore, I pray thee, let thy servant abide instead of the lad a bondman to my lord; and let the lad go up with his brethren" (Genesis 44:33). Judah's final words convinced Joseph that his brothers had been completely transformed, both inside and out. Judah said, "How can I face my father if Benjamin isn't with me? I couldn't bear to see my father in such sorrow" (CEV) "Oh, don't make me go back and watch my father die in grief" (Genesis 44:34); the Message version clearly expresses his deep emotions.

His Cup Was Full, Mine Is Empty

Joseph had no clue as to why he was prompted by the Holy Spirit of God to put their money back in their sacks' mouths and why he felt led to have his empty silver cup put in Benjamin's sack. His obedience would paint a picture that points to many dimensions of Jesus' finished work at Calvary. The prophet Isaiah said that God gave David as a witness, a leader and a commander to the people. (See Isaiah 55:4.) It is in much the same way that Joseph was given as a witness, a leader and a commander to the people. Their witness is of Christ and His finished work in typology and shadows. The corn that the brothers came to buy represents the food that keeps the spirit alive even in times of famine and scarcity. Jesus is referring to Himself when He tells His disciples "Verily, verily, I say unto you, except a corn of wheat fall into the ground and die, it abideth alone: but if it die, it bringeth forth much fruit" (John 12:24). The background to this story is that certain Greeks (Gentiles) who had come up to Jerusalem to worship at the feast of the Passover, presumably did not find any spiritual joy or fulfilment, so they wisely decided to seek out Jesus.

They had come to Philip the Apostle with the life-changing cry: "Sir, we would see Jesus" (John 12:21). By revelation, they had discerned that the religious traditions and observances of the Pharisees, scribes and Sadducees could never satisfy the hunger in their souls or the thirst in their spirits; only meeting with Jesus could do this. After all, Jesus had prophesied to the woman at the well that the time had finally come when true worshippers would worship the Father in spirit and in truth. (See John 4:23-24.) He had also told Thomas He was the Way, the Truth and the Life and that no one could get to the Father except by Him. (See John 14:6.) So, on a general and global level, unless Jesus was willing to fall to the earth and die, like a grain of wheat planted in the soil, he would abide alone. If, however, He chose to die, His death would bring forth much fruit, many sons like Him. On a more specific and individual level, unless the Word of God like a seed of grain falls into the ground of the hearer's heart and dies, it will never be more than one grain, but through its death it brings forth much fruit.

Putting all these together, the "corn of wheat" is nothing but the message of Christ, which in a nutshell is:

- Christ was crucified

- Christ died

- Christ was buried

- Christ was quickened

- Christ was raised/resurrected
- Christ is seated at the right hand of God in all authority

The sack full of corn is the storehouse or repository of revelation knowledge, wisdom and understanding, which is none other than the Bible, the Word of God. The money at the sack's mouth is Isaiah's picture of buying without money. Your money will always be returned to you because it is by grace you are saved through faith. It is a gift of God and is not by your achievements or human effort so that you have no bragging rights. On another level, the money at the sack's mouth is the secret treasures that are hidden in God's Word, which He has preserved for those who diligently seek Him. This is a picture of the things that accompany salvation, the things that are added to those who seek the Kingdom of God and His righteousness; the secret things that belong to those in covenant with God, and their offspring, the things that God by His glory has concealed and we by our honour as kings, do search out. (See Proverbs 25:2.) By far the more significant message, however, is that of Joseph's silver cup. Since we now know that Joseph's life is the most perfect Old Testament picture of the Lord Jesus and he felt obliged to have the cup put in Benjamin's sack, then it becomes obvious that the Holy Spirit had a message in mind when He inspired this action.

First though, it is expedient that we discover what some Old Testament types represent. Gold as a metal speaks of divinity and the nature of God. Silver always speaks of redemption, as richly exemplified by the atonement fee, which every adult Israelite (over twenty years of age) had to give for the ransom of his soul to the tune of half a shekel of silver. To show the equality of the value of every soul before God, this was a flat rate, and the rich were not permitted to give more and the poor were not permitted to give less! (See Exodus 30:12-15.) Incidentally, in Bible numerology, twenty is the number of redemption. So, the consistency of the message is quite striking–an adult of twenty years or older gives a half shekel of silver as a redemption price for his or her soul.

Moving on, brass or bronze is the metal that symbolises judgment. This is portrayed by the bronze (brazen) altar of Moses' Tabernacle, and the serpent of brass which Moses lifted up in the wilderness for the salvation of any who was bitten by fiery serpents. This occurred after the children of Israel complained against God and Moses, on their journey from Mount Hor toward the Red Sea avoiding the territory of Edom. (See Numbers 21:4-7.) With all these in view, the silver cup would therefore be the cup of salvation that belonged to our heavenly Joseph and from which He drank. The most instructive and pertinent point is that Joseph's silver cup was empty, having been drained of its contents by Joseph before it was placed in his brother's sack.

Jesus Himself clearly explains what this cup represents. In the Garden of Gethsemane earlier referred to, having left the others and going a little farther with Peter, James and John, Jesus Himself went yet a little farther, fell on His face and began to pray. His very words were: "O my Father, if it be possible, let this cup pass from me: nevertheless not as I will, but as thou wilt" (Matthew 26:39).

So Jesus refers to His impending crucifixion, death, burial and descent into the lower parts of the earth as "this cup." It is noteworthy that the word translated "cup" from the Greek (poterion) means a drinking vessel and by extension its contents. It also means figuratively--one's fate or lot in life. This is why he used the same word when the disciples were jockeying for positions of authority on His final ministry journey to Jerusalem. In fact, to aid their lobby, James and John, the sons of Zebedee had come with their mother to request that they would both sit one on either side of Him in His Kingdom. Jesus' answer was that they did not have a clue regarding the implications of what they were asking! He asked them, "Are you able to drink of the cup that I shall drink of, and be baptised with the baptism that I am baptised with?" (Matthew 20:22) Their rash answer was that they were able. If they had known what the cup symbolised, I am not so sure they would have been so quick to answer the way they did. Needless to say, James was the first of the twelve apostles to be martyred and John's Patmos exile was one of many aspects of "the cup" of the Lord that he had to drink. At the same Garden of Gethsemane, when Judas led a Roman military cohort to arrest Jesus, Peter drew his sword and cut off the ear of Malchus, the high priest's servant. Jesus immediately rebuked Him with the words, "Put up thy sword into the sheath: the cup which my Father hath given me, shall I not drink it?" (John 18:11)

Even earlier, at the Last Supper, Jesus had introduced His disciples to the cup of His communion. Paul would later explain that when we drink from the cup we ask God to bless, we are actually sharing in the blood of Christ. (See 1 Corinthians 10:16.) He then warns that you cannot drink from the cup of the Lord and at the same time from that of evil spirits or demons. (See 1 Corinthians 10:21.) Hebrews 2:9 makes it as clear when it says: "But we see Jesus, who was made a little lower than angels for the suffering of death, crowned with glory and honour, that He by the grace of God should taste death for every man." Our heavenly Joseph has, by drinking of and emptying the silver cup of salvation, tasted death for us all and has placed the empty silver cup as a central theme in every sack's mouth of every book of the Old and New Testament. The empty silver cup is a continual reminder that: "It is finished," and the work has been done.

Warning! Don't Accept Her Cup!

This empty silver cup of our heavenly Joseph is also a warning to accept no other cup than that of the Lord, no matter what others may do, or how attractive another cup might appear. In Revelation 17:3-6, we are introduced in the spirit to a woman who is the mother of prostitutes or figuratively idolatry. She has wooed, won to her side and overwhelmed the kings and inhabitants of the earth with her fornication (adultery and idolatry). Her name is MYSTERY, BABYLON THE GREAT, THE MOTHER OF HARLOTS AND ABOMINATIONS OF THE EARTH. This woman is said to be "drunken with the blood of the martyrs." Her pretentious claim to royalty and divinity are manifested in her purple and scarlet array decked out with gold, precious stones and pearls. Most significantly, however, is the fact that she has in her hand a golden cup, which is full of abominations (i.e. detestable idolatrous things) as well as the filth (moral impurities) of her fornication. She has successfully offered this cup to the kings and inhabitants of the earth and is now stretching it out toward you. From her name some clues emerge. Mystery (musterion) means to shut the mouth; a secret or "mystery" (through the idea of silence imposed by initiation into religious rites). This suggests that she utilizes religion and religious systems to win "converts," while our divine Joseph depends on relationship. She is also Babylon, which is defined as confusion and tyranny.

In her cup, therefore, is all the filth of your past, your shortcomings, failures and your inability to relate with God because you have sinned and come short of His glory. If you drink of her cup, your guilt and condemnation remain and as you continue to worship your past, death will reign in your life, and ultimately and finally separate you from God. The confusion comes from the fact that your spirit is aware that the price has been paid. The great whore working with your soul and the prevailing circumstances around you tries to convince you that you are still married to Adam, the old man, the sin nature. But you must realise that if the first Adam is not dead, you cannot marry the second and last Adam--to remarry would thus be bigamy. It is also important to realise that the great whore is going to be judged according to her works– "Reward her even as she rewarded you, and double unto her double according to her works: in the cup which she hath filled fill to her double" (Revelation 18:6). But her judgment will result from her attitude, which she tries to pass on to you, as evidenced by "how much she hath glorified herself, and lived deliciously (luxuriously and wantonly), so much torment and sorrow give her: for she saith in her heart, "I sit a queen and am no widow, and shall see no sorrow" (Revelation 18:7).

My soul is not a queen till it is married to the King of kings; it is a widow for its first husband is dead; and it knows sorrow because it is lamenting in repentance for the grief that its sins have brought upon the Lamb slain for its redemption and reconciliation to the lover of my soul. To accept her cup is to refuse to repent and to live and die in sin, in union with my old husband, Adam and his sin nature. When faced with the choice of a full gold cup of Mystery Babylon the Great and the empty silver cup of my heavenly Joseph, I know what my choice will be every time.

When Praise Redeems...

Judah is a picture of a true worshipper. Praisers and worshippers are interesting people. By their very nature, they are extreme people. Because they tend to be extremely sensitive in the spirit, they are susceptible to both positive and negative spiritual influences. They thus have to be properly harnessed and mentored. It was Judah who hatched the plot to sell Joseph when the others would have killed him. He was probably the one who hatched the plan to dip the coat in blood to convince their father that Joseph was dead. Ironically, it was another Judah, the son of Iscariot that hatched the plot for Jesus' betrayal! Now as the first Judah jointly organised the deception of his father, he suffered a similar fate at the hand of his daughter-in-law Tamar. Jacob recognised Joseph's coat and declared him dead.

Judah recognised his own seal, cord and staff, symbols of his authority, legal status and righteousness. He had traded these for the lust of the flesh. Upon seeing his items he declared Tamar righteous and himself unrighteous in not keeping his word to give her to his son Shelah in marriage. As Judah had been the spokesman for evil, God was giving him a chance to be restored by being the spokesman for redemption.

In conclusion, Judah's earlier lust and lack of self-control is placed in sharp contrast with Joseph's temperance and purity. How far Judah and his brothers have come and how much like Joseph they have become! This is apparent as they stand in awe before him, having learned to love their brother and father, regardless of his favouritism, and to bear their father's burdens.

CHAPTER NINE

THE UNVEILING

Here is a bold assertion that will withstand close scrutiny: before you have a personal encounter with the Almighty God through His Son Jesus Christ, all of your life is a series of events designed to bring you to the realisation that you desperately need Jesus in your life. Many of life's occurrences force on you the recognition that you have sinned and come short of God's divine standard of righteousness. The generalised morbid fear of death is an indication that we also perceive that our sinful nature has separated us from a holy God. Our mass addiction to alcohol, drugs, sex and promiscuity and worst of all, religion, is a glowing accolade to our vain efforts to minister palliatives which, only serve to numb this perception. We soon discover that only an encounter with Jesus will quench this thirsting of our souls. Upon recognising your spiritual bankruptcy and realising that Jesus is God's answer to reconciling you with Himself, you repent of your sins and invite Jesus into your life as your personal Lord and Saviour.

From the time Joseph set eyes on his brothers twenty years after they betrayed him, he orchestrated a series of events designed to bring them to a place of admission of their guilt, toward confession and repentance. In the realm of the spirit, it is only when an individual gets to this point that the Lord Jesus can reveal Himself to that needy person. Only when his brothers were proven and found to have undergone the needful changes did Joseph reveal himself to his brothers. Since he could no longer control his feelings in front of his servants he immediately ordered them to leave the room.

When he was finally alone with his brothers, he revealed his identity to them, but not before he wept so loudly that it caught the attention of the Egyptians and indeed the House of Pharaoh. Imagine the scene just before he revealed himself. He had just ordered his servants out of the room when he burst into uncontrollably loud sobbing. Picture all the brothers looking from one to the other and wondering what they had done this time after only just getting past the money in their sacks, their imprisoned sibling, the matter of the empty silver cup, the benevolence and volatility of this strange noble and all the other strange things that happened.

His next words were the very last thing they expected to hear. "I am Joseph; doth my father yet live?" (Genesis 45:3) Naturally, they were too troubled and frightened to answer. Joseph then invited them to come closer and when they nervously and hesitantly did so, he reiterated: "Yes, I am your brother Joseph, the one you sold into Egypt" (Genesis 45:4, CEV).

As the brothers hesitantly draw closer, what a glorious picture of a miserable sinner whose guilt, shame and condemnation have weighed him down so completely for so many years. What delightful tidings the graceful invitation bears: "Come unto me, all ye that labour and are heavy laden, and I will give you rest. Take my yoke upon you, and learn of me; for I am meek and lowly in heart: and ye shall find rest unto your souls. For my yoke is easy, and my burden is light" (Matthew 11:28-29). What a stunning portrayal of a tender-hearted Saviour who weeps for and over us when we are the ones who should be weeping for the heartache and misery our sin caused His loving, tender and holy heart. Truly we have a High Priest who is not untouched by the feelings of our infirmities. (See Hebrews 4:15), in other words He feels sympathy for our awful weaknesses.

The dismissal of the servants before the unveiling of Joseph is a picture of salvation as a very personal experience. You may be in a room or a church with a thousand other people but the call to Christ and the conviction that precedes it, are distinctively individual experiences. As Joseph's brothers were inclined to draw back from the guilt, condemnation and shame of their past actions, the sinner feels pretty much the same. Our heavenly Joseph however beckons with open arms: "Come near to me I pray you" (Genesis 45:4). This is a picture of the injunction to "Draw near with a true heart in full assurance of faith, having our hearts sprinkled from an evil conscience, and our bodies washed with pure water" (Hebrews 10:22).

God's invitation to you therefore is that you come with boldness, not timidity or anxiety or trepidation, because the blood from Emmanuel's veins has made a new and living way, which He has inaugurated for us by His death. "I am Jesus, whom ye delivered into the hands of sinful men to be crucified; but I rose again on the third day," is the gracious invitation of the Redeemer to the captive. As Joseph thus asked his brothers, the Lord Jesus in like manner asks the penitent, "Doth my Father yet live in your heart?" Can you find room for Him to rule amidst the clutter of your life? The word "live" (chay) also means fresh plant, fresh water or fresh year. Thus the implication of the question is whether or not you will like a fresh plant, let the fresh water of His Word cause you to enter a fresh year in your life that begins with God.

For This Purpose The Son... Was Manifested

I believe that the central message of the Joseph story is found in the next statement Joseph makes, "Now therefore be not grieved, nor angry with yourselves, that ye sold me hither: for God did send me before you to preserve life" (Genesis 45:5).

No wonder, Joseph was not moved by any of the circumstances that had bedevilled him, since he caught the revelation of his divine purpose. The Bible in Basic English lends more clarity to the text: "Now do not be troubled or angry with yourselves for sending me away, because God sent me before you to be the saviour of your lives" (Genesis 45:5 BBE).

Like every great character of faith in the Bible, Joseph understood that nothing could happen to him that was not orchestrated or permitted by God. The beginning of the Book of Job illustrates this point succinctly as the devil could do nothing without God's permission. (See Job 1:12.) God in turn would permit nothing that would destroy Job or even fail to ultimately work for his good. A second witness is found when the Lord Jesus told Peter that the devil had demanded him (for trial) so that the he could sift Peter as one would grains of corn or wheat. Happily, the text does not end there because Jesus then assured Peter that He had petitioned God on Peter's behalf so that his faith would not fail. (See Luke 22:31-32.)

So though his brothers had to accept personal responsibility for their evil acts and repent of them, Joseph knew his life and times were in God's hands.

He recognised that there was an apostolic mandate on his life: he was a sent one. Only two of the seven years of the great famine had elapsed. Another five years in which there would be neither ploughing nor harvest still lay ahead. For the second time therefore, Joseph emphasised that he was sent: "And God sent me before you to preserve you a posterity in the earth, and to save your lives by a great deliverance." Then to finally establish the fact, he testifies for the third time, "So now it was not you that sent me hither, but God: and He hath made me a father to Pharaoh, and Lord of all his house, and ruler throughout all the land of Egypt" (Genesis 45:7-8).

Likewise, the central theme of the gospel is the fact that Jesus was sent by God. "For God so loved the world, that He gave His only begotten

Son, that whosoever believeth in Him should not perish but have everlasting life." John the beloved, further quotes Jesus as saying "For God sent not His Son into the world to condemn the world; but that the world through Him might be saved" (John 3:16-17). So as Joseph was sent by God to be the saviour of his brothers' lives, so Jesus was sent by God to be the Saviour of His own brothers--the world with whom He shared the common bond of humanity.

After Peter and John's encounter with the Jewish leaders, the apostles acknowledged this fact: "For of a truth against thy holy Child Jesus, whom thou hast anointed, both Herod, and Pontius Pilate, with the Gentiles, and the people of Israel, were gathered together, for to do whatsoever thy hand and thy counsel determined before to be done" (Acts 4:27-28).

Jesus actually confirmed this to Pilate when Pilate claimed to have power to crucify or release Him: "Thou couldest have no power at all against me, except it were given thee from above..." (John 19:11). Joseph knew he was sent to preserve life. Jesus declared to His disciples who wanted to call fire down on a Samaritan village that would not receive Him: "For the Son of Man is not come to destroy men's lives, but to save them." (Luke 9:56). In fact, a central recurring theme in John's Gospel is Jesus' assertion that He was sent by God the Father. That Joseph's preservation of the physical lives of his brothers is a picture of Jesus' quickening of men's spiritual lives is attested to by the word Joseph uses for "preserve life" (Genesis 45:5), (michyah) which in the Hebrew means sustenance, and victuals; it also means the live flesh, the quick, to recover selves, and reviving. As God made Joseph "a father to Pharaoh, and Lord of all his house, and a ruler throughout all the land of Egypt," so He also made Jesus: "Lord of Lords and King of Kings: and they that are with him are called, and chosen, and faithful" (Revelation 17:14). Paul attests to Jesus' lordship when he declares that because Jesus was obedient to the will of the Father even unto death on the cross: "God also hath highly exalted

Him, and given Him a name which is above every name: that at the name of Jesus every knee should bow of things in heaven, and things in earth, and things under the earth; and that every tongue should confess that Jesus Christ is Lord, to the glory of God the Father" (Philippians 2:9-10).

Once Joseph was reconciled to his brothers, all that was left was for them to go to their father, letting him know that God had made Joseph lord of all Egypt, and inviting him to return to Egypt as quickly as possible. Joseph offered to give them land in a particularly fertile region of Goshen where they could live with their children, grandchildren, sheep, goats, cattle and everything else they owned. There he would nourish them and keep them from the ravages of the remaining five years of drought. "All of you, including my brother Benjamin, can tell by what I have said that I really am Joseph" (Genesis 45:12, CEV). They were to tell Jacob of all Joseph's great power and glory in Egypt and of all they had seen and then return quickly with their father.

Till Jesus' brothers, the Church, tell His Father (and ours) as well as the world of all of His power and authority and all we have seen of Him [and as a result have been changed into, (see 2 Corinthians 3:18; 1 John 3:2)] we will not bring His Father hither to the earth. Remember that it is God's ultimate goal to eternally dwell amongst men. Revelations 21:1-2 we see the picture of this when he saw at the culmination of the age, the holy city, the New Jerusalem, coming down from God out of heaven, prepared as a bride adorned for her husband.

"And I heard a great voice out of heaven saying, 'Behold, the tabernacle of God is with men, and He will dwell with them, and they shall be His people, and God Himself shall be with them, and be their God'" (Revelation 21:3). In 1 Corinthians 15:24 Paul explains that the end will only come after Jesus has "delivered up the kingdom to God, even the Father, when He shall have put down all rule and all authority and power."

Joseph in type had humbled himself and put down all authority and power as Pharaoh was the most powerful ruler at that time. He acknowledged that it was God who made him lord of all Egypt. Speaking in his messianic prophetic voice, he says to his brothers: "And there I will nourish thee..." (Genesis 45:11). At this point, Joseph and Benjamin embraced each other tightly and wept on each other's necks. Then Joseph turned to all his brothers and hugged and wept over them also. After all this, the fear of talking to Joseph had vanished, and they began to make up for lost time. Soon, as could be expected, news of this happy reunion reached Pharaoh and his officials, who were quite pleased. At that point Pharaoh instructed Joseph to tell his brothers to load their donkeys and return to Canaan to bring their father and families back to Egypt. This was because Pharaoh had decided to give them the best land in Egypt, which they could cultivate and enjoy. They were also to take some wagons from Egypt for their wives and children to ride in. Most importantly, they were to ensure that they brought their father back with them. If they were concerned about the possessions they would have to leave behind because of their relocation, Pharaoh assured them that they would be given the best of everything in Egypt, which would more than make up for whatever they left behind. Likewise Jesus assured His disciples of a hundredfold return to every disciple who gave up earthly possessions and relationships for Jesus' and the gospel's sake. (See Mark 10:29-30.)

This is a pivotal moment in the history of Jacob and his children. In fact, it could be said that this marks the birth of Israel as a nation because it is here that a phrase that would later become commonplace was first used—"And the children of Israel did so..." (Genesis 45:21). Joseph gave them wagons and provisions for the journey as Pharaoh had commanded. Pharaoh's generosity toward

Joseph's brothers is a testimony to Joseph's faithfulness, loyalty, dedication and integrity, in his service to Pharaoh. That Pharaoh was impressed with Joseph is quite obvious. No doubt, he had been pondering ways by which he could show his appreciation for Joseph's meritorious service. The appearance of his brothers and news of his father provided Pharaoh with the opportunity he so craved. When Joseph served with all his heart, he did not realise that his faithfulness would later benefit those connected to him. He also did not realise he would be the most perfect picture of Christ; he simply obeyed. This is what we ought to do, picture Jesus in all things, as well as serve in a way that will leave a legacy for our loved ones who have yet to embrace Him. And we do not have to die before they begin to enjoy the fruits of our labour and faithfulness.

In addition to Pharaoh's gifts, Joseph also gave his brothers gifts. He gave each of his brothers new clothes but gave Benjamin five times as many new clothes and in addition gave him 300 pieces of silver. This is the second time Benjamin received from Joseph five times more than his brothers. As is commonly known, five is the number of grace and mercy; Benjamin enjoyed grace in an unparalleled dimension. In a latter chapter we will discover the significance of this based on their mutual parenthood.

Three hundred is a picture of victory in the face of impossible odds as exemplified by Gideon's army of 300 winning men, each armed with only an earthen vessel, a torch and a trumpet. Having given pleasant gifts to his brothers, Joseph then sent ten donkeys loaded with Egypt's best products and another ten donkeys loaded with grain and bread and other items of food for the return journey. Ten (donkeys) is the number of the law and though the donkeys were laden with every good gift, Joseph was still aware that they would not have sufficed for the salvation of the parties concerned. It would take another ten donkeys to get the job done because twenty is the number of redemption. "Therefore by the deeds of the law there shall no flesh be justified in His sight…" (Romans 3:20). Once this was done, he sent his brothers on their way with the admonition that they were not to quarrel along the way. Why did Joseph tell his brothers not to quarrel along the way? There are a couple of conjectures. Perhaps now that he had reconciled with his brothers and was aware of his father's welfare, Joseph did not want anything to delay the eagerly anticipated reunion with his father. Another possibility is Joseph realized the fragile nature of his brothers' relationship, after so many years of disagreement.

Once they were on the road we can surmise that they probably conducted a verbal "post-mortem" examination of the entire situation, and might have been tempted to point fingers at one another. Joseph's admonition to his brothers to go and get their families is however, first a picture of Jesus who is described as the forerunner in the Book of Hebrews. (See Hebrews 6:20.) Like Jesus, Joseph had entered into a place of promise, a type of "that within the veil." And like Jesus, he had gone in as a forerunner for his brothers. We will later see Joseph interceding before Pharaoh for his family as though he were in Jesus' stead, a high priest forever after the order of Melchisedek. (See Hebrews 6:19-20.)

Joseph told his brothers to tell his father of all his glory. Yet as undeserving as they were, he was willing to share his glory with his brothers. In His high priestly intercessory prayers for His disciples through the ages, Jesus emphasized the fact that He was sent by God, ahead of His "brothers" for their salvation. Jesus prayed, "And the glory which thou gavest me I have given them; that they may be one even as we are one" (John 17:22). This is another reason why Joseph told his brothers not to quarrel along the way. They had to walk "in the unity of the Spirit and the bond of peace" (Ephesians 4:3). Joseph came into Egypt alone, but made a way for his brothers to enjoy that for which he had paid so dearly. However, they were to go back to Canaan and in turn bring their children, grand-children, wives, servants and other householders, thereby fulfilling Jesus' commandments concerning the believer: "The works that I do shall he do also; and greater works than these shall he do…" (John 14:12).

Rejoice! The Wagons Are Coming

Thus the brothers left Egypt and returned to the land of Canaan to meet Jacob. Can you picture the scene? The old man, when he last saw his boys, was resigned to the fact that Joseph was long dead, supposedly devoured by a wild animal; Simeon was imprisoned in Egypt and as good as lost; and Benjamin had also been taken away to be presented to some Egyptian demagogue and might never come back. In fact, from the way the last story sounded, the ruler was so temperamental that the possibility of actually losing all his sons in Egypt was a daunting and ever-present prospect. His heart was a picture of doom and gloom, despair and fear, isolation and desolation. To see his boys now falling all over themselves to give him good news was overwhelming. He could hear the words and the message conveyed, but his weary heart just could not decipher their contents. His delayed hope had filled his heart with so much despair that he had difficulty absorbing the flood of good news. Like David, we faint unless we believe. (See Psalm 27:13.) To convince Jacob, his sons gave him an account of everything Joseph had said to them. It was, however, only when he saw the wagons that Joseph had sent to him, that his spirit was revived. He then told his sons he had seen and heard enough to convince him that his son Joseph was still alive; he would thus go to see him before he died.

It would appear that every time Jacob struggled with his flesh, his faith and his conduct, he was referred to as "Jacob," and when he assayed to boldly apprehend God's covenant and its promises, he was referred to as "Israel."

Thus Jacob is a picture of the flesh and Israel a picture of the Spirit, and how both war in the life of a believer. Romans7 throws more light on this conflict. Paul concludes that this inward man--that is, his spirit (Israel), truly takes pleasure in the law of God, but he discovers a different law in his body parts (Jacob), fighting against the law of his mind and making him a prisoner of sin that tries to control everything he does. It is strangely ironic that when his sons told him Joseph was dead, Jacob was quick to believe it, yet now that he heard that he was alive, he was slow to believe it. This is because though: "we know that we are from God" and therefore have faith and fear no foe, "...the whole world lies under the sway of the evil one" (1 John 5:19, EMTV). People therefore, because of the fall and their sin-nature are wired to believe evil reports faster, than good ones. Moreover, when we are obsessively or idolatrously in love with anyone or anything, we live with the constant fear of losing them.

What a glorious note on which to end this part of the Joseph saga. No matter what you have been through, or how long it's been going on, I have good news for you--the wagons are coming! Your deferred hope is about to be realised, to become for you a tree of life. (See Proverbs 13:12.) Your dry bones are about to live again and become for you a mighty protectorate, an army of sorts. (See Ezekiel 37:10.) Your sons who have been separated from you are about to send wagons to secure reconciliation. It is important to realise that God's providence may take you out of the land of promise, to sustain you somewhere else till the appointed time. So do not fear to relocate when the glory cloud shifts, knowing that at the appointed time, God is able to restore to you the years devoured by the locusts, caterpillars, cankerworm and palmerworm. (See Joel 2:25.) This is a prophetic word and confirmation for that person who is unsure at this time of what the will of God is for their lives in respect to relocation.

Remember when God calls you to give up something in your life it is never for less; it is always for more!

CHAPTER TEN

WHY TAKE ME IN IF I'M ONLY GOING TO COME OUT AGAIN?

And so begins Israel's journey to Egypt with all of his possessions. This marks the beginning of a sojourn that would last the better part of four centuries. For Israel, it is decidedly an ambivalent journey. Apart from the issue of his well-advanced years, he would no doubt be battling the family history that surrounds previous trips to Egypt. His grandfather Abraham the father of faith had without God's approval gone down to Egypt to sojourn there on account of a grievous famine in the land of his residence. That move saw the Pharaoh of that time take Sarai (as she was called then) into his harem, and but for the intervention of God, she would have been defiled. (See Genesis 12:14-20.) Many years later, God warned his father Isaac not to go down to Egypt in spite of the famine in the land. (See Genesis 26:2.) He was to remain in Gerar where God would bless him. Isaac did as he was commanded, then even sowed in that time of crisis and reaped a hundredfold in the very same year. He grew wealthier and wealthier by the day till he was very rich indeed. (See Genesis 26:12-13.) Now it was Israel's turn; was he to remain where he was like Isaac, or go to Egypt like Abraham? Ah! Decisions, decisions!

He was probably still mulling over these things in his mind when he arrived at Beer-sheba. Beer-sheba is a place replete with family history and bursting with symbolic overtones. Beer-sheba is the place where Hagar and her son Ishmael wandered in the wilderness dying from thirst when Abraham had, at Sarah's behest, sent away the bondwoman and her son. Spiritually therefore, Beer-sheba is a place where the works of the flesh will not find pasture or rest. Oh that God would bring us to Beer-sheba where our carnal desires would be starved to death! Beer-sheba is also the place where the Philistine

King Abimelech and his army general, Phicol, recognised that God was with Abraham and thus wisely decided to entreat his favour. In fact in Psalm 45:12 David prophesied that: "...The daughter of Tyre shall be there with a gift, even the rich among the people shall entreat thy favour" (Psalm 45:12), referring of course, to the Messiah. When our light shines brightly, men likewise see our good works and glorify our Father who is in heaven. (See Matthew 5:16.) The prophet Isaiah makes it clear that when natural Zion, which is a type of spiritual Zion, the Church, arises and shines, then Gentiles will come to her light and kings to her bright dawn. (See Isaiah 60:1-3.) They will be attracted to God's favour upon the Church and bring their wealth and gifts to secure for themselves this uncommon divine favour.

Abimelech thus wisely chose to make a covenant with Abraham, who then took the opportunity to make a report regarding the issue of his well, which had been violently usurped by Abimelech's servants. So a covenant was signed between Abimelech and Abraham, and the place was named Beer-sheba, which means "well of the oath." (See Genesis 21:31.) So in addition to being a place of covenant, Beer-sheba is also the place where the possessions that have been violently taken by the enemy are restored to you. May God bring you to your spiritual Beer-sheba, where the lost years and possessions of your past, violently taken from you are restored to you, in Jesus' name.

To commemorate this covenant, Abraham built an altar to God, El-Olam, the Almighty, the Everlasting God, and marked the spot by planting a tree. This is significant because right up to this time, whenever men or nations served a god, such deities were restricted by time, space, event or even the death or annihilation of the worshipper(s). However, Abraham declared that his God was the Eternal One, the intergenerational God who would be served by his sons, their sons and indeed eternal generations. In fact, after passing his great test when this same God called upon him to offer up Isaac the son of promise upon the altar of sacrifice, Abraham returned to, and dwelt at Beer-sheba. (See Genesis 22:19.) Not surprisingly therefore, Isaac faces pretty much the same things his father Abraham faced at Beer-sheba. Two wells were violently taken from him, God also appeared to him and established His covenant with him as with his father before him, and he in turn builds an altar there. As expected, before long, you guessed it, Abimelech king of the Philistines, and Philcol, his army general and one Ahuzzath, his friend, after initially sending Isaac away from them, were now desiring covenant with him to entreat his favour because they could see that God was with him. After this covenant, there was also a restoration.

After Jacob had fled from the wrath of his offended brother, Esau, he ran from Beer-sheba toward Haran. In between at Bethel, he had his encounter with God in a dream. This however was many, many, years prior. The cycle would not be complete, till Jacob had his own encounter at Beer-sheba. Getting to the well of the oath and seeing the altar his forefathers had erected and the tree of remembrance they had planted no doubt stirred Jacob to offer sacrifices "unto the God of his father Isaac" (Genesis 46:1). The passage of time and the many vicissitudes of Jacob's life had caused him to forget that at Bethel, God had moved from being merely the God of Abraham and Isaac to being his God also. God therefore had to remind him of his position and status and to give him a rhema (that is, a specific word) in relation to his move to Egypt. God assured Jacob: "Fear not to go down into Egypt, for I will there make thee a great nation..." (Genesis 46:3). This then is the affirmation of a promise made to Abraham after he believed in the Lord; and God counted it to him for righteousness. (See Genesis 15:6.) That promise now established at the mouth of a second witness, declared unto Abram, "Know of a surety that thy seed shall be a stranger in a land that is not theirs, and shall serve them; and they shall afflict them four hundred years; and also that nation, whom they shall serve, will I judge: and afterward shall they come out with great substance" (Genesis 15:13-14). It must be fascinating to be the generation that not only sees, but brings prophecy to pass. God's final statement to Jacob carries an obvious reference to death, burial, resurrection, and ascension, which is of course, the message of Christ. "I will go down with you into Egypt; and I will also surely bring thee up again: and Joseph shall put his hand upon thine eyes" (Genesis 46:4).

Knowing that God would not and did not leave our Saviour's soul in hell nor suffer His Holy One to see the corrupting influences of decay, must be one of the most comforting thoughts of the scriptures. This is because we were crucified in Christ Jesus, making not just His death ours, but also making His life, His resurrection, His quickening and His ascension, all ours. This is what the prophet Isaiah saw in the Spirit when he prophesied: "Thy dead men shall live, together with my dead body shall they arise" (Isaiah 26:19). This is why he could further admonish in view of our impending resurrection that we should "awake and sing, ye that dwell in dust for thy dew is as the dew of herbs, and the earth shall cast out the dead" (Isaiah 26:19). Death holds absolutely no terror to the believer because as Joseph would be by the side of Jacob at his death and would comfortably and ceremonially close his eyes as he makes the transition into the presence of God, so our heavenly Joseph who has conquered death, hell and the grave, will lovingly close our eyes as He leads us out of this life into the eternal presence of His God and our God, His Father and our Father.

Assured of a future resurrection, Jacob could now rise up from Beer-sheba, the well of the oath, with God's oath resonating in his spirit, as he headed for Egypt. "Yea, though I walk through the valley of the shadow of death, I will fear no evil: for thou art with me; thy rod and thy staff they comfort me" (Psalm 23:4), was David's testimony in similar circumstances. So Jacob's sons put him in the wagon the king had sent, and they put their little children and their wives in the other wagons. Armed with their animals and everything they possessed,

Jacob's sons, daughters, grandsons, and his granddaughters indeed, his entire family set off for Egypt. The next eighteen verses of the text outline the names of all of Jacob's sons and their progeny. With the exception of historians and people of their ilk, few people have the stomach for enduring let alone studying genealogies. However, the student of God's Word must neither skip them nor rush to skim through them. Paul wrote to his spiritual son, Timothy that all scripture is God-breathed and profitable. (See 2 Timothy 3:16.) Patient study of even difficult texts will reveal hidden nuggets of truth. In fact, gold nuggets and other precious stones are never found on the surface. So let us leap into troubled waters and see if we can actually fish in the storm.

"And these are the names of the children of Israel, which came into Egypt, Jacob and his sons" (Genesis 46:8). The text begins as it lists each of the children and their own offspring.

As firstborn, Reuben is listed first. Reuben has four sons; Hanoch, Phallu, Hezron and Carmi.

Simeon has six sons namely Jemuel, Jamin, Ohad, Jachin, Zohar and Shaul. Where there is nothing to report with Reuben's sons, Simeon's last born is said to be the son of a Canaanite woman. The Bible is as instructive in what it leaves unsaid as it is in what it outlines. Many questions arise from this information. Why did Simeon have a son by a woman from the region with which God expressly forbade marital ties? Were all his other children from the same woman? Was this the consequence of an extra-marital affair, a liaison with a concubine, or the demise of his first wife? Was this why it was Simeon who was held in prison when the brothers first came to Egypt to buy food? To all these conjectures, the Bible gives no answer. However, one thing is clear: God's displeasure is unequivocal on the issue of His covenant children being unequally yoked with unbelievers, whether in the Old or New Testament. So whatever the circumstances, He felt the same displeasure with Simeon that he had when Judah went down from his brethren.

The sons of Levi were three – Gershon, Kohath and Merari. Why Levi's last born was called "bitter" no one really knows! (Is this the same root word from which we get the name Mary or Mara?) It is instructive that those who have been dealt bitter blows by fate tend to be intense God-seekers, God worshippers and intercessors. The severity of her affliction was what drove Hannah into the depths of God where she discovered His need for a prophet and keyed into it with her desire for a son. Remember it was said of her, "And she was in bitterness of soul, and prayed unto the Lord, and wept sore" (1 Samuel 1:10).

Judah is next in line, and if you recall we explored his family line earlier. Recall that he had five sons in total but Er and Onan were killed by God in the land of Canaan for their wickedness. So Judah was left with Shelah, Pharez and Zerah. Pharez on his part already had two sons, Hezron and Hamul.

Issachar had four sons called Tola, Phuvah, Job and Shimron. The name Tola means worm and immediately points us to a messianic declaration: "But I am a worm, and no man; a reproach of men, and despised of the people" (Psalm 22:6).

Matthew Henry in his comments on Genesis 46:13, quotes Bishop Patrick as observing that though Tola was considered a worm probably because when he was born he was a very weakly little child, yet there would later spring from him a prolific and great people, as evidenced by the record in the first book of the Chronicles of the kings of Israel. (See 1 Chronicles 7:2.) There is also some conjecture that his third son is the same legendary Job who was the object of great suffering and the object of the Biblical book of the same name. There is however no biblical support for this viewpoint, other than the shared name. One thing is clear though, and that is the fact that there was something special about Issachar's sons. It would later be said of the tribe's leaders that they had an understanding or expert knowledge of the times and what it was best for Israel to do, and so all their brothers were under their order. (See 1 Chronicles 12:32.)

Zebulun, the sixth and last of Leah's sons, had three sons. Sered, Elon and Jahleel. These first six sons of Jacob and their sister, Dinah, that Leah bore to Jacob in Padan-aram making the total number from this branch of the family thirty-three. Next, we see Jacob's children by Zilpah, the maid Laban gave to his daughter Leah. Gad had seven sons, Ziphion, Haggi, Shuni, Ezbon, Eri, Arodi and Areli. Asher had four sons, Jimnah, Ishuah, Isui and Beriah, and one daughter called Serah. Asher's last son Beriah had two sons of his own, Heber and Malchiel. Altogether, Zilpah's branch therefore accounts for sixteen souls.

The account progresses with these words: "The sons of Rachel Jacob's wife" (Genesis 46:19), are listed, of course, as Joseph and Benjamin. This statement under divine chronicling lends credence to Jacob's attitude that the only woman he really considered as his wife was Rachel, and the only sons he was truly drawn to were Joseph and Benjamin.

This is not surprising as Leah was never on his radar, let alone in his plans for a wife. It was the trickery and facetiousness of Laban that caused Jacob to end up with a second wife for whom he had absolutely no attraction, desire or inclination; a woman who was so physically and sexually neglected that she had to use her son's mandrakes (flowers reported to have magical power) as a bargaining tool with her rival Rachel to get Jacob to even contemplate spending another night with her! (See Genesis 30:15-16.) As for the maids Zilpah and Bilhah, they were nothing but pawns in the power play between their two mistresses. They were the grass that bore the brunt in the epic battle between two elephants.

Joseph, as we have discovered, had two sons in Egypt, Manasseh and Ephraim, born to him by Asenath the daughter of Poti-pherah, priest or prince of On. For reasons which we shall explore a little later, Benjamin is by far the most prolific of Jacob's children, with ten children of his own, namely Belah, Becher, Ashbel, Gera, Naaman, Ehi, Rosh, Muppim, Huppim and Ard.

So Rachel's branch of the family accounts for fourteen souls.

Dan has only one son, Hushim, and his brother Naphtali has four; Jahzeel, Guni, Jezer, and Shillem. Dan and Naphtali are of course the sons of Bilhah, the maid Laban gave to his daughter Rachel and she accounts for seven souls.

So not counting Jacob himself and his four wives, sixty-six of Jacob's offspring went into Egypt. Adding to that number Jacob's two grandsons born there, the number of Jacob's family who ended up in Egypt were seventy in number. Now Jacob had sent Judah ahead of him to Goshen to ask Joseph primarily for directions and that Joseph should meet him there. Why did Jacob choose Judah to run this errand that was of such vital significance to him? No doubt, because he had proven reliable in the recently-concluded matter of returning Benjamin as he had promised and indeed as a bonus returning Simeon and even Joseph though technically he could not lay claim to the credit of bringing these things to pass. Another reason is that praisers are leaders because praise reveals the mind of God, which always puts you at an advantage. Asaph caught this revelation when he said: "In Judah is God known: His name is great in Israel" (Psalm 76:1, KJV). It is praise that exposed Lucifer to understanding God's heart, and that made him arrogantly believe he knew all that there was to know about God and could therefore, at the worst, compete with God, and at best, usurp His place.

When faced with three mighty and impregnable armies Jehoshaphat called upon the Lord, and God gave him the assurance of victory. After consultation with the people, he appointed singers unto the Lord who would extol the beauty of God's holiness, dancing and singing before the army and enjoining all to "Praise the Lord, for His mercy endureth forever" (2 Chronicles 20:21, KJV). Thus as Jehoshapat, a type of Judah, went before the way and the rest of the camp, God set ambushes against the three mighty armies of Ammon, Moab and Mount Seir, and they all ended up dead. Thus for the believer, praise (Judah) is your secret and most potent weapon. This explains why the Psalmist tells us to enter God's gates with thanksgiving and His courts with praise. (See Psalm 100:4, KJV.)

Jacob could have sent a son, any son ("see a son-Reuben") or he could have sent "a hearing" –Simeon, or he could have sent the one to whom he was "attached"--Levi. He could have sent the one that would bring a reward--Issachar, or the one who was a "habitation"; surely he could have sent the "Judge" (Dan) or his "wrestling" (Naphtali); he could have sent a "troop" (Gad) or "happy" (Asher). Needless to say, sending Judah got the job done properly: "Some trust in chariots, and some in horses: but we will remember the name of the Lord our God" (Psalm 20:7). To remember the name of the Lord is to praise Him for who He is. Jacob and his family entourage arrived in Goshen, while Joseph harnessed his chariot and sped down to Goshen for the long-awaited reunion with Israel, his dad. When they meet, Joseph puts his arms around Israel's neck and weeps for a very long time. Israel then says to Joseph, "Now that I have seen you and know you are still alive, I am ready to die" (Genesis 46:30). Joseph then addresses the entire company comprising his brothers and father's family, and tells them he plans to go to Pharaoh to tell him that his family has arrived from the land of Canaan. He would inform

Pharaoh that they had always made their living by raising livestock. Naturally, he would conclude that they had brought their flocks, herds and everything else they own, along with them. Joseph then instructs them that should Pharaoh send for them and inquire about their profession, they were to inform him that they were shepherds from an illustrious and long heritage of sheep-rearers. "If you tell him this," Joseph reasoned, "he will let you settle in the region of Goshen" (Genesis 46:34, CEV).

As usual, because Joseph had knowledge and understanding he was operating at a higher level of wisdom. He knew sheep-rearing was a taboo with Egyptians and that they did not like to be around anyone who raised sheep. He was also aware that Goshen was among the most fertile of Egyptian territory. Having thought it through he had no doubt that Pharaoh would assign them the land of Goshen for their possession and use. This must explain why he chose to meet them in Goshen. Apart from the fact that they were already there, and so he would not need to look for some other place, the logistical nightmare and socio-cultural consequences of moving them and their flocks and herds to another location, would have been unappealing to Pharaoh. Thus Joseph had secured the best Egypt had to offer without upsetting the establishment. In fact, his wisdom made it appear that it was Pharaoh's idea and that his generosity had secured the decision.

What a lesson for managers and supervisory personnel: make your boss look good and let him take credit for your good ideas and efforts and you and yours will ultimately benefit. Joseph had the authority and goodwill to simply relocate his family and then inform Pharaoh as an afterthought. Joseph however, would never usurp or abuse his authority in this way. Thus he always exemplified the principle of accountability.

Note how Christ-like he was: "Who existing in the form of God, counted not the being on an equality with God a thing to be grasped..." (Philippians 2:6, ASV). If we all as believers adopted this attitude of humility, then no matter what degree of power we operate under, we would never be corrupted, and even absolute authority would not drive us toward evil. Joseph completely reflected Christ by demonstrating what Jesus' most important present day ministry is-- intercession. By His intercession, Jesus was able to invite us to the saving knowledge of our heavenly Father; He then showed us the Way to this God who is our Father; He Himself being the Way, the Truth and the Life. (See John 14:6.) Then He saved us completely and even now constantly makes intercession for us so that we do not fall. And even if we do, His prayers provide a way of restoration. (See Isaiah 55:12, Hebrews 10:21 & Hebrews 6:14.) This is what the Book of Hebrews alludes to when it says of Him: "Wherefore He is able to save them to the uttermost that come unto God by Him, seeing He ever liveth to make intercession for them" (Hebrews 7:25, KJV).

Joseph had access to and knew the very mind of Pharaoh. Like Mordecai did with Esther, Joseph tutored his wards not only on how to gain access to, but to enjoy the favour of the King. Because he had passed that route himself, Joseph could teach his brothers the way. Remember how the Prophet Isaiah prophesied that upon seeing the travail of the Messiah's soul, God would be satisfied. Furthermore, by His knowledge, God's righteous Servant, Jesus, would justify many by bearing their iniquities. God would therefore cause Him to have a heritage ("divide Him a portion") with the great so that He would divide the spoils of war with the strong i.e., believers who become partakers of the blessings Christ secured. Let us hear it from the horse's mouth: "Therefore will I divide Him a portion with the great, and He shall divide the spoil with the strong; because He hath poured out His soul unto death: and He was numbered with the transgressors; and He bare the sin of many, and made intercession for the transgressors" (Isaiah 53:10-12, KJV). Although his brothers were transgressors, Joseph divided the spoil of victory with them and spoke to Pharaoh on their behalf in intercession. Notice also that in the chronicling of the genealogy of Joseph, he is numbered among the transgressors!

Joseph was a picture of our Great High Priest who made His way through the heavens into the very presence of God. He was thus teaching his brothers as Jesus taught us, to hold fast their profession (notice the word play here as it relates to their profession as shepherds and the profession of their faith). Like us, Joseph's brothers had a high priest in him, who was not unable to sympathise with their weaknesses. Rather, they had one who was tempted in every way that they were and yet did not sin! (See Hebrews 4:14-16, KJV.) They, like us, could therefore boldly approach Pharaoh's throne of grace so that they could "obtain mercy and find grace to help in time of need." How powerful and awesome this message of grace is. We who deserved death are now able to enjoy both eternal and abundant life. We who should have been eternally incarcerated are granted unhindered, direct and continuous access to the King of kings. We who should be bankrupt, penniless, naked and ashamed, are being given the best of the land. Instead of the desert we get Goshen; instead of guilt, condemnation and judgment, we have an Advocate with the Father (See 1 John 2:4), an Intercessor at His Right hand Who ever liveth to make intercession for us, who come to God by Him.

In conclusion, it is ironic that "every shepherd is an abomination unto the Egyptians." Yet without the ministry of Joseph, a type of the Good Shepherd, Egypt would not have survived that period in its history. Not only did the ministry of this shepherd secure Egypt's survival, it actually accounted for an era of tremendous wealth and consolidation of the power, authority, influence and prosperity for both that Pharaoh and his people. These same people who were an abomination would provide the workforce for Egyptian nation-building for the next four centuries. If shepherds are an abomination, then the Egyptians were cutting themselves off from the Good Shepherd who "giveth His life for the sheep" (John 10:11). This means that the Judas "anointing" would prevail in their lives and they would have to hang themselves for their own iniquities rather than turn their lives over to the Good Shepherd whom they had foolishly, and by human traditions, made an abomination unto themselves.

So the next time someone despises you or treats you like an abomination, remember, you may yet be the key to their survival. The greatest tragedy is not what people think of you, but how much you let their thoughts affect, mould or change your opinion of yourself. They may not know your worth but you must under no condition forget your identity and your divine purpose. Is it not written, after all, that the Stone, which the builders rejected, has now become the cornerstone? (See Matthew 21:42.)

Why, we may be tempted to ask, would God allow His people to be in a land where their customs were anathema? Spiros Zodhiates in his notes on the issue observes that: "Throughout its history, Egypt had a hatred for foreign things. Their very language depicts foreigners as a lower class of humans. In addition, the particular manners and customs of the Jews were totally disgusting to the Egyptians."

He further explains that "the Jews had hair and beards, while the Egyptians, both men and women, shaved all their body hair. This attitude of superiority is reflected in Pharaoh's instructions to basically 'leave everything behind because we will give you good Egyptian stuff.' (Genesis 45:20, KJV.) God had carefully chosen Egypt as the one place where Israel could grow into a nation. The Egyptian abhorrence for the Jews would limit the danger of intermingling, either racially or religiously (a problem which would lead to much trouble in Canaan). The size and prosperity of Egypt would allow the Hebrew people to become numerous while still being a minority in the country. The later invasion of the Hyksos, an eastern people, led to the enslavement of the Jews, which served to make them physically strong" (Pg. 72-notes on Genesis 46:36, Key word SB).

God knows why you are where you are and what purpose it will serve in your life. You may not understand it now, but learn to trust the Lord with all your heart and do not depend on your own limited understanding; indeed in all your ways acknowledge Him and He will bring it to pass, by directing or making your paths smooth. (See Proverbs 3:5-6.)

CHAPTER ELEVEN

THE LAW OF THE FIFTH

Genesis 47 begins with Joseph going to inform Pharaoh that his father and his brethren, their flock, herds and entire possessions had come out of the land of Canaan and were already in the land of Goshen. This was Joseph again operating in his high priestly capacity on behalf of his undeserving brothers who, however, shared blood ties with him. It was the blood ties that compelled him to go where they had neither right of access, nor relationship ties to make intercession for them with "the great king." By this access, Joseph then invited his brothers to state their case before, and make their request to Pharaoh. What a precursor of our calling and our relationship with Christ, which is outlined in the admonition, "Let us, then, hold firmly to the faith we profess. For we have a great High Priest who has gone into the very presence of God--Jesus, the Son of God" (Hebrews 4:14, GNB). Jesus' preparatory work, leads to a further injunction "Let us therefore come boldly unto the throne of grace, that we may obtain mercy and find grace to help in time of need" (Hebrews 14:16, KJV). The Contemporary English Version (CEV) makes this point more relevant: "So whenever we are in need, we should come bravely before the throne of our merciful God. There we will be treated with undeserved kindness, and we will find help."

Joseph consequently took five of his brothers and introduced them to Pharaoh. It is important to realise that everything Joseph did was done with great forethought and wisdom. As he had so well thought through and chosen Goshen as their port of arrival, so he thought through and decided on how many of his eleven brothers he would present before Pharaoh. If he had brought all of them, it would have appeared like a power play to Pharaoh and his court, and this might have incurred Pharaoh's judgment. Remember that in Bible numerology eleven is the number of judgment. This is evidenced by the fact that there were eleven judgments on Egypt in the days of Moses and Aaron; the judgment of the flood coming upon the world occurred in the eleventh generation; and the eleventh child of Jacob was called Dinah, whose name means judgment. The judgment of the rebellious but united people of the earth is found in no other place than Genesis chapter eleven in the story of the Tower of Babel! If however Joseph had taken only one or two, he would have understated their numbers and misrepresented the situation. So after careful consideration, he took five of his brothers. No doubt, he would have wisely handpicked the brothers with the best temperaments, probably avoiding the volatile, intemperate, rash, and undiplomatic ones. Spiritually, picking five of them speaks of the grace by which the believer is saved, while repudiating his works of righteousness and walking in faith. Joseph was preaching to us through his brothers that whatever we get from God is a gift, which of course precludes boastful arrogance and smug self-righteousness. Also, this number is a subtle reference to a principle that Joseph would soon introduce us to: "The Law of the Fifth." As Joseph anticipated, Pharaoh's first question to Joseph's brothers is: "What is your occupation?" Isn't it wonderful to have a High Priest, an intercessor who knows his onions! As schooled, the brothers informed Pharaoh that they were practicing shepherds from a proud heritage of shepherds. Remember that the whole account of Joseph begins with him at age seventeen with his brothers looking after their father's flocks. It was also said of their great-grand father, Abraham (while he was still Abram) that he was very rich in cattle. (See Genesis 13:2.)

In the preceding chapter we discovered that the greatest biblical leaders were shepherds, with Moses, David and the Lord Jesus himself attesting to this fact. The diligence of the shepherds around Bethlehem at the time of Christ's birth is also telling and instructive in its own inimitable way. Joseph's brothers explained to Pharaoh the terrible famine in Canaan and requested to live in Egypt in the land of Goshen. Many times, we slave, work and labour and never seem to be rewarded. Nevertheless, on the appointed day your time will come. Ironically, it was Joseph's brothers who were now about to reap the benefits of the many seeds that Joseph had sown. Pharaoh was delighted to agree to their request. He told Joseph his father and brethren were welcome to dwell in the "best of the land," which, especially for grazing purposes, was Goshen. Furthermore, because of Joseph's exemplary service, Pharaoh was willing to employ any of Joseph's brothers who were especially good at their work, to look after his own livestock. If they were cut from the same cloth as Joseph, Pharaoh reasoned, then obviously, Pharaoh's sheep and goats would do as well as Egypt was now doing under Joseph's leadership.

What Joseph did next is one of the most significant but overlooked aspects of his story–"And Joseph brought in Jacob his father, and set him before Pharaoh: and Jacob blessed Pharaoh" (Genesis 47:7, KJV). At that time, Pharaoh was the supreme ruler, and yet Jacob blessed him! Pharaoh was the then world's most influential king, but Jacob blessed him! Pharaoh was wealthy beyond measure, but Jacob blessed him! Pharaoh was even considered by his citizens to be a deity, but Jacob blessed him! Jacob understood the importance and power of the covenant God made with his grandfather Abraham, passed on to his father Isaac and passed on to him instead of his twin brother who despised his birthright and then lost the blessing. In the covenant, God stipulated to Abraham: "In thee shall all families of the earth be blessed" (Genesis 12:3, KJV). When speaking to Isaac God assured him: "In thy seed shall all the nations of the earth be blessed." But when speaking to Jacob, He modifies it slightly, saying: "In thee and in thy seed shall all the families of the earth be blessed" (Genesis 28:12, KJV). The phrase "and in thee..." (Gen28:14) was an aspect of the mandate that gave Jacob the authority and boldness to bless a sovereign who was supposed to be doing him and his family a favour.

On many levels, the things Jacob had been through with people like his brother Esau and his father-in-law Laban had dented his self-confidence and given him a bit of a complex. This slips through in his response when Pharaoh, obviously in awe of his age and his apparent health and well-being, asked him how old he was. This is probably because Egyptians had a much lower life expectancy and never looked this strong, healthy and grand in their old age. Jacob answered, "I have lived only a hundred thirty years, and I have had to move from place to place. My parents and grandparents also had to move from place to place. But they lived much longer, and their life was not as hard as mine" (Genesis 47:9, CEV). He was still alive and well so how did he know whether he would not exceed the lifespan of his forebears? (The sorrows and hardships he had undergone probably made him feel that way.) However when it came to spiritual issues, he was acutely aware of his position and status as a chosen one, a prophet and a patriarch, and "a greater than Pharaoh." So like Apostle Paul, he magnified his office (see Romans 11:13, KJV); hence his blessings upon Pharaoh. This explains what could have been a contradiction in terms since Pharaoh was considerably wealthier than he was in worldly terms. Hebrews 7:7, CEV says: "Everyone agrees that a person who gives a blessing is greater than the one who receives the blessing." The Good News Bible says it this way: "There is no doubt that the one who blesses is greater than the one who is blessed." In God's eyes Jacob was definitely greater than Pharaoh, and had the spiritual authority to bless him. Jacob's love and adoration of God was in such dramatic contrast with his brother, Esau's, who despised his birthright .For this reason God loved him and chose him over his brother, who lost his birthright privileges. No wonder Esau was called a profane person and a fornicator. Indeed, when it was time for Esau to marry, he took not one but two "wives of the daughters of Canaan," the very people God forbade His people from marrying. We dealt with this thought when taking a look at Judah. This greatly displeased his parents, Rebekah and Isaac. His spiritual bankruptcy became obvious when he felt the only way to improve his situation was to marry Ishmael's daughter. In fact, Genesis 36 chronicles Esau's family line to show how he became inextricably integrated with the heathen inhabitants of the land in such a short time. His penchant for carnal living, his open rebellion and his contempt for sacred things did not come as a surprise to God, and it was for that reason that He rejected him from his mother's womb. Jacob would gladly take his place in the lineage of the founding patriarchs, and this made him eminently qualified to bless Pharaoh twice before leaving his presence.

Jesus was still the Christ, the Messiah, the King of kings and Lord of lords, even when he was born in a manger. Even with earthly parents of very modest means, He still blessed those around Him. He indicated that a man's life does not consist merely in the abundance of what he possesses. (See Luke 12:15, KJV.) Many of us devalue ourselves and do not know our spiritual worth. We will not bless the world around us because we think that we are not as financially buoyant as they are. Yet we hold the key to their welfare through the power of our tongues. Jesus taught His disciples that spiritual blessings are superior to and more to be desired than material ones. This, of course is not to suggest that they are mutually exclusive or that there is anything wrong with material or physical blessings. Rather, we as children of God have the key through preaching the gospel and exemplifying its message in our lives to impart God's spiritual blessings, of which we are custodians, to a lost and dying world.

Back to our story; we are told: "Joseph obeyed the King's orders and gave his father and brothers some of the land in Egypt near the city of Rameses" (Genesis 47:11, (CEV). He also made food available for them and their families from the youngest to the oldest.

Then the famine became very severe in both Egypt and Canaan and this caused terrible suffering among the peoples of these lands. As the famine intensified, the people had to spend more and more of their money on the grain that Joseph had wisely stored up in anticipation of the famine. Unlike contemporary politicians, Joseph did not keep away even a small part for himself, but put all the resources into Pharaoh's treasury. Soon, as could be expected, everyone ran out of money. The Egyptians then came to Joseph and said, "Give us more grain! If you don't, we'll soon be dead, because our money's all gone" (Genesis 47: 15, CEV).

"And Joseph said, Give me your cattle, I will give you grain in exchange for your cattle if your money is all gone" (Genesis 47:16), BBE). They did this for the whole of that year bringing their horses, donkeys, sheep and goats in exchange for food. The very next year, they came back to Joseph confessing that they were now devoid of money, livestock and other animals and had nothing left to bargain with except themselves and their land. To prevent their lands from coming to desolation and them from dying of starvation, therefore, they offered to become the king's slaves. They also offered him their land, all in exchange for seed to plant and grain to eat. So Joseph obliged them and bought all the land of Egypt for Pharaoh because the Egyptians all gave up their land in exchange for food on account of the severity of the famine. This is how all the land became the king's property. Joseph then made them slaves, town by town all across the borders of Egypt. He however made one exception to this general rule: he did not take the land belonging to the priests, because the king gave them a regular food allowance. The priests therefore had no need to give up their land. "Then Joseph said unto the people, 'Behold, I have bought you this day and your land for Pharaoh: lo, here is seed for you, and ye shall sow the land. And it shall come to pass in the increase, that ye shall give the fifth part unto Pharaoh, and four parts shall be your own, for seed of the field, and for your food, and for them of your households, and for your little ones.' And Joseph made it a law over the land of Egypt unto this day, that Pharaoh should have the fifth part; except the land of the priests only, which became not Pharaoh's" (Genesis 47:23-24& 26).

"Bought With A Price"

To those with a 21st Century westernised mindset, what Joseph did would be considered repugnant and anti-democratic. Hasty generalizations, however, fail to see the deep spiritual lessons he was trying to impart.

First, he was exemplifying the fact that the king was gifted with foresight, a picture of God's omniscience. The storehouses scattered across the major cities of Egypt were indicative of Pharaoh's national presence and symbolic of God's omnipresence. Second, Joseph's political astuteness was apparent in his strategy to gather grain directly under Pharaoh's control. This undermined the influences of the many autonomous provincial nobles while strengthening Pharaoh's position, authority and most importantly, his power. This is symbolic of God's omnipotence manifested as Jesus spoiled principalities, powers, wicked spirits in the heavens, all typified by the now impotent provincial lords. But more significantly, the whole issue of taking all the money, livestock, animals and land that belonged to the people, in exchange for grain was God's message to humanity that we ought to get our priorities right. Grain, which is a type of the Kingdom of God and His righteousness, is to be valued and sought above money, livestock, animals, land, clothing and shelter. Egypt was a wealthy land and its inhabitants decidedly affluent. With prosperity also comes arrogance and a false feeling of self-sufficiency and the "self-made-man" syndrome. No doubt, they took credit for the excellent work of their hands by which they prospered. Of course, they felt like their money could "answer all things" (Ecclesiastes 10:19, KJV), and be to them "a defence" (see Ecclesiastes 7:12, KJV) in their time of trouble.

When the famine began, everyone resorted to their money to bail them out. But soon even their savings were exhausted and this is conveyed to the reader in the most evocative and picturesque of expressions--"Money failed in the land of Egypt and in the land of Canaan" (Genesis 47:15). When this happened the people were still willing to barter with their animals. But God stripped them even further, down to the bare essentials till they were willing to be slaves to Pharaoh. When we come to God or receive an invitation to do so, He will strip us of the things we use as crutches if we will not forsake everything, take up our cross daily, and follow Him willingly. We must then recognize that all we have left belongs to the Lord and we are His bond-servants. We realize that we are not independent but accountable to God. We also discover what all the rest of creation knows and does, the art of living by faith. A recurrent theme in the Psalms and exemplified in Psalm 145 is that: "The eyes of all wait upon (God) and (He) giveth them their meat in due season" (Psalm 145:15). Incontrovertibly, by the end of the seven years of famine, the Egyptians and Canaanites had learned the lesson Apostle Paul taught his son Timothy: that true faith (godliness) does make your life rich but only if you are content with what you have. This is because we come into the world with nothing and will definitely leave the same way. Paul's conclusion therefore was that we should be satisfied just to have food and a roof over our heads. The Egyptians reached this point, and God expects us as believers to get there too. Another crucial lesson taught by the wisdom of Joseph is that we were bought with a price and are to glorify God with our bodies and spirits, which belong to God, even as Apostle Paul told the Corinthian church. (See 1 Corinthians 6:19-20.)

A Royal Priesthood

There is a subtle but potent message in the Joseph story, which could very easily be missed or overlooked. When Joseph bought all the land of Egypt for Pharaoh, we are told that the only land he did not buy was the land that belonged to the priests. There are two main reasons for this. The first is the obvious one and it is stated that they did not have to sell their lands because the king gave them an allowance to live on. The second is a bit less obvious. Joseph, you will recall, was married to the daughter of Poti-pherah, the priest of On. The message here is that Jesus is the great High Priest of our profession. Peter said that as saints, as believers, we are a chosen generation, a royal priesthood (the Good News Bible says we are "the King's priests"-- how awesome!) By reason of this connection Jesus is sympathetic toward us, ("for we do not have a high priest who cannot be touched with the feelings of our infirmities") (Hebrews 4:15).

Also no matter how bad things get around us, we have a portion (please note that word) assigned to us by our great King. So we will never have to be slaves to anything or anyone except our Master, Jesus. Besides it is written: "In famine He shall redeem thee from death; and in war from the power of the sword" (Job 5:20). It is also written that God will deliver the souls of those that fear Him from death and keep them alive in famine. (See Psalm 33:19.) And again it is written that the upright "shall not be ashamed in the evil time; and in the days of famine they shall be satisfied" (Psalm 37:19). It is a measure of the goodness and grace of our God that He sustains not just the priests who belong to Him, but also the rest of the people who have ignorantly or rebelliously refused to make a commitment to Him, for "He is kind to the unthankful and to the evil" (Luke 6:35). Just as Joseph would not harm the priests because he was, in a manner, one of them, God calls us to live in peace and unity as being part of one another. As an old African adage declares that one dog will not eat another dog, so we as Christians must not be guilty of spiritual cannibalism.

Apostle Paul admonishes the Galatian Church to fulfil the entire law as encapsulated in the commandment "Thou shalt love thy neighbour as thyself" (Galatians 5:14). He also warns: "But if ye bite and devour one another, take heed that ye be not consumed one of another." The CEV puts it a little more clearly "but if you keep attacking each other like wild animals, you had better watch out, or you will completely destroy one another" (Galatians 5:15).

The Law Of Portions

Perhaps the greatest lesson Joseph was trying to impart on a global level was one he had learnt on the many legs of his journey to his current position as second- in- command in the world's most powerful nation. This, of course, is the lesson of stewardship and accountability. We saw him operate and excel as a steward over his father's flock at an early age. Then we saw him remain faithful as a steward in Potiphar's house till he became the overseer of Potiphar's entire business empire and household. In contrast to Judah, we saw Joseph remain faithful as a steward over his sexuality when he refused to abuse the sacred trust over his body by rebuffing his master's wife's advances. In prison, he was faithful with the care of his fellow prisoners, the affairs of the jail and the welfare of the butler and the baker, who were committed to his care by the captain of the guard.

Joseph was even a faithful steward with his God-given gift of interpretation of dreams. He never tried to use it to secure an advantage for himself. Now as prime minister, controlling the nation's resources and power, he neither misappropriated public funds nor the king's resources. Joseph was now poised to go to the next level. God never blesses you without expecting you to be a blessing. He never saves you without expecting you to serve; He never teaches you but that you may teach others. Zecharias prophesied this saying: "That He would grant unto us, that we being delivered out of the hands of our enemies might serve Him without fear, in holiness and righteousness before Him, all the days of our life" (Luke 1:74-75). In John 17:18 in the high priestly intercessory prayer Jesus prayed just before His crucifixion, He said "As Thou hast sent me into the world, even so have I also sent them into the world." Joseph had come to know the God of Abraham, Isaac and Jacob. He knew that each of them had discovered something unique about God that set them apart from others. Jacob gave us the revelation that Jehovah is the "God of Abraham" as well as the "fear of Isaac." (See Genesis 31:42. The Prophet Jeremiah on the other hand reveals that Jehovah is the "Portion of Jacob." (See Jeremiah 10:16 & 51:19.) This latter revelation which Jacob walked in, he taught Joseph, and now that Joseph is acting on an international stage, he imparted the same revelation, not just to Egypt but to all of mankind through the ages from that time forward. "For the Lord's portion is His people; Jacob is the lot of His inheritance" (Deuteronomy 32:9). Moses declared this in his farewell to the children of Israel on the very day of his death. His point was that God had divided the nations of the earth into portions, allotments and inheritances, and had chosen Israel as His own portion. Israel was then to go out and evangelise the nations and bring them to the saving knowledge of their great God. But when Israel rejected Christ, the mandate passed on to the Church. Since God's relationship with Israel and the Church is based on covenant, as Israel (both natural and spiritual) is the Lord's portion, the Lord likewise is Jacob's (Israel's) portion.

When he interpreted Pharaoh's dream Joseph told Pharaoh that his dream was a picture of life on earth. There will always be years of abundance and years of famine; years of economic boom and prosperity, and years of recessions and financial setbacks. It will present us with many opportunities for victories and promotions, but also diverse challenges and adverse situations. Life is lived out in times and seasons as the preacher taught, and the key to success is to understand the formula of portions. Joseph advised him: "Let Pharaoh do this, and let him appoint officers over the land, and take up the fifth part of the land of Egypt in the seven plenteous years" (Genesis 41:34).

After introducing it to Pharaoh and executing it as Prime Minister Joseph then introduced it to the rest of Egypt. Having bought them as slaves for Pharaoh, Joseph told them to divide all their income into five portions. "And it shall come to pass in the increase, that ye shall give the fifth part unto Pharaoh..." (Genesis 47:24). So one-fifth, or 20% was the king's portion. So we must ask the question: as believers who operate within the confines of this principle, who is the King of our lives? Who has bought us with a price and called us to show forth His praises? Who paid for our lives with his own blood? Jesus Christ is our King of kings and so it is to Him that we bring not just our tithes, which account for 10% of our earnings, but also our freewill offerings, which account for another ten per cent. This is implied, as the tithe is known to be 10% and here Joseph was asking for 20%. Everything, we have now, our jobs, cars, home, wives, husbands, children and our very lives belong to our King. Yet He has given us every resource that is His by right. In the same way He instructs us: "Use these resources, increase by them, be blessed by them but bring 20% back to Me." This, the Lord's portion, therefore is the evidence of His ownership and represents a type of ground rent or occupier tax. Now having given this twenty per cent, it does not mean that you can now indiscriminately spend the balance to satisfy your generation's consumerist passion, ambitions, etc. Even what remains must be divided into four other portions.

He continues "... and four parts shall be your own, for seed of the field..." Genesis 47:24, KJV). "Seed of the field" is your investment portion. If everyone invested 20% of their monthly income without fail, no crisis would ever take them by surprise. Even churches, organizations and businesses should adopt this proven divine strategy. This investment portion ought to be reinvested into the soil that yields fruit in your life. You must plough back some funds into self-development and work-enhancement, and this includes ongoing education in your field, training on new developments and techniques and the purchase of relevant equipment. Practically, this means a teacher should invest in teaching aids, charts, audio-visual equipment etc. A lawyer must invest in law journals, legal volumes and encyclopaedias, etc. And even if you do not already have your own office, because you are still in training or are a clerk at a law firm, this is a good time to start the process. An anonymous wise man once said, the best time to dig a well is not when you are thirsty or when there is a drought, but in the time of abundance. From experience also, we have all discovered that you do not do your food shopping when you are hungry. Otherwise you buy a lot of unnecessary items. As a pastor or minister, you should invest in books, messages, inspirational music on compact discs or iPods, Bibles, commentaries, dictionaries, concordances and so on.

If 20% of your income is insufficient to buy what you need for self-development, (some professional equipment is very capital intensive) put it into secondary investment like shares, bonds, stocks, merchandising and trading or other investment endeavours that mature over time. Before you do this though, make sure that you consult a professional financial adviser. Even if you own or inherited a vacant plot of land and do not have the resources to develop it immediately, plant seeds like palm kernels, trees like citrus, fruits like strawberries and vegetables like celery and broccoli. If it is located in or close to a commercial centre, convert it to a temporary car park, a car wash centre, till you have the time and resources to develop it. One final note of warning, from my experience, it is wise not to put your investment portion in a savings account that you can access at a whim. Instead put it where it will bring the highest yield but will require an elaborate or a time-consuming process and a harsh penalty to access it.

He also advised that the third portion was to be set aside "for your food." This is a rather straightforward instruction that requires little explanation. This refers to basic sustenance issues like your dietary, clothing and recreational needs. Cosmetics, medicines, supplements and your exercising regime such as gym membership will probably all fall into this category.

The fourth portion is "for them of your households." By this Joseph is probably referring to the things and personnel that pertain to your household services. This would include your mortgage or rent, your utilities, your domestic staff and resources you send home to members of your family. If you live in a house that is costing you more than 20% of your income, the law of portions demands that you move into a smaller place till such a time as you can afford it. The aim of this is to teach you to curb your lifestyle to the level of your income. The final portion is "for food for your little ones" (Genesis 47:24, KJV). Children are so important to God that He apportions one fifth of your resources to them. Yet to keep up with the Joneses, many people are spending far more than 20% on their children's education, training and welfare. If your children's school fees exceeds one-fifth of your income, they are probably in the wrong school! Does that sound harsh? Maybe, but think about it. For some people, the problem is that they have too many children in the first place. Some have the primitive mindset that God gives children and I must have as many as He gives me. "Moreover," they reason, "these children will look after me in my old age." I would imagine this only works if you looked after them in their young age! True, God gives the capacity to have children, but He also gives you the responsibility of looking after them, and more importantly, He generally gives you the choice of how many you will have.

This principle of fifths governs our lives and investments and if we diligently follow it, we will be that good man the Bible talks about who leaves an inheritance for his children's children. (See Proverbs 13:22, KJV). The Psalmist, David, while hiding in the cave of Adullam caught the revelation and recognized that the Lord was his refuge and portion in the land of the living. (See Psalm 142:5.) The Prophet Jeremiah's soul in his Lamentations caught the same revelation. (See Lamentations 3:24, KJV.) Jacob, however had an even deeper revelation of this principle, which God used to prosper him. He in turn, taught it to his son Joseph who in turn used it to enrich Pharaoh and brought deliverance to the land of Egypt.

One last word on portions; the infallibility of this law of portions is based on the fact that it originates with God who made Jacob His portion. Jacob in turn made God his portion and then dealt with the affairs of his life on the basis of this revelation and had good success. His son Joseph applied it with the same excellent results, and all that is left now is how well you will apply it to the same effect.

The Egyptians acknowledged that by his knowledge and application of this law of portions, Joseph had saved their lives and they were therefore glad to be the king's slaves. Joseph then made it a law, which was in force even up to the time that Moses chronicled the history of all these events--that Pharaoh was to have the fifth part of the agricultural yield as an annual tax. The only exception of course, was the land of the priests, which did not come into the king's possession. Meanwhile, the fledgling nation of Israel dwelt in Goshen in Egypt acquiring property there and becoming very prolific in numbers and in wealth. And Jacob who had complained to Pharaoh of a hard and short life, lived another seventeen years in the land of Egypt and did not pass on to glory till he was 147 years old. Seventeen is the biblical number for victory. So Jacob lived the rest of his life in victory. According to his precipitous and ill-conceived statement to Pharaoh, he indeed did not live as long as either his father or grandfather did. Death and life are in the power of our tongue and we will receive the fruit of what we say. (See Proverbs 18:21, KJV.) So be careful what you say!

When Jacob realised the time of his transition to glory was imminent, he called in his son Joseph and said: "If you really love me, you must make a solemn promise not to bury me in Egypt. Instead, bury me in the place where my ancestors are buried" (Genesis 47:27-30, CEV). Naturally, Joseph acceded to this request, but Jacob made him swear an oath to this effect and Joseph duly did this. The chapter ends with Jacob bowing down in worship and prayer while supporting himself on the head of the bed or on his staff as rendered by the writer of Hebrews. (See Hebrews 11:21, KJV.) Adam Clarke in his Commentary on the Bible suggests that the simple meaning of this verse is that the elderly and feeble Jacob was probably reclining on his bed when Joseph came in, then sat up while conversing with him and swearing his oath and promise. This done, "He bowed himself upon the bed's head-- exhausted with the conversation, he again reclined himself on his bed as before" (Adam Clark – Commentary on the Bible-Notes on Genesis 47:31). On the other hand, it could mean that Jacob bowed to Joseph's staff as Joseph had prophesied through his dreams. It could also mean that he supported himself on his staff while bowing his head in "adoration to God, who had supported him all his life long, and hitherto fulfilled all his promises." Here again Joseph pictured Christ who only did the things that were pleasing unto the Father. We as believers are likewise admonished by Jesus when He says, "He that hath my commandments, and keepeth them, he it is that loveth me: and he that loveth me shall be loved of my Father, and I will love him, and will manifest myself to him" (John 14:21, KJV).

CHAPTER TWELVE

AT CROSS PURPOSES

Bearing the preceding events in mind, we see that Jacob's life is fast coming to an end. He had sent word to Joseph and clearly made his last wish known. When Joseph learned that his father was sick he set off with his two sons, Manasseh and Ephraim to see their grandfather, and say their final goodbyes. It is worthy of note that as is typical in Hebrew custom, the older son is listed first. Joseph's arrival is duly announced to Jacob by an anonymous source and Jacob mustered his failing strength and sat up in his bed. He then recounted how the Almighty God had appeared unto him in Luz (located in Canaan) and blessed him. God had promised to make Jacob fruitful, to multiply him and to produce from him a great family of nations. God would also give "this land" (Canaan) to Jacob's descendants as their heritage forever.

Strangely, Jacob next refers to Joseph's two sons but in reverse order. Referring to the younger before the elder, was in complete violation of Hebrew social mores and protocol. He declared that Joseph's two sons who were born in Egypt before he came there were to become his in the line of inheritance having the same rights as Jacob's own children. Any other children that Joseph gave birth to after Ephraim and Manasseh would be Joseph's and would derive their own inheritance from their first two siblings. It is no coincidence that Joseph now witnessed his father adopting Joseph's two sons. Joseph was without equivocation, a man of the Spirit and it is written, that, "As many as are led by the Spirit of God, they are the sons of God" (Romans 8:14). Joseph was always led by the Spirit of God like our Great Heavenly Joseph of whom it is written: "And Jesus being full of

the Holy Ghost returned from Jordan, and was led by the Spirit..."
(Luke 4:1).

As spiritual sons of the living God, if we would be sensitive to the promptings, dictates and leadership of the Holy Spirit, we would be infinitely more productive, blessed and effectual. As Joseph keyed into the mind of his father, even so Jesus said: "Verily, verily, I say unto you, the Son can do nothing of Himself, but what He seeth the Father do: for what things soever He doeth, these also doeth the Son likewise" (John 5:19). The hour is approaching and indeed is literally here when true believers will begin to manifest as sons of God because they can see what the Father is doing in any and every situation and are reflecting Him effectively by doing the same things at the right time and in the right way!

Jacob continued his account with the bitter-sweet reminiscence of his journey from Padan (Mesopotamia), and the death and burial of his beloved Rachel, Joseph's mother, in Canaan on the road to Ephrath, also known as Bethlehem. He was thus implying that what he was now doing was partly to honour the memory of Rachel.

Now Jacob was well-advanced in years and his eyesight was failing. He therefore did not recognise his two grandsons as they stood before him. "Who are these?" he asked. Joseph answered that they were his sons whom God had given him there in Egypt. Jacob then asked Joseph to bring them to him so that he could bless them. As Joseph did this, Jacob embraced and kissed them, his heart overwhelmed with joy. This was because for many years he had assumed Joseph dead with no hope of ever seeing him again, now ironically, he had lived long enough to see not just Joseph, but even his children! Then Joseph extricated his sons from their grandfather's laps and prostrated before his father with his face to the ground. Upon rising up, he prepared his sons for the promised blessings holding Ephraim in his right hand and directing him towards Jacobs's left hand and Manasseh in his left hand towards Jacobs's right hand. He did this purposely to ensure that the right order was maintained. The deliberateness of Joseph's action tells a story that is concealed within the lines of the text. The first thing to note is that Joseph was well conversant with the custom of laying on of hands as a means of imparting patriarchal blessings. He also knew that under the law the first- born, the beginning of a man's strength, was entitled to a double portion of all that his father had. (See Genesis 49:3 & Deuteronomy 21:17.) More significantly however, Joseph was aware of the drama that had surrounded his father's life and the issue of the birthright in relation to his uncle Esau. It was probably common knowledge and the subject of regular debates that if his grandfather Isaac had not been dim of sight, his father Jacob would not have been able to execute the subterfuge of pretending to be Esau, without Rebekah's interference. Ironically, now that the shoe is on the other foot, metaphorically speaking, Jacob himself, who is nearly blind in his old age, has Joseph to make sure he blesses his sons in the manner of tradition.

Most significantly, by adopting Joseph's two sons as his own, Jacob was publicly declaring that the rights of the first-born had bypassed all the other sons and rested upon Joseph. This raises some theological difficulties for avid Bible scholars. Mosaic law clearly states in Deuteronomy 21:15-17: "If a man have two wives, one beloved, and the other hated, and they have born him children, both the beloved and the hated, and if the firstborn son be hers that was hated: Then it shall be, when he maketh his sons to inherit that which he hath, that he may not make the son of the beloved first before the son of the hated, which is indeed the firstborn. But he shall acknowledge the son of the hated for the firstborn, by giving him a double portion of all that he hath: for he is the beginning of his strength, the right of the firstborn is his." Now if this is not an accurate reflection of the situation of Jacob and his two wives, I do not know what is. Without doubt, Leah was the hated wife and Rachel the beloved. Yet it was the hated wife who had birthed not just the first-born but also the next four sons. (We have already addressed the subject of his partiality toward Rachel and her sons in the previous chapter.) The difficulty is how Jacob who intended to give the double portion to Joseph was going to justify his actions without running afoul of the law. But I precede myself and will address this issue in the next chapter.

Back to our story: Joseph had set his two boys before Jacob expecting him to observe the social protocol. Israel however did a very strange thing – stretching out his right hand, he laid it on the younger son, Ephraim's head and his left hand on Manasseh's head. It is written that he guided his hands "wittingly" for Manasseh was the first-born. This suggests that contrary to Joseph's assumption Jacob did this after careful consideration. In other words, he crossed his arms. In this pose, Jacob blessed Joseph by the God whom his grandfather Abraham and his father Isaac worshipped. Jacob prayed that the same Almighty God who had sustained him all his life and delivered him from all evil, would bless Joseph's boys. Abraham, Isaac and Jacob's names would live on because of the boys and they in turn would have many children and descendant-nations as well.

At this point, a new drama was to unfold. Joseph was decidedly unhappy when Jacob put his right hand on Ephraim's head. So, he tried to remove his father's right hand from Ephraim's head and place it on Manasseh's. And while doing this he told his father he had made a mistake. "This is the older boy," he said, "Put your right hand on him" (Genesis 48:18, CEV). However his father refused declaring that he was crossing his arms on purpose. "Son, I know what I am doing. It's true that Manasseh's family will someday become a great nation. But Ephraim will be even greater than Manasseh, because his descendants will become many great nations" (Genesis 48:19, CEV). Israel then blessed his grandsons but put Ephraim's name first to show that he would be greater than his big brother. The nature of the blessing was that people in the future would call down divine blessings on each other by praying that God blesses them as much as he blessed Ephraim and Manasseh. At the end of the blessing he turned to Joseph. "Joseph, you can see that I won't live much longer. But God will be with you and lead you back to the land he promised our family long ago." Israel then reiterated the fact that Joseph was getting the double portion blessings of the firstborn: "Moreover, I have given to thee one portion above thy brethren, which I took out of the hand of the Amorite with my sword and with my bow" (Genesis 48:21-22). Of course he was referring to the fertile region of Shechem. Israel was thus signifying that the blessings of the firstborn were manifest not only in abstract and future-bound blessings, but also in concrete physical possessions like land, money, livestock, natural, human and indeed, every other resource.

"The Older Will Serve the Younger"

Ephraim and Manasseh were born in Egypt of an Egyptian mother and as grandsons they had no right of inheritance in Jacob. But because of their relationship with the beloved son Joseph, they enjoyed gracious access to unimaginable privileges. This is a picture of us as Gentiles who, unlike the Jews, have no direct physical blood bonds with the living God. But through our relationship with His beloved son, Jesus Christ, we inherit unsearchable riches and a joint inheritance. Paul captures it rather succinctly when he says "Therefore being justified by faith, we have peace with God through our Lord Jesus Christ. By whom also we have access by faith into this grace wherein we stand, and rejoice in hope of the glory of God" (Romans 5:1-2).

As Joseph's sons, Ephraim and Manasseh are Abraham's seed after the flesh and are therefore heirs according to the promise. Yet Paul tells us in Galatians 3:29: "And if ye be Christ's then are ye Abraham's seed and heirs according to the promise." And in Romans 8:17 he tells us that as children of God we are heirs of God and joint heirs with Christ. (See Romans 8:17.) The issue of the blessing of the boys carries spiritual significance on many levels. It strongly emphasizes the fact that God has no grandchildren but desires and delights in a personal relationship with "whosoever" chooses to believe. It also points to the fact that when God chooses to bless whoever He chooses to bless, HE does not need the permission of those around Him and will supersede traditions, culture or religion to get those blessings to His chosen ones. For Ephraim to get the blessings of the first-born, there had to be a crossing of Israel's hand. In doing this, Israel's arms formed the shape of a cross thereby taking us to Calvary. In like manner, for us to get the New Testament blessings of sonship and inheritance, there had to be the cross. But who were we in competition against? Who was the older or first-born son who had the birthright but was bypassed that we may be blessed? It goes back a long way.

"...Jacob Have I Loved, But Esau Have I Hated"

Apostle Paul admonishes the Church in Rome to remember what happened to the twin sons of Isaac and Rebekah,--Esau and Jacob. Even before their birth, before they had had the opportunity to make good or bad choices, the Lord had told Rebekah that the older son would serve the younger. This God said, to show His sovereignty and to outline the fact that it was not because of anything either of them had done. This indeed is what God meant when He said, "Jacob have I loved, but Esau have I hated." This statement troubles a lot of people because they think it portrays God as whimsical, unpredictable, irrational and even wicked. Yet to me, this statement is not indicative of the variable nature of God's judgment, as it is of the unconditional nature of His love. After all, it is "Not by works of righteousness which we have done, but according to His mercy He saved us, by the washing of regeneration, and the renewing of the Holy Ghost" (Titus 3:5).

In the New Covenant, Esau is described as immoral and ungodly, a ("fornicator, or profane person.") (See Hebrews 12:16.) He is thus a picture of the unregenerated or unsaved man. Jacob, on the other hand, is described as "a plain man, dwelling in tents" (Genesis 25:27). The word "plain" is a Hebrew word ("tam") that means complete, usually (morally) pious, and specifically gentle, dear. It also means coupled together, perfect, undefiled and upright. We do not need to wander far to realise that this is a picture of the believer who is complete in Christ, spiritually undefiled by reason of the washing of Christ's blood, and considered upright by virtue of his relationship with God through Christ.

On another level, Esau, as the firstborn would typify the Pharisees and Sadducees of Jesus' day who believed they were morally superior to the publicans, tax-collectors and indeed everyone else, especially the Gentiles as they believed they were the natural seed of Abraham. Yet their evil works and lack of faith disqualified them and gave precedence to even the vilest offender who came to Jesus by faith. Jacob is a picture of the Church of the living God, the Body of Christ; called and chosen, though not qualified by natural birth for the blessings of the first-born. Being also a trickster, he was also not qualified by conduct. In the end, just like us, Jacob was only saved by grace through faith. It was God's gift and so he could not boast.

Yet, we in the Church must also be careful and watchful for the leaven of the Pharisees, which is hypocrisy lest we be hated of God and the people we look down on so arrogantly and disdainfully, be preferred above us!

Abraham Also Had Two Sons

Many times, we forget that even Father Abraham had two sons and the younger was preferred and the older was subject to, and served the younger. In Galatians 4:22-23 we see: "It is written that Abraham had two sons, the one by a bondmaid, the other by a freewoman. But he who was of the bond woman was born after the flesh; but he of the freewoman was by promise."

In Galatians 4:30 we find an allegory, where Hagar speaks of Mount Sinai in Arabia as an image of the present city of Jerusalem, which is in slavery (bondage) with her children. In contrast to this, there is a heavenly Jerusalem, which is free and is the mother of us all. It is clear that Paul is equating Hagar and Ishmael to the legalistic orthodoxy of the Judaic leaders who had had Christ crucified and were at that time actively persecuting the Church. And to connect it back to Israel passing the double portion blessing to the junior son, Apostle Paul reminds us that the Scriptures say "Cast out the bondwoman and her son: for the son of the bondwoman shall not be heir with the son of the freewoman," (again referring to Galatians 4:30.) And Apostle Paul's conclusion shows that the younger is greater than the older and will be served by him. And in the end he triumphantly declares: "So then, brethren, we are not children of the bondwoman, but of the free" (Galatians 4:31). Alleluia!

God Had Two Sons

This recurring theme of the younger being greater than the older and the older serving the younger is important because it points to two other sons of a Father. God is the Father in question. His first son was Adam, who was given authority and dominion over the earth; the certificate of occupancy was in his name. By an act of disobedience and grand treason Adam handed over his rights to Satan. Adam thus introduced sin and its consequent product, death, into the world. "Even those who didn't sin precisely as Adam did by disobeying a specific command of God still had to experience this termination of life, this separation from God. But Adam, who got us into this, also points ahead to the One who will get us out of this" (Romans 5:14, MSG). So here Adam is clearly seen to be a type (figure) of Christ. Furthermore, Apostle Paul tells the Corinthians: "For as in Adam all die, even so in Christ shall all be made alive" (1 Corinthians 15:22).

The final reference shows the correlation between Adam and Christ and how God has exalted Jesus above Adam: "And so it is written, The first man Adam was made a living soul; the last Adam was made a quickening spirit" (1 Corinthians 15:45). Thus, the first son disobeyed unto death, and the second Son "humbled Himself, and became obedient unto death, even death of the cross. Wherefore God also hath highly exalted Him and given Him a name which is above every name: that at the name of Jesus every knee should bow of things in heaven, and things on earth, and things under the earth, And every tongue should confess that Jesus Christ is Lord to the glory of God the Father" (Philippians 2:8-11).

As previously mentioned Israel declared that Ephraim and Manasseh were his and that Israel (the nation) would bless one another in them. Israel stipulated also that Joseph's other sons would get their inheritance through Ephraim and to a lesser extent through Manasseh. In doing and saying all this, he was again illustrating a Messianic typology. This is because in like manner, "The Father loveth the Son and hath given all things into his hand" (John 3:35). Because of this blessing and the pre-eminence bequeathed on Jesus by the Father and because the nation of Israel is blessed in Joseph's sons, so the believer is blessed in Christ. John 16:23 puts it this way, "Verily, verily, I say unto you, 'Whatsoever ye shall ask the Father in my name, He will give it you.'" As the crossing of the hands elevated the undeserving, so the hands on the cross still elevate the undeserving.

Today, God Still Has Two Sons

Perhaps the most dynamic and relevant picture that the blessing of Joseph's sons evokes is that of two other sons that God currently has–natural Israel, and spiritual Israel. Jews and Gentiles, birth sons and adopted sons, a cultivated olive tree and a wild olive tree, demonstrate the natural or fleshly circumcision, and the circumcision of the heart. Romans 11 best explains the status of God's two contemporary sons. Israel is God's firstborn son. When God sent Moses to deliver His people from the bondage of Egypt, God told Moses: "And thou shalt say unto Pharaoh, 'Thus saith the Lord, Israel is my son, even my firstborn'" (Exodus 4:22). God confirms this by a prophecy to the Prophet Jeremiah: "They shall come with weeping, and with supplications will I lead them: I will cause them to walk by the rivers of waters in a straight way, wherein they shall not stumble: for I am a father to Israel, and Ephraim is my firstborn" (Jeremiah 31:9). Notice how that act of Israel crossing his arms has elevated Ephraim, so much that the entire nation of Israel is called after him on this and many other occasions. God did not turn His back on His people, Israel. As an aside, one of the reasons why it is impossible for God to turn His back on anyone is because He has no back! It is our spirit that is made in the image of God. In fact, in the midst of His throne, if the living creatures have eyes in front and behind, how much more the One seated thereon! Rather God's people turned their back on Him. God therefore used this as an occasion to save the Gentiles and by this provoke Israel to jealousy and thus win them back. God's desire is to befriend and to woo Israel back again.

Paul compares the Gentiles to branches of a wild olive tree grafted into a cultivated olive tree, which is Israel. Israel's rebellion and unbelief have caused them to be cut off, but one day they will be grafted back to their roots and made a part of that tree again, when they begin to believe on the One whom God sent for that purpose. Thus we the adoptees are enjoying the benefits of the double portion.

We therefore cannot afford to be arrogant, boastful or petulant. So where Jacob's 'cross' was a tool of separation, Christ's cross is a tool of unity.

Listen to Apostle Paul's argument as he elucidates the point to the Ephesian Church: "For by grace are ye saved through faith, and that not of yourselves: it is the gift of God. Not of works lest any man should boast. For we are His workmanship, created in Christ Jesus unto good works, which God hath before ordained that we should work in them. Wherefore remember, that ye being in time past Gentiles in the flesh, who are called Uncircumcision by that which is called the Circumcision in the flesh made by hands; that at that time ye were without Christ, being aliens from the common wealth of Israel, and strangers from the covenant of promise, having no hope, and without God in the world: But now in Christ Jesus ye who sometimes were far off are made nigh by the blood of Christ. For He is our peace who hath made both one, and hath broken down the middle wall of partition between us. Having abolished in his flesh the enmity, even the law of commandments contained in ordinances, for to make in Himself of twain one new man, so making peace; And that He might reconcile both unto God in one body by the cross, having slain the enmity thereby" (Ephesians 2:8-16).

Step Into The Jordan

So like Ephraim, you may have received the double portion blessing, you may be favoured and anointed, but remember it was not yours by right but by the grace of the Father, through the cross. Now that you are in your possession, your inheritance, your promised land, you cannot rest till every one of your brethren enters into theirs. Like the children of Reuben and Gad who had their inheritance on the opposite side of the Jordan from their brethren, we must declare as they did, "We will not return into our houses, till the children of Israel have inherited everyman his inheritance" (Numbers 32:18).

Our ministry is the ministry of reconciliation because God did everything necessary by sending Christ to reconcile us to Himself. Yet we cannot do it in our strength, power or wisdom, but by God's Spirit. The best picture is that of Joshua, another typical picture of Christ Jesus, leading the Children of Israel from Shittim and going to possess the land of promise but facing the obstacle of the Jordan. Like Joshua's officers, we are to go unto the people and urge them to sanctify themselves because the Lord wants to do wonders among them.

As Jesus' royal priesthood, we are to take up our own Ark of the Covenant, which is the message of the cross, the declaration of the finished work of the Christ and go before the people. We are also to stand on the brink of everything that represents sickness, lack, poverty, depression and death in their lives. Thus we are to cause every Jordan, every Red Sea in their lives to part. With our feet firmly planted in victory over the things that held them bound, we are to stand steadfast till all our brethren have passed over on dry ground, "till all the people are passed clean over Jordan" (Joshua 3:17). What a wonderful choice of words God's wisdom has chosen! The word "clean" (tamam) means both to complete, accomplish and perfect as well as to literally be clean, upright and whole! Glory to God, we have the key to the people's Passover. Apostle Paul encapsulates this thought when he admonishes Titus, reminding him that our Saviour Jesus Christ, "gave Himself for us, that He might redeem us from all iniquity, and purify unto Himself a peculiar people, zealous of good works" (Titus 2:14).

CHAPTER THIRTEEN

A BLESSING FOR EVERYONE

Having dispensed the double-portion blessing to his favoured son, it was now time for Jacob to administer blessings to the rest of his sons. He therefore sends for them urging them to gather themselves together so that he can prophesy to them concerning their futures. "Assemble and listen, O sons of Jacob," he reiterates poetically, "listen to Israel your father" (Genesis 49:1 ESV). By referring to himself as Jacob and Israel, he was making it clear that he was going to address them as a father to his individual sons in the natural realm, which the name Jacob signifies. He was however also going to prophesy to their progeny by addressing them as representatives of their tribes and the nationalities that would emanate from them. This is what the name Israel signifies. So whenever the name Jacob is purposely chosen and utilised, it speaks of the individual, the natural, the carnal, the fleshly, the temporal and the finite. Israel, on the other hand, signifies the corporate, the national, the spiritual and the enduring. The God of Jacob is the God of grace, who blesses even the undeserving, the supplanter, the trickster. The God of Israel, however, is the God of covenant who will never fail but will keep covenant to children's children to a thousand generations of those who fear and walk with Him. (See Deuteronomy 7:9 & Psalm 103:7.)

Indeed, we see both elements of grace and covenant, at work in the blessings that Israel would pour out upon his sons. In this, he immediately typifies God who invites the sinner, the undeserving to freely enjoy His grace. Note that He did not wait for us to cry out to Him or to change, but "God commendeth His love towards us, in that, while we were yet sinners, Christ died for us" (Romans 5:8, KJV). Once we respond to the God of Jacob, He invites us into a new covenant relationship. "For this is the covenant that I will make with the house of Israel after those days, saith the Lord; I will put my laws into their mind, and write them in their hearts: and I will be to them a God, and they shall be to me a people" (Hebrews 8:10, KJV). Of course, all this is "through the blood of the everlasting covenant" (Hebrews 13:20, KJV).

Being the firstborn, Reuben is the first to be addressed by Israel. "Reuben," he declares, "thou art my firstborn, my might, and the beginning of my strength, the excellency of dignity, and the excellency of power" (Genesis 49:3, KJV). Reuben was thus being hailed as firstborn, the firstfruit of his father's strength. He was pre-eminent in dignity and pre-eminent in power, an honoured and respected leader, to whom rightly, the dignity of the priesthood, the power of kingship and its kingdom, as well as the birthright should have been bequeathed. Now we are aware that the blessings of the firstborn had already been given to Joseph. Someone reading this may say "Wait a minute! How do you know that what Jacob did with Joseph and his sons, was to impart the blessings of the firstborn and not just any old blessings or even just special blessings?" Israel's next pronouncement gives a potent clue: "Unstable as water, thou shalt not excel; because thou wentest up to thy father's bed; then defilest thou it: he went up to my couch" (Genesis 49:4, KJV). The CEV gives it more clarity for the modern man: "Uncontrollable as a flood, you slept with my wife and disgraced my bed. And so you no longer deserve the place of honour."

In fact, when the Chronicles of God's people were being written, it was clearly stated: "Now the sons of Reuben, the firstborn of Israel, (for he was the firstborn; but forasmuch as he defiled his father's bed, his birthright was given unto the sons of Joseph, the son of Israel: and the genealogy is not to be reckoned after the birthright" (I Chronicles 5:1). We will later discover that the rights to kingship went to Judah as outlined in the very next verse: "For Judah prevailed above his brethren, and of him came the chief ruler; but the birthright was Joseph's" (1 Chronicles 5:2).

Subsequent to all this, the tribe of Reuben never rose to any renown in Israel either in numbers or achievement. Indeed they were amongst the first to be whisked off into captivity in Assyria. (See 1 Chronicles 5:26.) Even in his dealings with his brothers and with his father when he tried to negotiate taking Benjamin on the second trip to Egypt, Reuben exerted little or no influence. It is instructive that the Messianic line of kingship did not come from the tribe of Reuben. God warns believers everywhere, the youths (in age and in the faith) who are more susceptible to youthful lusts and even the mature believer, who faces the same temptations to beware of giving in to such temptations. In the beginning, God said to our first father, "Be fruitful, and multiply, and replenish the earth, and subdue it: and have dominion" (Genesis 1:28). The primary meaning of dominion is to reign and rule over, as a king does. Fruitfulness and multiplication have to do with sex and your sexuality. You cannot subdue and have dominion over your environment and circumstances till and unless you can subdue and have dominion over your sexuality. This is because God connects sex with dominion. Therefore if God does not have control of your sexuality He does not have control over you.

Because Reuben had sexual sin in his life Jacob described him using the word "unstable," which is used elsewhere by Apostle Peter, to refer to dissolute, depraved, debauched and licentious false teachers out to seduce true believers. (See 2 Peter 2:14.) Now that it was time for the blessing, Jacob could not give it to him because no one who is wise will elevate an unstable person to a position of authority. Note also, that when Reuben committed this transgression, his brothers may not have known. But as Jesus said when warning His disciples about hypocrisy: "There is nothing covered that shall not be revealed; neither hid, that shall not be known. Therefore whatsoever ye have spoken in darkness shall be heard in the light; and that which ye have spoken in the ear in the closets shall be proclaimed upon the housetops" (Luke 12:3, KJV). Now at this point, everyone was aware of his disgraceful act.

If only we as believers, as well as politicians, televangelists, pop and movie stars and indeed every member of the human race would realise that we cannot get away with anything. In effect, every action, good or bad has an inevitable consequence. We may get by for a season but one day, "be sure your sin will find you out" (Numbers 32:23), and you will reap what you sowed, more than you sowed and later than you sowed!

Israel then proceeded to jointly address his next two sons, Simeon and Levi. They are brothers, Jacob observes, not just because they share the same parentage, as indeed do Reuben, Judah, Issachar and Zebulun. More significantly, they were brothers in crime sharing a similar negative temperament of anger, stubbornness, deceitfulness, vengefulness and cruelty. They used their swords as weapons of violence and derived pleasure from killing a noble in anger. Jacob speedily dissociated himself from their plans and deeds at his death just as he did when the events happened. After cursing, not them, but the ferocity of their anger and the cruelty of their wrath, Israel proceeded to pronounce his judgment--he would divide them in Jacob and scatter them in Israel.

As a result of this prophecy, the two tribes never ever really had their own territory but were attached to other tribes. In spite of all this, grace still prevailed and the privilege of the priesthood still passed on to Levi. Here again, the character of God shows through because He never deals with us according to our just desserts but according to the "multitude" of his tender mercies.

The lesson for the contemporary believer is the devastating effect anger can have on a person's destiny. There is hardly a crime, a negative reaction, a stirring up of trouble that did not have its origin in uncontrolled anger. Anger, in turn, births stubbornness or rebellion against God's injunctions, as well as deceitfulness and, worst of all, revenge. God therefore permits us to be angry but never to the point of sin. (See Ephesians 4:26.) No matter the provocation, we must be like God who is "ready to pardon, gracious and merciful, slow to anger, and of great kindness" (Nehemiah 9:17, KJV). As a person who was quick-tempered in my youth the entrance of God's Word has enlightened me and completely changed my disposition. I meditate on Scriptures like "Be not hasty in thy spirit to be angry: for anger resteth in the bosom of fools" (Ecclesiastes 7:9, KJV). Since one of my avowed goals in life is to find wisdom and walk in it, I will not allow myself to meditate on anything that could draw me into sin. Also, Proverbs 16:7, CEV tells us: "Controlling your temper is better than being a hero who captures a city."

If only Simeon and Levi had heeded the wisdom of Proverbs 22:24, KJV) that says: "Make no friendship with an angry man; and with a furious man thou shalt not go. Lest thou learn his ways and get a snare to thy soul." They fed off each other's anger to their peril instead of each other's virtues to their mutual benefit. In every situation therefore we are to: "cease from anger, and forsake wrath: fret not thyself in any case to do evil" (Psalm 37:8, KJV). Finally, James 1:19, KJV says: "Wherefore, my beloved brethren, let every man be swift to hear, slow to speak, slow to wrath." One last point before we move on to the next son: there is no doubt that what Shechem did to Dinah was despicable and her brothers had a right to be angry. The Bible does not, however, permit us to react the way they did. Again you have heard it said that "Revenge is a dish best served cold." But I say unto you: "Revenge is a dish best left off the menu." Vengeance belongs to the Lord and He will justly repay His transgressors.

Next Israel moves on to bless Judah. Judah means praise and his birth, elicited praise to God from his mother. He, in turn, would be a praiser and his brothers would praise him. Judah's tribe would comprise successful warriors who would exercise dominion over the other tribes—in fact, more illustrious and numerous than them all. Jacob also compares Judah to a lion at different stages and in different postures. He is like a cub returning from a successful hunt; like a content lion stretching out and lying down, and like a lioness that no one dares to disturb. Judah's dominion and right of rulership symbolised by the sceptre would continue till the time of Shiloh, which is a poetic name for the Messiah. Israel on his deathbed was thus much like Abraham, and like Isaac before him, who saw the Lord's Day at a great distance. (See John 8:56.)

All of these scriptures are fulfilled in King David who was the natural type of the Messiah, revealed to be the Lion of the tribe of Judah. (See Revelation 5:5.)

In fact, it was unto Jesus that both Jews and Gentiles gathered. This Scripture and its prophetic fulfilment are best epitomised by blind Bartimaeus. Jesus had come into Jericho and was on His way out with His disciples and a great number of people. Hearing the huge crowds, this prophecy of Israel's over Shiloh must have resonated in Bartimaeus' spirit: "The sceptre shall not depart from Judah, nor a lawgiver from between his feet, till Shiloh come, and unto him shall the gathering of the people be" (Genesis 49:10, KJV). Recognising that this was Jesus of Nazareth, he immediately caught the revelation, made the connection and cried out in faith, "Jesus, thou Son of David, have mercy on me" (Luke 18:38, KJV). The censure and rebuke of many could not douse the fire of the revelation as he cried out even louder and more persistently till he got the attention of Shiloh to whose sceptre of rulership the people were gathering. Israel concludes his extravagant blessings on Judah by promising him a land replete with choice vines and luxuriant pastures. References to the foal and ass's colt are a picture of Jesus' triumphant entry into Jerusalem, which is the Lord's choice vine in typology. Jacob also makes a reference to "the blood of grapes." The word 'blood' apart from its natural meaning figuratively means in the Hebrew, bloodshed, and 'grapes' figuratively means to bear fruit. Thus the shedding of Jesus' blood while pronouncing judgment upon the wicked, declares fruitfulness and jubilee for the believer. (See Isaiah 63:1-3.) Here the wine and the blood of grapes point to the New Testament ratified in Jesus' blood.

Judah's eyes were red with wine and his teeth were white with milk, which speak of the natural blessings of abundant wine and milk. But it also on a deeper spiritual level means his revelation (eyes) would come by the Holy Spirit (New Wine) (see Acts 2:13 & 16) and in his mouth (teeth) would abide the sincere milk of the Word (see 1 Peter 2:2), which would also account for his phenomenal growth. It is interesting to imagine how Judah felt after hearing the words spoken over his older siblings .Hearing Israel recounts their past misdemeanours, Judah, who had many gruesome skeletons in his closet, must have been quaking in his boots. Expecting judgment, instead Judah received mercy, thanking God that: "Mercy rejoiceth against (that is triumphs over) judgment" (James 2:13).

At this point Israel turns to Zebulun and prophesies over him. The seacoast would be his inheritance and his progeny would be merchants, sailors and marine traders. It is pertinent to note that Israel said nothing concerning that time in relation to Zebulun, nothing about his situation, nothing about his deeds and character except that implied by his seafaring interests. To prophesy into a man's future is a risky business unless you are instructed by God to that end. "When a prophet makes a statement in the name of the Lord, if what he says does not take place and his words do not come true, then his word is not the word of the Lord: the words of the prophet were said in the pride of his heart, and you are to have no fear of him" (Deuteronomy 18:22, BBE).

Some two to three centuries after that, Israel's prophesy was fulfilled, after the land of Canaan was divided and "... Their border went up toward the sea ... and reached to the river..." (Joshua 19:11). A skeptic might say, "Oh, come on! Surely somebody remembered Israel's words and made it happen that way." This might have been the case, except that Joshua apportioned the inheritance of seven of the tribes and he did it by casting lots! So, Israel was a prophet keyed into the mind of God. Thus the division of this lot to Zebulun was by divine instruction and guidance. However, what Zebulun did with his sea coasts and waterways was up to him. Happily, he aligned with his divine destiny and excelled at the use of the resources made available to him.

Today, the saint must grab God-given opportunities and maximise the use of divinely- apportioned giftings and resources. Paul tells Timothy: "But watch thou in all things, endure afflictions, do the work of an evangelist, make full proof of thy ministry" (2 Timothy 4:5, KJV).

Issachar is next to get Israel's blessings. He is likened to a strong donkey reposing between two saddlebags; he saw that rest was good and the land pleasant, so he bore the burden of servitude and became a slave labourer. Israel is predicting that people from this tribe would be active, patient and given to agricultural pursuits. Rather than exert themselves to secure their liberty, they would rather pay exorbitant taxes. He is a hireling by name and by disposition. Two images come to mind in relating Issachar's position to the child of God. The first is the donkey on which Jesus rode into Jerusalem in victory. The two saddlebags are the Lord's burden and His people's burden. Submitting to tribute is the equivalent to surrendering to our Christian duties of tithing, worshipping, praying, evangelising, home and prison visits and so on. The second picture is captured by Jesus' injunction: "Come unto me all ye that labour and are heavy laden and I will give you rest. Take my yoke upon you and learn of me, for I am meek and lowly of heart: and ye shall find rest unto your soul. For my yoke is easy and my burden is light" (Matthew 11:28-30, KJV). All the elements of Israel's words over Zebulun are present here--the labour, the two loads (yoke and burden), rest, a pleasant land, bowing one's shoulder willingly. How amazing!

Even though he was the son of a bondwoman, Jacob said that Dan would preside over one of the tribes of Israel, and would be the judge of his people. He further compares him to an adder, a poisonous snake by the path that bites a horse's heels so that its rider is thrown off backward. The snake referred to here has the characteristics of a chameleon, which, if trodden upon unwittingly, responds by biting the trespasser. This implies that the majority of Dan's conquests and victories would be secured not as much by force or superior firepower, but more by cunning and strategising. We see this in their dealings on the matter of Laish, (see Judges 18), and in the life of Samson who single-handedly with great power and not a little cunning "discomfited" the Philistines. This also meant they were more susceptible than most to yielding to satanic influences and promoting false worship. The message for the Church from Dan's blessing is captured in Jesus' instructions to the twelve disciples when He sent them out with authority over unclean spirits and to heal the sick: "Behold, I send you forth as sheep in the midst of wolves: be ye therefore wise as serpents, and harmless as doves" (Matthew 10:16, KJV). By using this analogy, God is asking us to be completely aware of the enemy's devices but to only use the Lord's methods, to outwit the enemy by counterbalancing the extreme cunning of the serpent with the simplicity of the dove and vice versa, till we reach a happy and fruitful equilibrium.

After this Israel prophesies over Gad, "A troop shall overcome him but he shall overcome at the last" (Genesis 49:19). Gad's name means "troop" and indeed, they turn out to be a very warlike tribe. The Gadites, who attached themselves to David while he was in the fort in the wilderness, were men of might and men of war, battle-ready and skilful with shields and spears. They also had faces like lions and the agility of gazelles" (Chronicles 12:8). Indeed, they faced incursions and many fierce battles with their neighbours the Ammonites and the Moabites. Certainly, as the prophet foretold they lost many battles, but by the end of Saul and David's days they had totally eradicated these enemies. Indeed "they overcame at the last." The word for today is that we may be going through hell and high water; we may even have been defeated several times by many of life's trials. We can however celebrate ahead of time for we know the end of the story--we win the war! Alleluia! "We shall overcome at the last!"

Concerning Asher Israel foresees: "His bread shall be fat, and he shall yield royal dainties" (Genesis 49:20, KJV). This means he will have a land abundant in wheat, pleasant fruits and oil. By his very position, his products are good enough to grace the table of kings. These lowlands of Carmel were amongst the most fertile land in Canaan, and even Solomon furnishes Hiram with wheat and oil from this territory. (See 1 Kings 5:11.) Our lives are that most fertile of lands designed to yield wheat, (the message of Christ's death) and oil (the promises of the Holy Spirit to a hungry world).   We also have what it takes to grace the King of kings' table.

Naphtali is the next to receive his father's blessing. Israel's pronouncement is that "Naphtali is a hind let loose: he giveth goodly words" (Genesis 49:21). This literally means that Naphtali has the gift of the gab and would overcome more by fair words than by the use of violence. Like the hind or the deer, those of his tribe are agile and nimble, eloquent in prose and in poetry and are of an artistic temperament. The story of Deborah and Barak and their defeat of Jabin and the song they sang gives a good picture of the character and nature of the tribe of Naphtali. (See Judges 4:5.)

Naphtali is a picture of Christ as the Lion and the Lamb, the Mighty Warrior and the Prince of Peace, the Weeping Shepherd and the

Whipping Son. As His sons and ambassadors we must know when and with whom to be gentle and when and with whom to be aggressive. We must be equipped and ready to defeat His enemies and then sing a new song to His praise and glory.

"And Now For Something Completely Different"

Since this story is about Joseph, particular attention must be paid to what Israel has to say to him. Israel himself has conducted this ceremony like a classical masterpiece. Having gone through several varied and interesting movements, he brings the masterpiece through a "coaxing diminuendo" to a "counterpoint crescendo" (Piano and Drums by Gabriel Okara), in his prophecies over his dearly beloved favourite son, Joseph. Indeed like any literary or drama musical production worth its salt, the benediction ends with Joseph's blessings being a kind of coda, which serves as a summation of the preceding themes i.e., the blessings of his older siblings. Israel affectionately and gratefully declares, "Joseph is a fruitful bough, even a fruitful bough by a well; whose branches run over the wall" (Genesis 49:22). Historically and prophetically, the first thing Israel says about Joseph has to do with his exceeding fruitfulness. He is literally compared with a fruitful vine, and the reason for his good success is that he is planted beside the water source, a well and is productively self-sufficient. His blessedness is further highlighted by the fact that his branches "run over the wall." After prudently gearing up for the vast harvest of Egypt, he benevolently spreads it beyond his own enclosure and feeds not just his own family, but Egypt and other nations as well. This would also be a characteristic feature of the twofold tribe he spawned, who regularly overshot the boundaries assigned to them, and were much more influential than almost any other two tribes put together.

This extraordinary increase was evident in the census in the Book of Numbers. (See Numbers 1:33-35.) Even Joshua acknowledges this: "And Joshua spake unto the house of Joseph, even to Ephraim and Manasseh, saying, Thou art a great people, and has great power: thou shalt not have one lot only" (Joshua 17:17). Likewise, Moses in his farewell blessings to the tribes, said: "His glory is like the firstling of this bullock, and his horns are like the horns of unicorns: with them he shall push the people together to the ends of the earth: and they are the ten thousands of Ephraim and they are the thousands of Manasseh" (Deuteronomy 33:17). This is again as typical a picture of our heavenly Joseph as you will find in the account. The Lord Jesus Christ tells us He is "the true vine," and we are the branches. (See John 15:1, KJV.) In fact the central theme of this entire discourse is fruitfulness. The believer who abides in Christ and lets Christ work through him will yield "much fruit," because as Christ put it, apart from Him we can do nothing. Our heavenly Abba Father is the well, and Jesus, like Joseph, is planted by this well: "If ye keep my commandments, ye shall abide in my love, even as I have kept my Father's commandments, and abide in His love" (John 15:10, KJV).

Indeed it is to Jesus that the Psalmist refers in the very first Psalm, which is yet another picture of the fruitful bough beside a well, with branches running over the wall. Compare "And he shall be like a tree planted by the rivers of water, that bringeth forth his fruit (that word again) in due season, his leaf also shall not wither; and whatsoever he doeth shall prosper" (Psalm 1:3). If Jesus is the fruitful bough and His Father the well, then we are the branches that march over the walls of limitation to bring the rich harvest we enjoy in Christ to a starving world. We bring forth abundant and abiding fruit because we "consider the lilies" (Matthew 6:28), as Jesus taught us to. The lily grows from a bulb with roots planted into moist soil. If it can find an underground water source, its roots draw from it even when there is devastating famine all around. We must also take root downward in the dark moist soil of the crucifixion, death and burial of Christ. We bear fruit upwards (see Isaiah 37:31), as we drink in Christ's quickening, resurrection and ascension to God's right hand. Truly, without our Joseph, we can do nothing.

Israel continues his blessing by recalling some events in Joseph's history – "The archers have sorely grieved him: But his bow abode in strength, and the arms of his hands were made strong by the hands of the mighty God of Jacob; (from thence is the Shepherd, the stone of Israel)…" (Genesis 49:23). The archers represent enemies from within and without who attacked him fiercely, provoked him sore, persecuted him persistently, harassed him severely and hated him perfectly, without a cause. This is referring to the hatred by, and the conspiracy of, his siblings to kill him, the hellish fury and subsequent dishonest accusation of Potiphar's wife, his unjust incarceration without a trial (fair or otherwise) and all the tests and tribulations he went through in spite of his integrity and innocence. Regardless of all these, his bow remained steady, that is, his faith did not fail. His arms remained limber; this means he maintained his integrity, focus and vision by enduring every hardship. All this was not in his own strength but by the hands of the mighty God of Jacob who was gracious to, and in covenant with him; by the hands of the Shepherd who provided for him, led him, fed him and protected him; by the hands of the Stone of Israel, his building block and his fortress. Prophetically, this refers to the persecutions the Jews have endured and their indomitable spirit. More significantly, however, Joseph here again aptly typifies Christ. Christ was shot at by his brothers, the nation of Israel, who hated him without a cause and would not speak peaceably with him; He was persecuted by the establishment, harassed and molested by the Gentiles, falsely accused by the Scribes, Pharisees and Sadducees; cruelly wounded at Calvary; yet he did not sin. For the joy that was set before Him, He endured the cross, despising its shame and now, as Joseph, was, He is set above all things. He is exalted far above all dominions, thrones and every name that is named. (See Hebrews 12:2.) Of course, it was all achieved through the Father by His grace and covenant. Thus the One who was the Shepherd, made His Son the Good Shepherd; while the Stone of Israel made His Son the Chief Cornerstone, though rejected by the builders! (See Psalm 118:22 & Matthew 21:42.)

After choosing His twelve disciples Jesus warned them to expect the same kind of treatment meted out to Him. Followers of Jesus will be hated, persecuted, harassed, mocked, attacked and provoked. "The disciple is not above his master, nor the servant above his Lord. It is enough for the disciple that he be as his master, and the servant as his Lord" (Matthew 10:24-25). In fact, Jesus encapsulates it this way: "These things I have spoken unto you, that in me ye might have peace. In the world ye shall have tribulation: but be of good cheer; I have overcome the world" (John 16:33). So, like Joseph and his Antitype, we have a word spoken unto us, a vision, a dream that gives us a living hope and peace. The world will challenge this peace, this word with tribulations. But just as Joseph did not compromise because of the mighty God of Jacob, the Shepherd, the Stone of Israel who strengthened him, so we will not be moved and will maintain our joy, peace and most importantly our integrity in Christ.

Israel is not yet finished by any stretch of the imagination. All the said blessings would come "by the God of thy father, who shall help thee; and by the Almighty, who shall bless thee with blessings of heaven above, blessings of the deep that lieth under, blessings of the breasts, and of the womb" (Genesis 49:25). Joseph was going to have rain in the right season, fair weather and the positive influences of the heavens. He was also going to enjoy the blessings of the depths of the earth such as its springs and natural resources, not to mention fertile soil. The blessings of the heavens above could also be spiritual gifts and spiritual blessings. Blessings of the breasts and womb are blessings of fertility, numerous descendants, absence of barrenness and miscarriages and the wherewithal to conveniently nurse one's offspring. These blessings would extend even to his servants, livestock and other animals.

These blessings freely and unconditionally bequeathed on Joseph are almost identical to the ones listed in Deuteronomy 2:1-14. Because Christ fulfilled every demand and condition of the Law, all these blessings pass through Him to the entire world and can be accessed by faith in Him. Israel triumphantly attests: "The blessings of thy father have prevailed above the blessings of my progenitors unto the utmost bounds of the everlasting hills" "They shall be on the head of Joseph, and on the crown of the head of him that was separate from his brethren" (Genesis 49:26). Indeed, Israel's blessings were far greater than those of his forbears. This is because they were and still are, cumulative.

Abraham could only bless Isaac, and so Ishmael and Keturah's sons only received gifts after they had been sent away from Isaac. Isaac, in turn, only had enough blessings for Jacob, and when Esau came he could find no blessings for him. Yet here we find Israel with enough blessings for his twelve sons and even double for Joseph! Moreover, the quality of these blessings, were eternal "greater than the blessings of the oldest mountains and the richest of the ancient hills" (Genesis 49:26, GW).

These blessings would rest on the head of Joseph and on the crown of the one that was separate from his brothers. He was morally separate and from as early as seventeen took an evil report of his brothers to their father. Like Christ, too, no iniquity was found in him and no one could convict him of sin. He was separate in the things he suffered-- persecution and humiliation-- and the obedience he learned in the process. He was separate in his exaltation having passed the test of submission and humility with flying colours. He was also separate in his blessings and inheritance. In like manner, the heavenly Father separated His Son and gave Him a blessing above that of His fellows. "But unto the Son He saith, Thy throne, O God, is for ever and ever: a sceptre of righteousness is the sceptre of thy Kingdom. Thou hast loved righteousness and hated iniquity, therefore God, even thy God, hath anointed thee with the oil of gladness above thy fellows" (Hebrews 1:8).

Paul helps us to understand how we can key into this Abrahamic blessing which found full expression in Jesus typified by Joseph. "Know ye therefore that they which are of faith, (that is you and I) the same are the children of Abraham. And the scripture foreseeing that God would justify the heathen through faith, preached before the gospel unto Abraham, saying, "In thee shall all nations be blessed. So then they, which be of faith are blessed with faithful Abraham" Galatians 3:7-9). Paul concludes his argument by saying "And if ye be Christ's, then are ye Abrahams's seed, and heirs according to the promise." What a joy to know that the same blessings Israel pronounced on Joseph are also pronounced on me by my heavenly Israel through my heavenly Joseph, Jesus Christ. Indeed we are as Peter declared--that chosen generation, that nation of king-priests, a people purchased by Him to proclaim the excellencies of the One who took us out of darkness into His marvellous light. Once we were nobodies expecting judgment. Now we are God's people enjoying His mercy. (See 1 Peter 2:9.)

Finally, Israel concludes his patriarchal benediction with a blessing on Benjamin. "Benjamin shall ravin as a wolf: in the morning he shall devour the prey and at night he shall divide the spoil" (Genesis 49:27). A ravenous wolf hunts for prey day and night, using the daytime to hunt and devour his quarry, and the night-time to divide the plunder. Figuratively, this means Benjamin would be warlike in his character and in his ways. The veracity of this prophecy is ostensible in that tribe's many campaigns of war in the Book of Judges and the Books of Chronicles. On the matter of their wickedness in

Gibeah, they were even willing to take on all the other tribes. (See Judges 20.) Also, as a result of their martial prowess, they produced many skilled archers and artfully accurate stone-slingers. For reasons, which we will explore later, they were also predominantly left-handed.

Their illustrious ancestors include the second judge of Israel, Ehud who secured a great victory against the Moabites and was of course left-handed. Saul, the first king of Israel, and his valiant son Jonathan, the covenant friend and brother of David, were also from the tribe of Benjamin and did many exploits on the battlefield. Esther and Mordecai whom God used to save the Jews and to destroy their enemies were also Benjamites. But by far the most important ambassador of the tribe of Benjamin is Apostle Paul, previously known as Saul of Tarsus. Matthew Henry best illustrates how Paul fulfils the prophesy: "Blessed Paul was of this tribe; and he did in the morning of his day, devour the prey as a predator, but in the evening, divided the spoil as a preacher" (Romans 11:1, Philippians 3:5). It was said of Jesus prophetically by the Prophet Isaiah that He suffered the perils of the cross, justifying many and bearing their iniquities. The Father promised, "Therefore will I divide Him a portion with the great, and He shall divide the spoil with the strong" (Isaiah 53:12). Benjamin was warlike, strong and courteous and knew how to enrich himself with the spoils of his enemies. He would therefore be a foremost recipient of this Messianic blessing. The significance of all this to the church today is that Benjamin is the most perfect Old Testament type of the Church.

Jacob's first ten sons were the fruit of Laban's deception. Recall that Jacob had seen Rachel and had fallen in love with her and had contracted with her father to work seven years for her hand in marriage. At the end of the tenure, Jacob on the wedding night, got Leah instead and thus had to work another seven years to get Rachel. Rachel, who was barren watched her sister give birth to six children.

Her own maid, at her insistence, bore two children for Jacob and her sister's maid another two. In effect, it is no coincidence that the total fruit of that carnal, fleshly comedy of errors comes to ten. Ten in the Bible stands for the Law. Thus Jacob's first ten sons represent natural Israel under the Law. The Bible says, "For the law was given by Moses, but Grace and Truth came by Jesus Christ" (1 John 1:17). By many incontrovertible proofs we have shown that Joseph is the most perfect type of Christ. Benjamin is thus a type of the church, the same father with the ten brothers who are the Jews, but the only one who had the same mother in common with Joseph.

It is also no coincidence that Rachel's name means ewe, which is a mature female sheep. As everything brings forth after its own kind, Jesus is the Lamb of God that taketh away the sin of the world, (see John 1:29), and we are His people, the sheep of His pasture. (See Psalm 85:7, 100:3). Joseph was the eleventh son, yet in Jacobs's eyes, he was the firstborn and the dearly beloved. Another very important symbolic issue is the fact that upon the birth of her first son she prophetically called him Joseph meaning increase or addition. "God will add to me another son." Jesus was the Great Increaser or Adder in contrast to Adam who was the great decreaser or subtractor. Through Jesus' suffering as through Joseph's, many sons have been brought into glory. (See Hebrews 2:10.)

Another relevant symbolism is the fact that Benjamin was brought forth by, and, at Rachel's death. The ewe died and the son of her sorrows was born, then the father changed his name to the son of the right hand. Likewise, by the death of the Lamb of God, by the labours of "The man of sorrows acquainted with grief" (Isaiah 53:3), the church--the son of His sorrows was born. His Father and our Father has however, changed our name to the son of the right hand. This is because the Risen Christ was told to sit at His Father's right hand till His enemies are made His footstool. (See Psalm 110:1.) We are seated with Him in the heavens, (see Ephesians 2:16), far above principalities and powers, dominion and thrones and every known name. (See Ephesians 1:21.) We are Benjamin, the twelfth son. Twelve is the number of divine power, rule and authority. We have the authority of our heavenly Joseph to go into the world in His name and do exploits and make disciples of all men and all nations. Alleluia! Moreover, God the Father declared that the government of the earth would be on the shoulders of the Child who is born and the Son He gave us. Thus divine authority is given to the Son, the Head, but it is executed by the Body, and represented by the shoulders. The nations of the earth, their leaders and their people are the Lord Jesus' portion and His heritage. He asked them of His Father. As we, the mighty war-like Benjamites, win them over, Jesus shares the spoils of the war with us.

The weapons of modern day Benjamin's warfare are not carnal, however. They are neither fleshly nor bodily nor temporal and unregenerate. Rather they are God's powerful weapons, which ultimately subdue every thought to the obedience of Christ. (See 2 Corinthians 10:4-5) What then are these powerful weapons? Paul tells us: "For I am not ashamed of the gospel of Christ; for it is the power of God unto salvation to everyone that believeth; to the Jews first, and also to the Greek" (Romans 1:16). And speaking to Timothy, he further makes the link between God's power and the gospel. (See 2 Timothy 1:8.) He also suggests that we should focus on the things which are not seen, in other words the products of the message of Christ because these are eternal, in contrast to fixing our gaze on the things which are only temporal.

Benjamin's greatest weapon is his availability to convey the message of Christ. Christ and Him crucified should be the focal point of every spiritual warfare, the contents of the duffel bag of every divine messenger or ambassador of the Gospel, and the catalyst of every revival. Before Apostle Paul, the greatest of the Benjamite clan's messengers of the finished work of Christ came on the scene, several Old Testament types, some already mentioned in passing, did the same thing. The first illustration is when Eli was judge in Israel. His sons were devilish and he did not restrain them. Eventually, God's judgment came on them and in one day, word came back to Eli that both his sons were dead and the Ark of the Covenant had been taken into captivity. Incidentally, it was a Benjamite messenger that brought the news. Eli asked him, "What is there done, my son?" This could be read as, "What is finished, what has happened?" The Benjamite messenger told him his two sons were dead and the Ark of God was captured. As soon as Eli heard of the capture of the Ark, he fell over backwards, broke his neck and died for he was an "old man." This is so significant. Our old man, the man of flesh, of carnality and sin can only be disposed of, killed, when a Benjamite messenger comes with a declaration of the Finished Work. All other attempts would be like film, movie and pop stars going in and out of rehabilitation with no permanent heart change in their quest to be delivered from drug or substance abuse.

The second illustration is Saul, the first king of Israel. Saul was the people's choice, a man of valour, head and shoulders above everyone else, a perfect picture of a fleshly, carnal king. David on the other hand was a ruddy lad, unknown, unrecognised and unimpressive, yet, or perhaps, thus chosen by God, the picture of a spiritual eternal king. The biggest difference however between Saul and David is the vessels from which their oil of anointing came. Saul was anointed from a vial, an earthenware vessel made by man's hands. In this way, the oil of the Holy Spirit flowed through a man-made receptacle. David, on the other hand, was anointed by the same oil of the Holy Ghost poured through a ram's horn! A ram's horn is of course, the product of a dead animal sacrifice.

The message is very clear--the Holy Spirit anoints us through the death of Christ to rule and reign with Him (forever) as David did. This is what the psalmist Asaph means when he quotes God as making this demand: "Gather my saints together unto me, those that have made a covenant with me by sacrifice" (Psalm 50:5). Most times we have read this to mean our sacrifice. But our sacrifices cannot cut, secure or execute a covenant; only Jesus Christ's can. Neither indeed can the blood of bulls, goats nor the demonic child-sacrifices of the heathen nations, purge or sanctify. Even our sacrifices of praise, the fruits of our lips, of time, effort, money, worship and such are not acceptable unless they are filtered through the ram's horn of His great sacrifice on Calvary's tree, on Golgotha's brow. The Jews celebrated Jubilee every fiftieth year. This jubilee was declared nationally by a loud long blast of the message proclaimed through a ram's horn. Today, Jesus is the fulfilment of our Jubilee. By a loud long blast through the death of the pascal Lamb, we realise we are not slaves to sin anymore. Our debts are forgiven, our lost rights and mortgaged properties and consciences are restored. Glory to God through Christ Jesus!

The third illustration is Esther, another Benjamite. As important and commendable as Esther's role was in the salvation of the Jews and the elimination of their enemies, the real hero of the Book of Esther is Mordecai. He was the Benjamite messenger who schooled Esther in all she had to do to get the attention of the king and spend quality time with him. It is said of Mordecai "When Mordecai perceived all that was done...." (Esther 4:1). When he saw what was finished, he realised there was a decree of death on a whole race and that ought not to be. Paul likewise perceived there was a statute of death on the whole human race and taught us to touch the top of the King of king's sceptre of righteousness even as Esther did King Ahasuerus' sceptre and thereby found grace, mercy and favour, to secure life for those with a death-sentence hanging over them. The fourth illustration is Ehud, already mentioned. The children of Israel were being oppressed by a wicked king, they cried unto God and He raised up for them a deliverer, Ehud, a Benjamite. Ehud slew the Moabite king, Eglon with a two-edged dagger--a picture of the Sword of the Spirit-- the Word of God who is alive and powerful. (See Hebrews 4:12.) The account states that Ehud plunged the dagger into Eglon's belly and because he was very fat, the haft went in with the blade. More significantly, it is written "and the dirt came out" (Judges 3:22). The picture here is much the same as the previous ones. The Benjamite messenger has taken the Word of God, the message of Christ and plunged it into the flesh, thereby executing the old, fat man, the Adamic sin nature. Crucially, as the message of Christ comes into our hearts, all the dirt, the filth of the old nature is dislodged. What amazing grace! The final Old Testament illustration is one already discussed at length in a previous chapter. This is when Joseph put his empty silver cup in the mouth of Benjamin's sack.

All these Old Testament types of the Benjamite messenger are fulfilled in Paul the Apostle. Paul is the antitype of the Benjamite who tells us as Eli was told, that all that we produce, our sons in the flesh all that comes from the carnal man, leads to death. Paul explains that as the Ark of the Covenant was captured even so the Son of Man descended into the lower parts of the earth to incapacitate our old man. Paul is our Mordecai. We as the bride of Christ must listen to Him to learn how to spend time with our King of kings, and how to execute the enemies of our souls. In conclusion, Israel's benediction over his sons, ends thus: "All these are the twelve tribes of Israel; and this is it that our Father spake unto them, and blessed them, everyone according to his blessing he blessed them" (Genesis 49:28). This verse underscores the importance of personal responsibility and making the right choices. Our actions and character affect not just us, but tribes and nations that are yet within us. Is it not accounted unto Levi that even as he receives tithes, he paid tithes while still in Abraham. (See Hebrews 7:9.) The grace, goodness and mercy of God, and His immeasurable love also palpably resonate in this verse and indeed the entire account. In spite of the incestuous fornication of Reuben, the murderous rage of Simeon and Levi, the unequal yoking and whore-mongering of Judah and the overall "evil report" of the sons of the maids and all the others, God did not withhold His favour and blessings from them. Truly, "the Lord thy God, He is God, the faithful God, which keepeth covenant and mercy with them that love Him and keep His commandments to a thousand generations" (Deuteronomy 7:9). Yes, he rebuked where appropriate for as many as He loves, He rebukes and chastens. (See Hebrews 12:6.) However, "He will not always chide, neither will He keep His anger forever" (Psalm 103:9).

It is also glaring that Israel did not conduct this all-important exercise in the flesh, but was led by the Spirit, "not by might nor by power, but by my Spirit saith the Lord of hosts" (Zechariah 4:6). If it were a carnal exercise, Israel would probably have said a lot more about Benjamin and a lot less about Judah for example.

To bring this epoch-making event to a close, Israel gives the instructions for his burial, (which he had earlier shared with Joseph in private), to all his sons. "Then he gave them these instructions, 'I am about to join my ancestors in death. Bury me with my ancestors in the cave in the field of Ephron the Hittite" (Genesis 49:29). Israel could make this request because Abraham had had the presence of mind, foresight and wisdom to buy a cave located in the field of Machpelah (east of Mamre, in Canaan) with its adjoining fields from a Hittite Prince, by the name of Ephron. This had become the family's final resting place with Abraham and Sarah, Isaac and Rebekkah all interred there. Indeed, Israel even buried Leah there himself. Israel re-emphasises that the cave and the field had indeed been properly purchased from Ephron with the children of Heth as witnesses. Now Jacob was truly done, done with the blessings, done with the instructions and done with the journey of life. He had seen all the promises of God fulfilled. He was confident that as God had kept His promises for his life, He would do exactly the same with his progeny. Having mustered all his strength to sit up and bless his sons, "He gathered up his feet into the bed and yielded up the ghost, and was gathered unto his people." His attitude said he was "confident of this very thing, that He which hath begun a good work in you will perform it till the day of Jesus Christ" (Philippians 1:6).

What dignity in death! What confidence in the resurrection! What faith in the Promises of God as yet unseen! What confidence in the Messiah, Shiloh who was yet to come! What a picture of Jesus' words: "I am the resurrection and the life: he that believeth in me, though he were dead, yet shall he live: And whosoever liveth and believeth in me shall never die" (John 11:25-26). By "yielding the ghost," dying in peace, calmly exhaling his last breath, Israel showed his sons that death holds no terror for the believer. By referring to being gathered unto his people, Israel reiterates Jesus' teaching to the sceptical Pharisees that there is a resurrection and the saints triumphant are alive in Christ, as God is a God of the living not the dead. So those who have "died" in Christ have only transitioned into the Spirit realm, into the very presence of the living God.

Time To Pray

Dear reader, brother, sister, friend, perhaps you have been reading and enjoying this Joseph story so far till this issue of death came up and then your heart skipped a beat and then began to race like Usain Bolt. You hate thinking about death and no doubt, it sends involuntary shudders all the way down your spine. This is perfectly normal for those who have not made a commitment to Christ. It is the fear of death. It is a natural human reaction to have a morbid fear of the unknown. Something inside of everyone witnesses to them, that because they do not know God, the thought of facing Him at death holds nothing but looming dread. Even the atheist and the agnostic, the backslidden and the rebellious know deep down there is a God who made all things. They may choose to silence their hearts but in their more lucid and contemplative moments His existence is indisputable. Some think that by being openly aggressive, unpleasant and vehement in their attack of the "naïve and gullible" who foolishly believe in God, He will cease to exist, or we all will cease to believe in Him. But for you who have never really had the chance or heard the clear message, this is a clarion call.

The names of the first four sons of Israel represent the salvation process. Reuben's name means: "Behold, A Son." To be saved, you have to see Jesus Christ of Nazareth as the Son of the living God. It was of Him the Prophet Isaiah wrote, "For unto us a child is born, unto us a son is given; and the government shall be upon his shoulder and his name shall be called Wonderful, Counsellor, The Mighty God, The Everlasting Father, The Prince of peace. Of the increase of His government and peace there shall be no end, upon the throne of David, and upon His kingdom, to order it, and to establish it with judgment and with justice from henceforth even for ever" (Isaiah 9:6-7). Also when Jesus asked His disciples who men around were saying He was, they answered that some thought He was John the Baptist, others Elijah, still others Jeremiah, and yet others one of the prophets.

He then asked the disciples, "But who do you say that I am?" You see, Jesus is not as interested in what others say about Him as in what YOU say. Peter by inspiration, boldly answered, "You are the Christ (the Messiah), the Son of the living God."

Remember that Jacob's first four sons were the children of Leah. Leah's name means weary. Till you are weary from, and wearied by sin, you have no incentive to behold a son, the Son. Leah's second son was Simeon, which means "Hearkening" or in modern terms "hearing." Romans 10:17 (CEV) tells us: "No one can have faith without hearing the message about Christ. How then shall they call on Him in whom they have not believed? And how shall they believe in Him of whom they have not heard? And how shall they hear without a preacher? So then, faith cometh by hearing, and hearing by the word of God" (Romans 10:14-17). Leah's third son was Levi, which means "Joined." Once you have seen Jesus as Lord and believed the message, you follow on by opening your mouth and confessing what you believe. Once you do this, you are immediately joined to the Lord by faith in His Spirit as you become a part of the body of Christ. "...He that is joined unto the Lord is one Spirit..." (1 Corinthians 6:17). Leah's fourth son was Judah, which of course means "Praise." Having taken the first three steps, now, being born again, will you praise the Lord with sacrifices that are only now acceptable? The story says after this Leah left off childbearing. You will also leave off bearing in the flesh and, because instead you are led by the Spirit of God, you will begin to walk in the Spirit.

From this point, you can say of God, He is your Zebulun; "Lord, thou hath been our dwelling place in all generations" (Psalm 90:1). And as you continue to walk with Him in honesty and truth, He will be your Issachar, your recompense and your reward. Should anything come against you, God will be as Dan to that thing--He that judges will bring judgment to that thing, person or spirit. Indeed by Him you will be as Gad, that is run through a troop and by God you will leap over a wall. (See 2 Samuel 22:30). Asher will be your state of mind and affairs, for you will be happy and blessed and through all your Naphthalis, that is wrestlings, struggles, and fights in life, you will always come out as Joseph with increase and addition. And all this because you were once the son of sorrows (Ben-oni), but you are now the son of God's right hand (Benjamin).

So why not say this prayer out loud by yourself to God. He is near to those that call upon him with a sincere heart.

My Dear Heavenly Father,

I thank you for sparing my life till today. I can see clearly now that Jesus is your very own beloved Son. Having heard the message of His death, burial and resurrection, I believe that Jesus came in the flesh and died for my sins. On the third day, you raised Him for my justification, that is to forgive my sins and declare me not guilty before your heavenly throne. I hereby invite Jesus into my heart as my personal Lord and Saviour. By faith, I believe I am now joined to Him in my spirit and I am born again. Therefore, I will praise you now and forevermore. You are my shield, my protection from trouble and my King and Master forever. Thank you Lord, for I pray in the name of your dear Son, Jesus Christ. Amen

Now formalise your relationship with Christ by finding a believer to make this confession to. Next look for a good Bible-believing living church nearby which you will regularly attend.

CHAPTER FOURTEEN

"CAN THESE BONES LIVE?"

With the peaceful transition of Israel to glory, Joseph is overwhelmed not so much with grief (for we are not ignorant in relation to believers who die, so we do not sorrow, even as others who have no hope (1 Thessalonians 4:13), as with the pangs of temporal separation. He falls on his father's face, weeping and kissing him. Once he gets over the initial shock, Joseph commands the physicians in his service who were expertly trained in such matters to embalm his father's body. The process traditionally takes a period of about forty days. And because the Egyptian mourning period lasted about seventy days, Israel was mourned for another thirty days.

At the expiration of this period of mourning, Joseph conferred with Pharaoh's courtiers and leaders urging them to speak to Pharaoh on his behalf. They were to inform Pharaoh of Joseph's oath to his father to bury him in a place Israel had prepared for that purpose in Canaan; they were also to secure Pharaoh's permission for Joseph to make the journey there and then to return. They did this and Pharaoh promptly gave Joseph the royal go-ahead. The reason Joseph could not approach Pharaoh directly in spite of the cordiality that existed between them, was because he was already in mourning and dressed accordingly. It was forbidden for people in mourning clothes to stand before Egyptians and indeed most other oriental monarchs. It was also a glowing testament to Joseph's integrity, stewardship and trustworthiness, that Pharaoh was quick to grant the consent. Had Joseph been anything but completely reliable, Pharaoh would never have let him out of his sight on account of the political clout he wielded and the potential to use that influence for insurrection, rebellion or subversion, particularly in cahoots with other regional chieftains in and around Canaan. Even a sniff of disloyalty in the past would have made it impossible for Joseph to honour the obligation he had to his beloved father's deathbed wish. The fact that we will reap the fruits of our actions, good or bad can never be overemphasized. Joseph thus showed forth the heavenly Joseph of whom it is written: "For such an high priest became us, who is holy, harmless, undefiled, separate from sinners, and made higher than the heavens" (Hebrews 7:22).

Most assuredly, we see Joseph's exaltation, position and great favour in the quality of the entourage, that accompanied his father's cortege, described as "a very great company" (Genesis 50:9). Apart from all of Joseph's family, his brothers and his father's household, Joseph was accompanied by the king's highest officials; leaders in his palace staff, and leading men of Egypt. Not just that, but Pharaoh's military chariots and cavalry were also released to accompany and honour Joseph and his late father. In fact, only the children, cattle, sheep and goats were left behind in Goshen. It was without a doubt, a state funeral. One cannot help but parenthetically wonder if Potiphar was a part of this great company and how he and his wife (if they were still together) felt about Joseph's pre-eminence! Eventually the cortege comes to the threshing floor of Atad, which is on the east side of the River Jordan. There, Joseph commands the conclusion of the funeral ceremonies with seven days of mourning, as was then typical amongst the Jews. This mourning period witnessed such an intense outpouring of grief on the threshing floor of Atad that it attracted the attention and the comment of the resident Canaanites. They even decided to change the name of the place to Abelmizraim as a lasting tribute to the "grievous mourning" of the Egyptians.

It is a stunning first irony that of all people, Jacob the deceased and his covenant sons, Joseph et al, should be mistaken for Egyptians! As the chief mourner and most senior "Egyptian" official, Joseph would have been perceived as an Egyptian royal. This is not strange as his

Antitype Jesus, was often accused by the Jews of being a foreigner. In one instance, it is recorded, "Then answered the Jews, and said unto Him, Say we not well that thou art a Samaritan, and hast a devil" (John 8:48). And since Egypt can be said to be a type of the domain of the devil, they even accused Jesus of casting out devils by the prince of darkness, Beelzebub. (See Matthew 12:24.) The second irony is that the Egyptians should love, respect and honour Joseph, and by extension his father, Israel, so much that there would be such genuine fellowship in his suffering. It was because they knew him that they could so vicariously partake of his sorrow and loss in this manner. This level of intimate knowledge is what the Apostle Paul yearned and cried out for when he said of Jesus, "That I may know Him, and the power of His resurrection, and the fellowship of His sufferings, being made conformable unto his death…" (Philippians 3:10). It is worth noting, also the stark contrast between these Egyptians and those who would later oppress Jacob's seed. Since the formalities of mourning had been duly observed, it now fell to Israel's sons to inter him according to his avowed wish, burying him in "the cave of the field of Machpelah, which Abraham bought with the field for a possession of a burying place of Ephron the Hittite before Mamre." The importance of this fact, along with its natural and spiritual applications will soon be looked at a little more closely.

After Joseph had done the will of his father, he returned to his position of authority in Egypt with his brothers and the entire retinue that had accompanied him to the funeral. This points to Jesus' ascension to the right hand of the Father after He had done the will of the same Father. A death, his "funeral" and a large company of people was also involved with Jesus. With the passing away of their father Israel, Joseph's siblings feared that they would no longer have an advocate to stand between them and the fierce wrath and judgment they felt they deserved for their despicable acts in the past. They were at Joseph's mercy and they knew it! "What if Joseph still hates us and plans to pay us back for all the harm we did to him?" (Genesis 50:15, GNB). From the tests that Joseph carried out on their journeys to purchase food in Egypt, there is no doubt that Joseph's brothers had been regenerated having gone through genuine repentance. They however, were still not walking in perfected love. John the Beloved tells us, "There is no fear in love; but perfect love casteth out fear: because fear hath torment. He that feareth is not made perfect in love" (1 John 4:8).

They sent an emissary to Joseph to tell him that their father left clear instructions to Joseph to forgive his brothers their grave sin, for indeed, by their own admission, they had been evil and cruel toward him. They were also to go and seek Joseph's forgiveness personally, which they were now doing. To tug at Joseph's heartstrings and evoke his compassion, they used the name of the two most important people in his life, God, and their father: "…and now, we pray thee, forgive the trespass of the servants of the God of thy father." Joseph's tears flowed freely when he heard their supplication. Jesus also wept twice for sympathy, and on account of the misery, shame and repercussions of sin and the lack of faith displayed by His followers and disciples. (See Romans 12:19 & John 11:35.)

For the fifth time since Joseph received the revelation (by dreams) of dominion over his siblings, his brothers who had now come before his presence, immediately bowed down in front of him. "Here we are before you as your slaves" (Genesis 50:18). Here indeed was Joseph's sheaf standing upright and their sheaves standing round about and making obeisance to Joseph's sheaf: Jacob the "sun" after a glorious day, having gone to bed, and the "moon" his--mother having waxed and waned, here indeed were the eleven "stars" making obeisance to Joseph. It is highly unlikely that the conversation the brothers purported to have had with Jacob actually took place. If it had, Israel would have appealed directly to Joseph himself, either privately when he sent for him to bless his two sons, or publicly when he imparted the blessings to all his sons. Even if the conversation did take place, that Israel did not talk about it to Joseph is a clear indication that he was confident that vengefulness was not a feature of Joseph's character. After all, recall that in Joseph's early years, his father imparted to him every godly virtue he himself possessed. Going over Israel's biography, his meekness is outstanding. He yielded always to the dealings of God and never sought to vindicate himself or inflict revenge on anyone who offended him even when it was in his power to do so.

Joseph turns to his brothers quavering before him with fear and assures them to: "Fear not: for am I in the place of God?" (Genesis 50:19) This statement shows that Joseph was aware of the sentiment expressed by the Psalmist that vengeance belongs to God and Him alone: "O Lord God, to whom vengeance belongeth; O God to whom vengeance belongeth, show thyself" (Psalm 94:1). The literal Hebrew is calling on the "God of revenges" to "shine forth." Moses on his part in the law gives it as a commandment; "Thou shalt not avenge, nor bear any grudge against the children of thy people, but thou shalt love thy neighbour as thyself: I am the Lord" (Leviticus 17:18). Note the addendum to the commandment because it hides a revelation that we shall unveil shortly. On his part the preacher advises in the Book of Proverbs: "Say not, I will do so to him as he hath done to me. I will render to the man according to his work" (Proverbs 24:29). Finally, Apostle Paul outlines the New Testament position in the nineteenth verse of the twelfth chapter of his epistle to the Romans: "Dearly beloved, avenge not yourselves, but rather give place unto wrath: for it is written, Vengeance is mine; I will repay, saith the Lord."

The interesting irony is that just knowing that we should not avenge ourselves is not sufficient to prevent us from doing so. We need to know and have the antidote to retaliation, which is forgiveness. The only problem is that those who hurt us the most are often times,

1. Usually people closest to us and for whom we have done the most;

2. Those who do not deserve to be forgiven and

3. Many who do not ask for, or even care if they are forgiven!

In the text quoted above we learn that the power of forgiveness is the antidote to revenge and malice; and love is the motivation, the driving force that makes forgiveness possible. If you love your neighbour as yourself, there will be no basis for hurting him or wishing him evil even if he has wronged you. When God ends the instruction or indeed any instruction in the Old Testament with the phrase "I am the Lord," He is pointing the hearer to the fact that the truth highlighted is an inherent aspect of His character and nature. As John admonishes us therefore: "Beloved, let us love one another for love is of God and everyone that loveth is born of God, and knoweth God. He that loveth not knoweth not God, for God is love" (1 John 4:7-8). Apostle Paul reiterates that this "love of God is shed abroad in our hearts by the Holy Ghost which is given unto us," that is, at the point of our conversion, when we make Jesus Lord of our lives. (See Romans 5:5.) In effect, if we really know God, we will realise that He is love and has therefore loved us with a perfect and everlasting love. The epicentre of this love is the sacrifice of His only begotten Son for the forgiveness of our sins. God is 100% holy and the prophet Habakkuk tells us that He is "of purer eyes than to behold evil, and canst not look on iniquity" (Habakkuk 1:3).

The only way therefore that He can relate with fallen humanity is through the agency of the full and eternal atonement secured by the blood of the Christ. In the Old Covenant, the blood of bulls, goats, sheep, lambs etc., was a type of Jesus' blood, but it only had the power to cover over sins for a time. In the New Covenant, however,

God puts His law in the believer's "inward parts" and writes it in their hearts. Speaking by Jeremiah, God says, no man will need to teach the other the knowledge of God, for every saint from the least to the greatest would know God. The reason for this widespread knowledge of God is because "I will forgive their iniquity," God graciously declares, "and I will remember their sin no more" (Jeremiah 31:33-34).

The extent of the totality of the remission of our sins is reflected in the Psalmist's declaration that "As far as the east is from the west, so far hath He removed our transgressions from us" (Psalm 103:12). Jesus' blood cleanses us from all guilt, fear, condemnation, and from an evil conscience and gives us the boldness of access into the holiest of all (that is, the throne room of God) while bequeathing on us the privilege of fellowship with the Most High God. "I am the Lord" (Leviticus 17:18). This means He is the Lord who is love and therefore He loves you. You are the product (begotten) of His love, forgiven by His love, sustained by His love and encouraged to live by His love. Knowing God loves you with an everlasting love enables you to love yourself. In effect, the secret to a healthy sense of self-worth is the knowledge that you are loved unconditionally. Armed with this sense of security, significance and self-worth that God's sacrificial love imparts, you are then free to love your neighbour as yourself; to forgive him his trespasses toward you as God has forgiven you yours toward Him; and as you have forgiven yourself.

Please realise though that forgiveness is not an abstract, unattainable utopian ideal. The Physician Luke gives us practical insights into the process. He says: "Love your enemies, do good to them which hate you, bless them that curse you, and pray for them which despitefully use you" (Luke 6:27-28). This is the true definition of Christianity and what sets it apart from religion and the vain philosophies of men! "For if you love them which love you," Luke further postulates, "what thank have ye? For sinners also love those that love them. And if ye do good to them, which do good to you, what thank have ye? For sinners also do even the same. And if ye lend to them of whom ye hope to receive, what thank have ye? For sinners also lend to sinners, to receive as much again" (Luke 6:32-34). Moses records God concluding His instructions against unforgiveness with a spotlight on God's character of forgiveness, mercy and love in the statement, "I am the Lord."

Luke 6:35 also concludes by pointing to the divine propensity for grace, mercy and generosity: "But love ye your enemies and do good, and lend, hoping for nothing again: and your reward shall be great, and ye shall be the children of the Highest: for He is kind unto the unthankful and to the evil. Be ye therefore merciful, as your Father also is merciful." So when God calls you to forgive, He is not as interested in preventing you from retaliation, as He is in prompting you to walk in love. This is because walking in love, kindness, goodness, mercy and grace, is the most effective way there is of reflecting the character and nature of God. Besides, it will always prevent you from vengefulness! Joseph understood this very well, and there was no way he was going to walk contrary to the God–nature that was within him. Remember if you will that one of the seven things Jesus said on the cross was "Father forgive them; for they know not what they do" (Luke 23:34). Moreover, Joseph recognised that God works all things together for good to them that love Him and are the called according to His purpose. He knew he was a God–lover and one called to do God's good pleasure. This is why he told them "But as for you, ye thought evil against me; but God meant it unto good, to bring to pass, as it is this day, to save much people alive" (Genesis 50:20). Here Joseph was simply reiterating what he had said many years before when he revealed himself to his brothers, the second time they came to purchase grain at the onset of the great famine. In saying the same thing, he pictures Jesus Christ who is the same yesterday, today and forever. (See Hebrews13:8.) Jesus, in turn pictures the Father who says in Malachi 3:6 "For I am the Lord, I change not." Moreover, one of God's inviolate principles, as mentioned earlier is that of establishing His word at the mouth of two or three witnesses. Apostle Paul exemplifies this principle in all his epistles and tells the Philippians that this is why he repeats instructions, doctrines etc.: "To write the same things to you, to me indeed is not grievous, but for you it is safe" (Philippians 3:1).

Joseph was letting his brothers know like the Psalmist, that his times were in God's hand and He would deliver him from the hand of his enemies and those that persecuted him. (See Psalm 31:15.) The Sovereign God would also not permit anything to happen to him that did not ultimately serve His divine purpose. Even the things men consider as evil could never happen in the believer's life without God's express permission and that only if it serves God's greater purpose as we have said earlier on. So the brothers' goal was to harm Joseph, but God's intention was the salvation and preservation of the lives of countless people. Needless to say, in the end, the will of God prevails. This, of course, is a picture of Jesus' ministry and the conspiracy by the rulers, the princes of this world to dispose of Him by crucifixion. They, like Joseph's brothers, thought evil against the Christ, but "God meant it unto good, to bring to pass as it is this day, to save much people alive" (Genesis 50:20). Spiritually, Jesus repeatedly emphasized to the Jews, as Joseph did to his brothers that "God did send me before you to preserve life," and again "God did send me before you to preserve you a posterity in the earth, and to save your lives by a great deliverance."

The following scriptures show, Jesus says virtually the same thing to Nicodemus emphasizing that He was sent by God. (See John 3:17), also to the Jews at Jerusalem at the feast of the dedication, (see John 10:36) and to the disciples at sundry times. Apostle Paul testifies to the Galatians to this effect; (see Galatians 4:4-5.) John the beloved also confirms this in his first epistle. (See 1 John 4:9-10.)

As all these themes have been addressed previously, it is apparent that God is concluding this Joseph saga by tying all the loose ends together and showing where apparently unconnected events interlock. Joseph ends his consolation of his brothers with the exhortation and admonition against fear and the assurance that he would provide for them and their little ones. With kind and comforting words, he reassured his brothers, touched their hearts and set their minds at ease. Joseph lived to be one hundred and ten years old and in that time, he, his father's house (that is, his brothers and their progeny) and indeed the land of Egypt grew in grace, influence, wealth and strength. So Joseph gives meaning to the scripture that says: "For our light affliction, which is but for a moment, worketh for us a far more exceeding and eternal weight of glory" (2 Corinthians 4:17).

From his dream to his ascension to the throne it took thirteen years, though it seems like much longer. (See Genesis 37:2 with Genesis 41:46.) Those thirteen years of trials and tribulations are thus a "light affliction" when compared to the eighty years of rule and dominion and the even more weighty glory of the preservation of God's people as an eternal posterity, and more importantly, the fulfilment of the counsel and purposes of God. The prophet Isaiah says likewise of Jesus: "After a life of suffering, he will again have joy; He will know that He did not suffer in vain. My devoted servant, with whom I am pleased, will bear the punishment of many and for his sake I will forgive them" (Isaiah 53:11, GNB).

What is more, Joseph lived to see his great, great-grandchildren by his son Ephraim and his great-grandchildren by his other son, Manasseh. Joseph had the honour and joy of taking these successive generations upon his knees, and showering upon them his patrimonial blessings. His days had been prolonged and he had thus seen his seed. Of Jesus, whom he typified, the prophet Isaiah prophesied that: "He shall see His seed, he shall prolong his days, and the pleasure of the Lord shall prosper in His hand" (Isaiah 53:10). When Joseph realised that his life journey was about to end, he called his brethren and said to them, "I am about to die. God will definitely take care of you and take you out of this land to the land he swore with an oath to give to Abraham, Isaac, and Jacob" (Genesis 50:24, GW). The word used for brethren here is one described by Strong as "used in the widest sense of literal relationship and metaphorical affinity or resemblance" (Strong's Hebrew and Greek Dictionary). It also refers to kindred. So it is unlikely that all his eleven brothers were still alive as ten were actually older than he was. Also, since the message was one for the future, Joseph would most likely be talking to the newly emerging heads of tribes and the leaders of tomorrow. Joseph's words are words of faith. He assures them that God would, without doubt, visit them. The word "visit" is repeated in the Hebrew text for emphasis. Amongst other things it means to visit with friendly (as in this case, or hostile) intent, to care for and to remember. They therefore did not need to worry for God would take care of them in that season even in Joseph's absence, and would remember them in the future, long after Joseph was gone. Though for now, they had a good life and enjoyed the best that Egypt had to offer, it was not to be their focus because God had a better land, the land of promise in store for them. They were to set their affection on their spiritual heritage.

David typified this when he handed over the charge for the building of the Temple to his son Solomon with the words, "Moreover because I have set my affection to the house of my God, I have mine own proper good, of gold and silver, which I have given to the house of my God, over and above all that I have prepared for the holy house..." (1 Chronicles 29:3). In like manner, Paul encourages the believer to "Set your affection on things above, not on things on the earth" (Colossians 3:2).

What Joseph did here thus perfectly mirrors what Jesus would do just before His own death. It is written of that incident that: "When Jesus knew that His hour was come that He should depart out of the world unto the Father, having loved His own which were in the world, He loved them unto the end...Jesus knowing that the Father had given all things into His hands, and that He was come from God, and went to God..." (John 13:1 & 3). Jesus arose from the supper table, took off His outer garment and wrapped a towel around his waist. He then proceeded to wash the disciples' feet with water from a basin and to dry them with the towel. This was a deliberate symbolic gesture that spoke of humility in the face of divine elevation; setting an example for the disciples to follow; spiritual cleansing by the "washing of water by the word" (Ephesians 5:26), and an undying love for His disciples. It was an act of faith in the light of His soon-coming elevation after His crucifixion, death and resurrection. Joseph's instructions were an act of faith. He believed God would fulfil His promise to his father, grandfather and great-grand-father and bring their seed into the land of promise. Since faith without works is dead, Joseph decided to add action to His faith. He made the children of Israel (this confirms that he was not necessarily talking to his siblings) swear an oath. He reiterated that God would surely visit the nation of Israel at the appointed time. As at the first time, he repeats for emphasis the same word for "visit" as he did before. When the time of God's visitation came, Joseph enjoined them, they were to carry up his bones from "thence," that is Egypt, and inter them in the Promised Land. Wow! The spiritual implications of this are manifold and mammoth. That it was an act of faith is made clear by the writer of the Book of Hebrews, who included this incident in the Faith Hall of Fame. It is said of Joseph: "By faith, Joseph, when he died, (literally when dying), made mention of the departure (literally of the Exodus) of the children of Israel; and gave commandment concerning his bones" (Hebrews 11:22).

Since "no one can have faith without hearing the message about Christ" (Romans 10:17 CEV), it stands to reason that Joseph knew that his life was symbolic, and a type and a shadow. More importantly, he was by instruction signifying that he believed in a promised land, a promised rest for God's people, the immortality of the human spirit and resurrection of the dead. Responding to the Sadducees who were sceptical about resurrection, Jesus tells them that when God calls Himself the God of Abraham, Isaac and Jacob, He is not the God of the dead, but of the living. Thus this nomenclature proves God to be the God of resurrection. (See Matthew 22:33.) By referring to this in his instructions, Joseph is identifying with this God of the living not of the dead. So like Job, he knew that his Redeemer was alive and that He shall stand at the latter day upon the earth, "And though after my skin worms destroy this body, yet in my flesh shall I see God: whom I shall see for myself, and mine eyes shall behold, and not another; though my reins be consumed within me" (Job 19:25-27).

In giving the instructions concerning his bones Joseph was seeing in the spirit what Ezekiel saw when: "The hand of the Lord was upon (him), and carried (him) out in the spirit of the Lord, and set (him) down in the midst of the valley which was full of bones" (Ezekiel 37:1). Though the bones were exceedingly dry and brittle, by the Word and the Spirit (prophecy and the breath of God), they came alive and became a mighty army. God interpreted the vision thus: "Son of man, these bones are the whole house of Israel: behold, they say, Our bones are dried, and our hope is lost: we are cut off for our parts" (Ezekiel 37:11). That it has to do with resurrection soon becomes obvious when the Lord God says: "Therefore prophesy and say unto them, Thus saith the Lord God; Behold, O my people, I will open your graves, and cause you to come up out of your graves, and bring you into the land of Israel" (Ezekiel 37:12). The prophet Isaiah had a similarly very lucid picture of resurrection and gave voice to Joseph's vision when he said: "Thy dead men shall live, together with my dead body shall they arise. Awake and sing, ye that dwell in dust: for thy dew is as the dew of herbs, and the earth shall cast out the dead" (Isaiah 26:19).

All these are fulfilled in Christ. In the Book of Acts Luke puts it this way: "And we declare unto you glad tidings, how that the promise which was made unto the fathers, God hath fulfilled the same unto us their children, in that He hath raised up Jesus again; as it is also written in the second Psalm, thou art my Son, this day have I begotten thee" (Acts 13:32-33). The Matthew account finally shows us how Christ as the Antitype brings all these prophetic symbolic pictures to fulfilment: "And the graves were opened; and many bodies of the saints which slept arose, And came out of the graves after His resurrection, and went into the holy city, and appeared unto many" (Matthew 27:52-53).

And so having made the children of Israel promise to take his bones to the land of promise, as his father had made him swear to him, Joseph died at one hundred and ten years of age. He was then embalmed and put in a coffin in Egypt. If his father, benefitting from his favour and the grace upon his life, enjoyed what can rightly be termed a state funeral, imagine what Joseph's funeral would have been like had he opted for burial in Egypt. Instead, he was put in an ordinary coffin and stored in a room, there to remain for another three and a half centuries. It is interesting to note that faith outlives the faithful and acts of faith keep speaking even when their originator has long fallen silent in death. As the children of Israel looked at Joseph's coffin for succeeding generations, faith would be stirred up in their hearts and perseverance would be established and thus Joseph like Abel "being dead yet speaketh" (Hebrews 11:4). Could it be that Joseph's coffin was a memorial and one of the things that constantly reminded Moses of the Promises of God and His faithfulness toward them? After all, as they left Egypt in the great exodus, with all that Moses had to do and had on his mind, it is written: "And Moses took the bones of Joseph with him: for he had straitly sworn the children of Israel, saying, God will surely visit you; and ye shall carry up my bones away hence with you" (Exodus 13:19).

And so Joseph's story began with him feeding the flock with his brethren and ends with him feeding their faith even in his absence. It also ends with him dying, being embalmed and put in a coffin in Egypt. Likewise the story of our heavenly Joseph ends with His crucifixion and death. Joseph of Arimathea asked Pilate for Jesus' body and Pilate granted him permission to take it. Together with Nicodemus, they "embalmed" Jesus' body in linen clothes and a mixture of myrrh and aloes weighing a hundred pounds and they placed it in a newly dug sepulchre.

Not...

THE END...

but a new beginning...

EPILOGUE

What she held in her right hand to a modern observer could have passed for a table tennis bat. Upon closer look however, one would discover that it was made of molten bronze. In her typical conscientious manner, she noticed a bit of rust was developing around the handle and traces of it were already sending tinges of discolouration to the shiny oval surface two and a half inches above the handle. She made a mental note to herself to polish off the rust once she returned from the well a few hours later.

Ah, the well! she thought to herself. She hated going to the well because it opened up old wounds, stirred up deep feelings of resentment and insecurity. At the well, she always felt like a leper. As soon as the other women saw her coming, they nudged each other and began an intensive whispering campaign. The more polite among them simply avoided eye contact. Others more brazenly gave her hostile looks, tried to stare her down or even aggressively brushed past her spoiling for a fight. They whispered loud enough for her to hear and she had picked up names like "husband stealer," "serial polygamist," "adulterer," and "fornicator."

Her stunning facial features stared back at her from the brass plate that served her culture and generation as a mirror. She was beautiful, even to the point of being bewitching. She had a devastating effect on members of the opposite sex and she knew it. Wherever men gathered and she walked in, there was a muted turmoil as men tripped over themselves to be first to make her acquaintance. In her pre-adolescent years, she had been flat-chested, and had short hair; in other words, she looked like a boy. It did not help matters that she grew up around her older brothers and tried to match them in all their "wild" activities.

After her father died, her mother struggled rather unsuccessfully to deal with the difficulties, prejudices and challenges of balancing raising children and keeping a roof over their heads. She had therefore grown up as a "tomboy" with little adult supervision and because she had a strong desire for a father's love, had picked up a lot of unsavoury habits.

Rather suddenly, she hit puberty and discovered that she was sprouting appendages on her chest, and her figure was becoming curvaceous and decidedly different from her brothers'. Men of every walk of life, every age bracket and every culture began to greedily devour her with their hungry lascivious eyes and she soon discovered the power of the female anatomy on the opposite sex. Over the years, she would also discover the power of barter and how to effectively use her "assets" to get what she needed.

Yet all that "power" and its attendant benefits could not erase the yearning or quench the thirsting of her innermost being for the genuine love of a father. She could hear irregular, shallow breathing from the bed of fluffy quilts spread directly on the floor behind her. Without turning around she knew this was usually accompanied by rapid eye movement that testified that her...well...um...husband was coming out of a deep sleep. The look of satisfaction on his face also suggested he was having a sweet dream from which he would soon be rudely awakened. Hmm... did she say husband? She supposed she was employing that term in the loosest sense of the word. She had been trying to get this joker to do all that was needful to legalise their relationship but he just seemed uninterested. And why, she asked herself sardonically, did he need to pay through his nose for a thimble of milk when he could indeed have and freely milk the cow!

As attractive as everyone thought she was, she always felt deep inside like used and damaged goods. Who except this non-starter, this unemployed appendage whom she sustained, would want her?

Enough of the musing self-pity; there was work to be done and she needed to get to the well to fetch some water. It was about an hour before midday. She knew that no woman worth her salt went to the well at this time of the day. For the oriental woman, the evening meeting at the well was not just a matter of domestic exigency, but one of expectant social intercourse. It was at the well that all the latest gossip was shared. Because of her chequered marital history, she had for too long been the topic of discussion and had evolved a system of going to the well when other women were not there; to avoid their bitchiness. Suddenly, she recalled that when she woke up this morning, she had a strong premonition that something significant, a destiny-enhancing encounter was about to change everything. What it was; what form it would take, how it would play out, where it would lead--she had absolutely no clue. Oh well, here goes. She picked up her favourite designer pitcher and set off down the dusty dirt track toward a date with destiny.

He considered that in the last three days they must have covered about thirty-five miles. They were approaching the "City of Sychar" which in reality was a village snuggled against the slope on the southeast of Mount Ebal. The ruins of the ancient city of Shechem could be seen below as indeed could a little plain and what looked from where he was, like a well. Across the valley toward the south as though a mirror image of Mount Ebal, lay Mount Gerizim where the Samaritans had their temple for the worship of the One they called the God of Jacob. He pondered as he recollected the events preceding this journey. Is it possible that one could be fully cognizant of truth and yet blatantly and deliberately reject it? How could people gang together to promote their selfish agendas while ignoring the glaring principle of consequences and repercussions? Surely it is evident that the inevitability of day following night and vice versa, winter following summer and the reverse, cold co-existing beside heat, all point to the enduring principle that as long as the earth exists, harvest will invariably follow seedtime and what a man sows, that he shall reap. Jesus shook His head sadly as he pondered the latest attack and campaign of persecution against Him by members of the religious sect known as the Pharisees. He couldn't resist jokingly observing that "as far he sees" is "as far as he believes," and being not just short-sighted but actually spiritually blind, the Pharisee actually sees nothing and therefore knows and believes nothing!

The Pharisees had hounded him in regard to everything from their vacuous human traditions by which they nullified God's commandments, to issues of doctrine and controversies as to whether He really was the Messiah. He who made the very heart of man marvelled at the desperate wickedness to which man now turned it in his bid for self-gratification and glorification. He could not but laugh at the irony and futility of the creature trying to outwit the Creator, the finite mind, trying to outfox the Omniscient! Their latest controversy, born of jealousy, was over the fact that his ministry was growing because he was making and baptising more disciples than John, that greatest of all prophets, as acknowledged by all the people and reluctantly by the religious leaders themselves. Yet, Jesus thought to himself, it was His disciples, who did the actual baptisms. However, since the Pharisees would not relent till they had done some major mischief, Jesus decided to leave Judea and go again into Galilee because the time for open confrontation had not yet come. He considered that the shortest most direct and obvious route would be through Samaria. But He felt a twinge of sadness when he realised that 99.9% of Jews would rather take a far distant way around, through Perea and Decapolis than endure the taboo of dealing with the Samaritans. Needless to say the feelings were altogether mutual. A travelling Jew who was foolhardy enough to pass through Samaria was ignored at best and scorned as a matter of course. Services for which he was ready to pay were routinely denied him and definitely no courtesies or hospitable gestures were volunteered. If he had the misfortune of having night fall while in this territory, he could be sure he was at the mercy of the elements as well as brigands and marauders who roamed the countryside in search of someone to rob. His disciples, led by the impulsive Peter and the rambunctious sons of Zebedee whom he had fondly nicknamed "Sons of thunder" had reminded him that the Jews had no dealings with the Samaritans. And in case He had forgotten, they had further reminded him that the Samaritans were a polluted breed being half Jew, half Gentile. His gentle rebuke was all that stopped a history lesson on the origin of the Hebrew/Samaritan conflict and a religious lesson outlining why God, and right were on the side of the Jews. Yet, in spite of all the overwhelming natural arguments, Jesus felt a divine compulsion to go through Samaria. In fact, His heavenly Father and the resident Holy Spirit had made it clear that "He must needs go through Samaria." He had walked with the Father and knew that such promptings were a prelude to the miraculous and the unfolding of divine purpose.

The journey had been long, tedious, dusty and tiring; and opportunities for refreshments though few and far between, had presented themselves. Yet the compulsion to keep moving had remained strong till they came to a Samaritan city called Sychar. This city was noted for and reputed to be built around a famous well, known as "Jacob's well," where Jesus and the disciples had just arrived. Exhausted from His journey, Jesus sat on this well. The disciples decided, upon Jesus' prompting that this would be a good time to go buy food because the chances of success were more in that city than out in the country. The disciples left but not before the clown in their midst asked Jesus if he had heard the one about the three water holes in the ground. Jesus played along and said he hadn't. "Well, well, well!" the disciple said, bursting into hearty laughter, as they disappeared into the horizon.

She had completely mastered the art of "mincing." Her pitcher was balanced on her right shoulder, her head held upright and her neck displayed ostentatiously in a technique where it is elevated and extended as far as possible and highlighted with layers of chokers and chains. She took short steps heel to toe as was her custom as if wearing a ball and chain, and made her way toward the well. The sun was almost directly overhead and she found that walking in this kind of heat was energy-sapping. She could not wait to get back home. It was highly unlikely that there would be anyone at the well, but she could never be sure. Still lost in her trouble and heat-induced reverie, she did not see the stranger and was surprised to hear a soft male voice say, "Give me to drink."

Startled and unprepared, she quickly cursed herself for not being as prepared as she normally was when dealing with men. And indeed what a perfect specimen of a man this one was. Beyond his perfect physical attributes, however, there was something tender, compassionate and totally non-judgmental in his eyes. A furtive cursory glance was sufficient to highlight the ribbon of blue at the bottom of his garment, which together with his dialect clearly indicated that he was not just a Jew but in all probability one with religious authority. As such, his request seemed even stranger. Even every non-thinking person and his dog knew that the Jews and the Samaritans were avowed enemies and had no dealings whether social, cultural, economic or religious. They would not borrow from nor lend to each other, neither eat nor drink from or with the same crockery, cutlery and chalice, or even drink from the same well. Oh, she was not going to refuse him since he had the audacity, or could it be, blissful ignorance, to ask. But she was going to find out what made him tick--how he could so casually bypass the bigotry of several generations and establish an instant rapport.

"How can a Jewish man like you ask a Samaritan woman like me for a drink of water?" she queried. His answer was somewhat cryptic: "If you knew what God's gift is and who is asking you for a drink, you would have asked him for a drink. He would have given you living water." Immediately, she thought of running water, surely that's what he must mean. The well is deep, he has nothing to draw from the well with, so where, on earth was he going to get this "living water"? His manner was impressive and his words compulsive but somewhat incomprehensible. With each passing second, the stirring inside her soul grew greater. Was this great man going to direct her to a new and better spring of water somewhere in this region, which no one else knew about? If he did then he had to be greater than Jacob whom her race claimed as their forefather. Yes, technically, her people were made up partly of the remnant of the ten tribes and partly of people sent from Chaldea, still they claimed to be Jacob's descendants. She noticed that the stranger did not directly answer her question but inferred that Jacob's water could alleviate but not altogether remove thirst but his would be a wellspring of eternal life. Wow!

She did not fully understand what he was trying to say, but he had certainly piqued her curiosity, and she had to know more. After all this was the very first man she had ever known who had offered her something with no expectation of anything in return. Moreover, the idea of not thirsting ever again was like the much sought-after utopian dream everyone, especially women, had, hoping to stay forever young. His next statement burst her bubble of excitement: "Go get your husband and come back here with him." Her heart skipped a beat, then started pounding like it would burst from her chest. An accompanying swirl of guilt swooped over her soul kicking awake her slumbering conscience and convicting her of her behaviour. She wished the ground would open up and swallow her whole. He looked her straight in the eyes as if he could see into her very soul. But as much as she wanted to look anywhere but at him, she couldn't look away. Should she lie to him or duck the question? Too late! You could not lie to this man! Without knowing why she blurted out, "I have no husband." He did not hesitate in his own response, "That's right, you're telling the truth. You don't have a husband. You have already been married five times, and the man you are now living with isn't your husband". Remorse filled her heart immediately as she pondered the lifestyle she had lived. This man knew her heart; he knew the secrets of her life. No doubt, he was some kind of prophet and she could learn some heavenly truth from him. What better place to start than with the burning religious issues of her day--the controversy Jews and Samaritans had, as to which was the true place of worship, Jerusalem or here at Mount Gerizim. Moreover, it would take the spotlight from the very touchy issue of her marital misadventures and her now gnawing and restless conscience.

Jesus' answer was that the old dispensation of worshipping God in only one place, with special rules, was about to cease. In fact, He said God would soon be worshipped and celebrated anywhere and anytime by all people in and of the Spirit. Responding to her question He said: "God is a Spirit, and they that worship Him must worship Him in spirit and in truth". A light suddenly came on in the woman's spirit. This was not an intellectual thing. It was not an emotional thing. It was not even a volitional thing. She couldn't define it but she felt as if her dead spirit had begun to waken, confronted by this amazing man. She had heard that the Jews were expectantly awaiting the coming of their Messiah. Her people were also eagerly anticipating the Messiah whom they called The Converter and sometimes The Returning One. Because she was anxious to connect with this man she said, "I am certain that the Messiah, who is named Christ, is coming; when he comes he will make all things clear to us". This was the moment He had been waiting for. Jesus had skilfully and with divine wisdom brought this sinful woman to the point of receiving Him as Discerner, Forgiver, and now--Messiah. Jesus therefore said unto her "I that speak to you am he". At this point, the disciples returned with their arms overflowing with fresh fruits, vegetables and exotic Mediterranean foods. Their furrowed brows and quizzical expressions spoke volumes. The Rabbi was not only talking to a woman in public, but a Samaritan woman with a questionable past. Bursting with excitement she abandoned her water pot, ran off to the city-centres and invited the men of the city: "Come, see a man, which told me all things that ever I did: is not this the Christ?"

On the third day, Jesus departed from Sychar, looked back at the city and saw that a sense of serenity had descended upon it. His mission had been an unqualified success. The good news had been preached to the poor who had received it as hungry x factor hopefuls receive Simon Cowell's approval. Blind eyes had been opened, broken hearts had been healed, the captives had been set at liberty while addictions were broken from people's lives. Even those oppressed by evil spirits had been liberated. Jesus recalled that it was a divine compulsion that made him come this way, moved by the Holy Ghost. Now His constant friend and companion was explaining why. That well which had been the breeding ground of the revival of a whole city was located in a Parcel of land Jacob gave to his son Joseph. The irony was not lost on Jesus that Joseph by his obedience was that most perfect type of Jesus himself in the Law. He also remembered that Jacob bought the parcel of a field where he now spread his tent. He had bought it from the children of Hamor, Shechem's father for a hundred pieces of silver. Holy Spirit reminded him that Hamor's name meant "Ass" and was also symbolic of labour, toil, bondage or carrying heavy loads, while Shechem meant back or shoulder. Together, they discussed what they had inspired the Prophet Isaiah to pen: "And it shall come to pass in that day, that his burden shall be taken away from off thy shoulder, and his yoke from out thy neck, and the yoke shall be destroyed because of the anointing". They went on to talk about how the Assyrian's yoke ...would depart from off God's people and "his burden depart from off their shoulders" They also mused on divine arithmetic and the significance of hundred as the number of the elect.

They joyously reminisced and thanked Abba that He worked in Jacob to will and to do of His good pleasure. Jacob had therefore erected an altar unto God on that piece of land and called it El-Elohe-Israel, that is God, the God of Israel. So from that point that land was dedicated land. It didn't matter who dwelt in it afterward, it still belonged to God, the God of Israel. "After Jacob bought the land," Holy Spirit continued pensively, "At his death, he gave the same piece of land to his son Joseph as his inheritance."

"Aha" Jesus added catching the revelation. "No wonder Joseph asked that his bones be buried in Shechem in that same parcel of ground which had been bought for hundred pieces of silver."

The Holy Spirit went on, "We worked it so that it had a dual meaning and could also read one hundred lambs both of which picture the redemption you will achieve at Calvary."

Jesus smiled with understanding. "So that is why I had to pass through Samaria. The Samaritans were sitting on a time-bomb which was assembled by Jacob and whose fuse was lit by Joseph."

"Of course, you do remember the legal imperative which I quote 'qui quid plantata, solo solo cedit!" "That which is on the land belongs to the owner of the land," they said in unison. "The land was ours, paid for by the cost of redemption, the blood of the lambs or the silver pieces and as Joseph left it for his children, we have left it for ours-- they are elect represented by the number one hundred." Holy Spirit very reverently turns to Jesus. "The land was on layaway, and now the very same God to whom it was dedicated has come in the flesh. Hail, Emmanuel! Abba has exalted you and given you a name above every other. Indeed, the kingdoms of this world have become the kingdom of our God and You His Christ and You shall reign forevermore. Amen."

Jesus changed the subject. "But there was still the issue of what Joseph's bones represent."

Holy Spirit nodded. "Indeed, we inspired Joseph by faith to insist on his bones being carried from Egypt when the children of Israel were eventually delivered after four centuries of slavery."

Jesus couldn't contain His excitement. "When the leaders of Israel, after Joshua's death, buried Joseph's bones in this very plot, little did they know the spiritual significance of that act."

"Isaiah would later shed some light with his prophecy about you. Thy dead men shall live together with my dead body shall they arise. Awake and sing, ye that dwell in dust: for thy dew is as the dew of herbs, and the earth shall cast out the dead". "In effect, this speaks about resurrection. Joseph's bones therefore point to the Christ who would become the first begotten from the dead."

Jesus asked, "What about the issue of another set of bones, the dry bones Ezekiel saw in an open valley?"

The Holy Spirit explained, "They also speak of resurrection. In Ezekiel's case, God needed the prophet to prophecy to the dead bones, so that they could come alive again."

"Wow, what love, what grace, what compassion the Father has. The harvest was ripe and ready to be plucked. And Abba chose a woman, a Samaritan with a chequered history, a Gentile Samaritan woman, as the prophet to prophesy to the dry bones, the spiritually dead people of Samaria, that they may live again and indeed, they came alive! Glory be to Abba Father! Alleluia!" Jesus concluded.

As Sychar faded into the background, Jesus turned to his disciples and said, "Did you hear the one about the three wells?"

"No" they answered. "Well, well, well" Jesus joked. "The Living well sat on the old well so that out of the belly of the believer, a well spring, that is, rivers of living water, would flow."

Their expressions told Jesus they did not fully grasp what He had just said, but he was not worried. After His death, on the Day of Pentecost, when Holy Spirit would soon come, He would teach them all things, guide them into all truth, remind them of things Jesus had taught them and show them things to come.